The Cuban Filmography,
1897 through 2001

The Cuban Filmography,
1897 through 2001

by Alfonso J. García Osuna

McFarland & Company, Inc., Publishers
Jefferson, North Carolina, and London

Library of Congress Cataloguing-in-Publication Data

García Osuna, Alfonso J., 1953–
    The Cuban filmography, 1897 through 2001 / by Alfonso J. García Osuna.
       p.   cm.
    Includes index.

    ISBN 0-7864-1275-5 (library binding : 50# alkaline paper)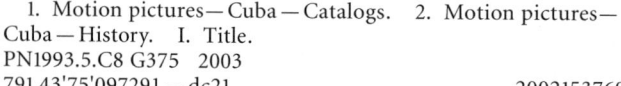

    1. Motion pictures—Cuba—Catalogs.   2. Motion pictures—Cuba—History.   I. Title.
PN1993.5.C8 G375   2003
791.43'75'097291—dc21   2002153760

British Library cataloguing data are available

©2003 Alfonso J. García Osuna. All rights reserved

No part of this book may be reproduced or transmitted in any form or by any means, electronic or mechanical, including photocopying or recording, or by any information storage and retrieval system, without permission in writing from the publisher.

Manufactured in the United States of America

McFarland & Company, Inc., Publishers
  Box 611, Jefferson, North Carolina 28640
    www.mcfarlandpub.com

For Elvira and Xavier,
always my inspiration

Contents

Preface
1

Introduction
5

A History of Cuban Film
9

The Films
49

Conclusion
185

Bibliography
189

Index
207

Preface

To write about Cuban cinema is to write about the fate of a Euro-American medium in a world of alien experience. It is not only a world where traditional institutions like marriage and family have suffered a profound change, but also one that has lost the traditional distinction of class; a world without a significant history or a substantial past; a world that left behind the horror of capitalist society not for the socialist innocence it dreamed of, but for new and special guilts associated with unfulfilled dreams; a world doomed to play out the old mistakes of the First World. In the end, Cuban cinema is only finally Cuban in spirit; its appearance is an event in the history of the Cuban imagination, as, indeed, is the very invention of Cuba itself.

As a researcher of Spanish medieval and Renaissance literature writing a book on Cuban film, I believe it is especially appropriate and important to acknowledge my debts to the film savants who have guided my way. Although scholarship is based on private research and the interpretive efforts of the individual, I owe much to current film researchers and historians. At the same time, I owe a very real debt to my colleagues at the City University of New York and to my Cuban friends who shed light on the fascinating world of Cuban social history. It is thanks to them that this work took shape. I must also acknowledge the pioneering work of Paulo Antonio Paranagua, who directed the edition of *Le Cinéma Cubain* (Paris: Centre Pompidou, 1990), a work that contains a wealth of information that has considerably assuaged the task of gathering facts, names and dates. The publications of the Cuban Institute for the Cinematic Arts and Industry (ICAIC) and Michael Chanan's *The Cuban Image* have also proved very helpful in this regard.

For the encouragement, advice, and invigorating conversations with colleagues and friends during the various stages of my research and writing, I wish to thank especially: Ronald Schwartz, consummate film sage, who has led my way in the world of film; Prof. Rodolfo González and Drs. Leconte, Pollack and Lolo of Kingsborough; my parents Alfonso and Encarna, lovers of Cuban culture; my brother Raúl; Jorge and Iraida Méndez, and the librarians at Hofstra University and Kingsborough College who made my toil easier. I would also like to acknowledge John Harris and Mary Corlis, at New York's Museum of Modern Art, for their help in gathering information and stills, and especially Mary Pérez, of ICAIC, who constantly provided me with new information and missing data, taking time off her busy schedule to respond cheerfully to my persistent queries.

I have attempted to include herein all significant films produced on the island of Cuba from 1897 through December 31, 2001. I fully realize that the word "significant" is very subjective and that any act of choosing is open to disagreement, yet I expect any casual observer would understand my method. The inclusion in this text of the hundreds of very short documentaries shot in Cuba, for example, many dealing with subjects such as the proper techniques for breast-feeding or better ways to manufacture screws, would make this book unfeasible and impractical. Also, if one were to include all foreign films in which a Cuban technician, writer, director, musician or actor participated, we would have to restyle this new gargantuan project as an "encyclopedia." In this regard I've included some of the most interesting films in which the ICAIC has worked with foreign companies and has had a major role in the films' production, and important foreign films that have been shot in Cuba or otherwise have Cuban themes.

Aside from a couple of notable exceptions, I have generally avoided films shot by Cuban-born individuals outside of Cuba; those productions belong in the filmographies of the countries in which they were undertaken.

The presentation of each film is accompanied by the following information: (1) Original title of the film; (2) English translation of the title, where applicable (feature films are given their official English title, documentaries intended exclusively for internal consumption do not have English titles—in those cases I've given a literal translation of the Spanish); (3) Director; (4) Production company or companies; (5) Year of release; (6) Black and white or color; (7) Total running time; (8) Writing credits (when film is based on an outside source, like a novel); (9) Animation (when it is a cartoon); (10) Music (when the music has been written for the film); (11) Cast; and (12) A synopsis and short critical evaluation.

As is customary in both Spanish and English, the initial articles (in Spanish *el, la, los, las, un, una, unos, unas*) are ignored in alphabetizing. In Spanish titles, only the first letter of the first word is capitalized, unless proper names are included.

Introduction

The word "Cuba" has many meanings. When contemporary academics, for example, use the word to talk about the culture associated with it, they are referring to a vast bibliography of creative work, criticism and interpretation that in many ways depends on the confrontational polemic that has attached itself to its image. It seems that to talk about Cuba means the necessary taking of sides on the ideological plane. When I use the phrase "Cuban film," I can hardly expect to extract the polemical content inherent to it; I can only explain what I have in mind when I utter the words. I see Cuban film as a visual tradition available to a large public, a body of works that in some way preserves and even defines the identity of the nation and proclaims its ideals, but also broods over its problems and defects. It is the unkempt image of a nation bludgeoned by its history and its ideals.

Ever since the bloody wars of independence and the foundation of the republic, ideals have been a major part of the world that surrounds the population of the island; the differing interpretations of them have brought the nation much pain and heartbreak. We cannot properly separate the story of these ideals from the story of Cuba itself, any more than we can separate the heartbeat from the heart.

This book is not about ideals or ideology. Cuban film is worth our thoughtful consideration not because it reflects certain ideals or defends a specific ideology, but because in its images is especially apparent the enduring identity of a people.

Introduction

Between cinematography and Cuba there are peculiar and intimate connections. An innovative form of culture and a new nation, their beginnings roughly coincide. Cubans are living not only in their century of independence and revolution, but also in the age of film.

The revolutionary government has known, since its inception in 1959, that its international reputation could be enhanced through a medium with mass appeal like film. This comes from the knowledge that, in a way, many of the notions of greatness once associated with a great national literature have been transferred to film. Ironically, this shift is part of the "Americanization of culture" that many Cuban intellectuals continue ritually to deplore.

But is there, as certain critics insist, a "Cuban film," a specific variety of the medium? If we turn to these critics for a definition, we find that the terms associated with Cuban cinematography derive from a standard view of Cuba as an "anti-culture," an eternally maintained preserve of confrontation and action against the bourgeois, technocratic, capitalist values that emerge from the Western tradition. This view equates Cuba with a sort of primitivism and ends in finding in Enrique Díaz Quesada the same values as in Tomás Gutiérrez Alea; this is more a symptom of Western cultural malaise than a useful critical distinction. It is tempting to insist on the pat rebuttal that, far from being anti-culture, Cuba is merely a branch of Western culture, and that there is no "Cuban film," only the local variants of standard American kinds of productions. Certainly no single major innovation has been invented in Cuba. Yet the peculiarities of their variants seem more interesting and important than their resemblances to the parent forms.

There is a real sense in which Cuban films are immediately distinguishable from those of the United States or Europe. In this sense, they seem not primitive, perhaps, but innocent, naive in a disturbing way, almost juvenile. This may be due precisely to the rejection of immoral Western perspectives that justify exploitation and injustice; in a compulsive way, many a Cuban filmmaker returns to a limited world of experience, of simple good vs. evil, black and white situations bred in a world of unquestionable truths. Even when the filmmaker questions these truths he does not invalidate them.

Merely finding a language, learning to convey a message in a land where the old conventions have been trashed, where there is no more dialogue between social classes, no continuity of expression — this exhausts the Cuban filmmaker. For, especially in the last decade of the twentieth century, he or she inhabits a country at once the dream of social engineers and a fact of history; he lives on the last horizon of an endlessly retreating vision of socialist innocence — on the last "frontier," which is to say, the margin where utopian theories and the fact of human fallibility come face to face. To express this situation and to live by it in a society in which, since the fall of Communism, a vague hope for a better "future" has become the chief effective religion, is a complex and difficult task.

A History of Cuban Film

For Cuba, 1897 was a momentous year. Amidst widening repression by Spanish authorities headed by General Valeriano Weyler, the growing conflict in the countryside and United States saber-rattling, Havana residents enjoyed plays and musical comedies in the various venues that give city life a semblance of normality. Federico Villoch's anti–American satire *Guau guau o la toma de Haway* (Bow-wow or the Taking of Hawaii) and his zarzuela (musical comedy) *La cruz de San Fernando* (Saint Fernando's Cross) were very popular in theaters like the Cervantes, which catered to male-only crowds.

On Sunday, January 24, 1897, an event took place that would change the face of Cuban culture forever. On that date, moving pictures were shown in Havana, in a theater at 126 Paseo del Prado, next to the famous Tacón Theater. A year after it was unveiled in Paris, Gabriel Veyre, the Lumière Bros. representative for Latin America, presented the new Cinématographe Lumière. Although the Edison Kinetoscope had been introduced two years earlier, on January 16, 1895, Monsieur Veyre's business acumen allowed him to capture wider popular attention for his product. Veyre arrived in Cuba at a very dramatic time: The insurrection against Spain had spread throughout the island, and the Spanish authorities were concentrating the population around Havana to keep people from helping the rebels. The mortality rates in these earliest of concentration camps were appalling. Under these circumstances, Veyre began his shows with his Cinématographe, charging 50 cents per ticket for adults, 20 for children and military personnel. A couple of weeks later, on February 7, Veyre would have the distinction of filming the first movie ever made in Cuba: *Simulacro de incendio*. The film shows firemen going out on a call, rescue vehicles, the water pump. Two nozzles were hoisted and placed, ladders were coupled and hoses were mounted. The whole production was organized for the benefit of Spanish actress María Tubau, on tour in Havana at the time. A large portion of the film's success was its particular appeal: The "actors" playing the parts were instantly recognized by Havana moviegoers as their neighborhood storekeeper, the beauty salon operator, the civil servant from the corner office house.

Other shorts shown by Veyre, as reported in the daily *La Unión Constitucional* of February 2, 1897, were titled *Un duelo a pistola en México* (Pistol Duel in Mexico) and *Carga de los rurales en México* (Charge of the Police in Mexico). These are the same films that were produced and shown in Mexico as *Un duelo a pistola en el bosque de Chapultepec* (Pistol Duel in the Chapultepec Forest) and *Carga de los rurales en la villa de Guadalupe* (Charge of the Police in the Town of Guadalupe). Produced by Lumière Bros. technicians in Mexico between August 1896 and January 1897, these were the first films ever made in Latin America. Other titles offered to the awed public were the shorts *Partida de cartas* (A Card Game), *El tren* (The Train), *El regador y el muchacho* (The Boy and the Sprinkler), and *El sombrero cómico* (The Funny Hat).

In 1898 the Cuban actor José E. Casasús bought a Pathé projector and other equipment and sallied forth on a tour of the island, showing a number of films to people who only recently had learned of the existence of electricity. We can only imagine their astonishment. Interviewed in the 1950s, he claimed to have introduced film to Cuba; while this is not entirely true, he was the first Cuban to make a film, *El brujo desapareciendo* (The Disappearing Warlock), the second film ever produced in Cuba.

This same year of 1898 the American presence, begun in 1895 with the Kinetoscope and later continued with Edison's Vitascope, was again affirmed when operators of the Edison Vitograph landed in Cuba with Teddy Roosevelt's Rough Riders. These technicians turned out shorts showing various firefights, the Battle of San Juan Hill, shots of the Morro Castle and of the savage naval battle of Santiago between the Spanish and U.S. fleets. This last battle, though, was in reality filmed in New York using model ships, water tanks and special effects. These films are known collectively by the title *Fighting with Our Boys in Cuba* (30 min.) and *The Naval Battle of Santiago de Cuba* (2 min.).

Also in 1898, French filmmaker Georges Méliès turned out another short accomplished with special effects, *The Explosion of the Cruiser Maine*. Méliès was thus able to profit from the wide international repercussions the event was having.

During this first phase of introduction, several locales in Havana began to cater exclusively to film: Panorama Soler, Salón de Variedades o Ilusiones Ópticas, Paseo del Prado #118, Panorama, and Vitascopio de Edison. The Irijoa Theater was the first theater to show films on a regular basis, and the first movie theater, the Floradora, was built by Cuban entrepreneur José E. Casasús, a venue that later came to be known as the "Alaska."

Film became a stable business concern in Havana before the beginning of World War I, with the theater Polyteama as the number one moneymaker. Traveling projection teams brought film to the interior of the island as well. In 1901, while the U.S. Congress was passing the Platt Amendment (giving the United States the right to intervene in Cuban affairs) and Tomás Estrada Palma was being elected as the nation's first president, the Alhambra Theater was showing the popular *Pinturas vivas o el Cinematógrafo parlante* (Living Pictures or the Talking Film), by Olallo Díaz.

The period from 1904 to 1909 was traumatic for the new republic. In an attempt to give a voice to the workers' aspirations, Marxist ideologue Carlos Baliño founded the Workers' Party in 1904. The following year was marked by the murder of Enrique Villuendas, the most important figure of the political opposition to the government, and the reelection of Tomás Estrada Palma. This is the year the movie theater Actualidades opened its doors for the first time, the oldest active cinema hall in Cuba. In 1906, while an uprising against the government of Tomás Estrada Palma brings war (La Guerrita de Agosto) and U.S. intervention, Francisco Rodríguez and Enrique Díaz Quesada opened their film distribution company, the Moving Pictures Company. Díaz Quesada also shot the oldest documentary extant in Cuba, *El parque de Palatino* (Palatino Park), as well as *La Habana en agosto de 1906* (Havana in August of 1906), and *La salida de palacio de Don Tomás Estrada Palma* (Tomás Estrada Palma Leaving the Presidential Palace), a short subject propaganda film in support of the president. Owing to the growing popularity of film in Cuba, Havana's newest leisure park, the "Coney Island," contained a movie theater.

In 1907 the island's population surpassed the 2 million mark. As massive immigration from Spain changed the face of the nation and workers were striking for the eight-hour workday, Díaz Quesada shot *Un duelo a orillas del río Almendares* (A Duel on the Shores of the Almendares River), the first known work of fiction in Cuban film, and *Un turista en La Habana* (A Tourist in Havana), a classic of tourist promotion. At the same time, legendary Cuban musician Gonzalo Roig was learning his trade playing the piano in Havana movie houses. In 1908, Charles E. Magoon, head of the U.S. intervention administration, organized the Cuban National Army and the Rural Guard while Evaristo Estenoz created the Independent Association of Colored People, an organization dedicated to the defense of Cubans of African descent. On April 29 of this same year, Spaniards Pablo Santos and Jesús Artigas opened the first film distribution company on the island, Compañía Cinematográfica Habanera, the same Santos and Artigas who directed a renowned circus. They bought and sold film material and replacement parts. Also in 1908, Díaz Quesada shot *Un cabildo en Ña Romualda* (City Hall in Ña Romualda), a film that delved for the first time into Afro-Cuban matters.

The next year, 1909, saw the coming to power of José Miguel Gómez and the end of United States military intervention. Musical legends Guillermo and Jorge Anckermann rented the Molino Rojo theater and presented comic sketches like *La segunda república reformada* (Reformed Second Republic), *Las cosas de Cuba* (Things Cuban) and *Todo por honor* (All for the Sake of Honor). In film, Díaz Quesada shot *Los festejos de la Caridad en Camagüey* (The Feast of the Virgin of Charity in Camagüey), *Toma de posesión de José Miguel Gómez* (José Miguel Gómez's Inauguration) and *Salida de Mr. Magoon de Cuba* (Mr. Magoon Leaves Cuba). This same year an anonymous filmmaker shot *La leyenda del charco del Güije* (The Legend of the Güije's Puddle), and Havana's first outdoor movie theater, the Miramar Gardens, opened its doors. The Miramar Gardens was centrally located in the intersections of Prado and Malecón avenues and quickly became the preferred meeting place for Havana's high society.

The years preceding World War I and the war years were very trying for Cuba. Growing interracial tension obliged the government to prohibit all organizations that based membership on race. The magazine *Minerva*, supporter of racial equality and integration, was first published in 1910, and so was *Bohemia*, the longest-lasting magazine in Cuban history. More movie theaters opened in Havana: on January 15 the Polyteama Grande, on February 5 the Polyteama Chico, and in May the Salón Norma, billed as "the only establishment that provides mahogany armchairs and tiers." As labor laws came into effect on May 29 restricting work hours, Cuban movie theaters like the Miramar Gardens pioneered the "permanent viewing" concept, where the film enthusiast may enter the theater at any time through the abrogation of restrictive showtimes. Enrique Díaz Quesada teamed up with distributors Santos and Artigas to make the process of making films more effective.

In 1910 Díaz Quesada shot the documentaries *Los funerales de Morúa Delgado* (Morúa Delgado's Funeral), recording the obsequies for that patriotic black Cuban intellectual, and *Los cruceros Cuba y Patria entrando en el puerto de La Habana* (The Cruisers "Cuba" and "Patria" Entering the Port of Havana). He also shot *El sueño de un estudiante de farmacia* (The Dream of a Pharmacy Student), filmed at Havana's famed Droguería Sarrá. Both *Los funerales* and *El sueño del estudiante* were presented by Santos and Artigas in the most popular new movie theater in Havana, the Polyteama Grande. On March 26 the Montecarlo movie theater showed Díaz Quesada's *Criminal por obcecaión* (*Blindly Criminal*), a 17-minute work of fiction starring the underemployed actors from the Albisu Theater (film had put many theater actors out of work). On August 23 of this same year, 1910, Díaz Quesada filmed *Juan José*, a 36-minute social drama based on a popular play. The public at the Polyteama Chico also witnessed, on August 6, 1910, the projection of the French film *La Prise de la Bastille* (The Storming of the Bastille), which, at one hour and forty minutes, was the longest-running film ever presented in Cuba.

The next year (1911), while black Cubans staged a bloody insurrection against the white Havana government and Gonzalo Roig composed the classic song "Quiéreme mucho," the indefatigable Díaz Quesada shot *Vuelo del aviador McCurdy sobre la Habana* (McCurdy's Flight Over Havana), which was shown at the Payret and Actualidades cinemas. By 1912 and in response to the Morúa amendment to the Constitution prohibiting institutions based on race, there was a generalized revolt by black groups in the eastern part of the island that got a violent and bloody response. Black insurgents massacred white farmers while the Cuban National Army, in a bloody counterinsurgency action, crushed the aspirations of the black population. The melee brought in the U.S. Marines. This is the year General Mario García Menocal was elected president and Ernesto Lecuona, Cuba's leading composer, directed his first concert. As Federico Villoch and Jorge Anckermann produced their political satire *La casita criolla* for Havana's theater goers, young filmmaker Enrique Díaz Quesada released his *Festival infantil de Bohemia* (Bohemian Children's Festival). The projection was accompanied by an official ceremony in which the mayor of Havana and the vice-president of the Republic helped distribute presents to the poor children of the capital. The event was held under the auspices of the magazine *Bohemia* and was officially sanctioned by the government. Back to contemporary events, Díaz Quesada shot *La campaña o Salida de tropas hacia Santiago de Cuba durante la guerra racista* (Troops Leave for Santiago de Cuba During the Race War), and *Epílogo del Maine* (Epilogue for the Cruiser Maine). Although it is difficult to say that Díaz Quesada was making "political" or "official" film, it is true that his allegiances were firmly on the side of the government and that official support was very important to his success. The appearance of the magazines *La gaceta teatral y cinematográfica* (February 17, 1912) and *Cuba cinematográfica* (November 1912), edited by Santos and Artigas, attest to the ever-growing importance and popularity of film.

In 1913 Cuba's sugar production surpassed the 2 million ton mark, putting $106 million in the nation's coffers. The nation now produced 12 percent of the world's sugar. The United Fruit Company, an American concern, invested $82 million in Cuba and began to introduce large numbers of Haitian workers into Cuba. Ernesto Lecuona won the first prize awarded by the National Conservatory, and the Cuban National Museum was inaugurated. In April of 1913 a new movie theater was opened, the Nueva Inglaterra, with its own confectionery and capacity for 150 moviegoers, quite large for the time. This same year Enrique Díaz Quesada shot *Manuel García, rey de los campos de Cuba* (Manuel García, King of the Cuban Countryside), the first full-length work of fiction in the history of Cuban film. The film is based on a real-life Cuban Robin Hood, who in the nineteenth century took from the rich and gave to the poor. The legend of Manuel García proved fruitful: In the forties and fifties it became the subject of a good number of radio daily-installment novels, and the movie had a remake in 1941. The original film was shown at the Polyteama Grande and Chico on August 6, 1913; it had taken some six months to shoot. The anticipation was great: The press kept a close eye on the developments and advance tickets were sold to eager high society film enthusiasts. Díaz Quesada also shot promotional short subject films such as *Industria de la caña de azúcar* (The Sugar Cane Industry), *Los carnavales de Cienfuegos* (The Cienfuegos Carnivals), and *Toma de posesión del general Menocal* (General Menocal's Inauguration). The following year, in April of 1914, Jesús Artigas traveled to Europe in order to purchase films. He stopped in Madrid, Barcelona, Paris, Berlin, Milan, Rome, London and Copenhagen. European films thus began arriving in Cuba in greater numbers than ever before. But Artigas' march through the old continent would be abruptly stopped by the beginning of the First World War. Also in 1914 the Cuban government decided to issue a national currency shortly (to replace the dollar and the Spanish peseta), and a ferry company first linked Havana to the U.S. on a regular basis. Díaz Quesada expanded and further exploited his excellent relationship with the Army with the film *El capitán mambí o libertadores y guerrilleros* (The Mambí Captain or Liberators and Guerrilla Fighters), inspired by the Cuban War of Independence and the role played in it by the patriot Manuel Sanguily. This film, made expressly to manifest the heroic nature of Cuba's struggle against Spain, evidences the major role film had in the nation-building process in Cuba. The film was a great success, and Sanguily himself commented, after seeing it: "In order to depict and render the sublime aspects of the history of the fatherland, there is no better medium than film" (*Bohemia*, Nov. 14).

The birth of the Cuban "peso" marked 1915, as Spanish and Italian anarchists were deported from the island and labor strikes slowed down the economy. Theatergoers were treated to Guillermo Anckermann's political satirical sketch *El país de las botellas* (The Country of No-Show Jobs), and the Teatro Nacional (previously known as Tacón) opened its doors. The town of Matanzas, east of Havana, opened a brand new movie house, a space dedicated exclusively to film. In Havana, Enrique Díaz Quesada filmed the boxing match between Jess Willard and Jack Johnson on April 5, 1915, and he obtained material support from General García Menocal's government for his film *La manigua o la mujer cubana* (The Countryside or the Cuban Woman). The story is based on the participation of women in the War of Independence, and it was supplemented by an original score by famed musician J. Mauri. Attending the premiere were 3,225 people, paying a whopping 80 cents per ticket. *La manigua o la mujer cubana* set records both in attendance and in the price paid per ticket. Six new movie theaters opened this year in Havana, bringing the number in the capital to 40 and to 300 on the island, a considerable number for a country of two and a half million people. In 1916, amidst the electoral fraud that returned García Menocal to the presidency, the Virgin of Charity was made patroness of Cuba and the variety periodical *La farándula* was first printed. Enrique Díaz Quesada shot *Inauguración de la estatua del general Maceo* (Unveiling of General Maceo's Statue), *Un mensaje al general Calixto García* (A Message to General Calixto García) and the full-length historical feature *El rescate del brigadier Sanguily* (The Rescue of Brigadier Sanguily).

This last film was the subject of much preparation and research. In their effort to be historically accurate, the producers got their hands on Brigadier Sanguily's saddle and the orthopedic apparatus used by the soldier, raised the red and gold Spanish colors on the Morro Castle, and did much homework to avoid mistakes. This intricate production needed the consent of the highest authority, President Menocal himself. He gave his permission to the producers personally in the language of Cuban grandiloquence: "I take this opportunity to congratulate you on the high degree of development that the cinematographic arts have attained in Cuba with this film, as well as for the validity of its subject and the inspired choice of scenario. It can only bring forth, in our youth, a spirit of national pride, the firm foundation on which to build the future of the Republic" (*Bohemia*, Oct. 1915). The producers, of course, used this letter in their profuse publicity barrages.

As a direct result of the First World War, U.S. productions now replaced European ones in Cuban movie houses, while native production seemed to be involved in the construction of a national ego ideal, if one is to judge by the subject matter of most films. From time to time, the national press would print opinion columns that were hostile to the film industry, such as one published by the *Diario de la Marina* in February of 1916. In it, a distinguished upper crust dame, prominent member of the Society of Family Mothers, requests the constitution of censure paradigms for the film industry. This industry, she claims, is a "school for corruption and perversion."

The following year, 1916, marked the conspicuous general decline of European screenings in Cuba. The Caribbean Film Company began to distribute American films produced by the Famous Players–Lasky Artcraft Company as well as other firms that later fused to form the Paramount Pictures Corporation. To keep up with the times, the Campoamor Theater adopted a policy of showing only U.S. films, and even Pathé distributed Yankee productions, like Louis Gasnier's *The Mysteries of New York* (1915).

In the year of the "Chambelona," 1917, an armed uprising staged by the Liberals against the electoral fraud kept their candidate, Alfredo Zayas, from being elected president. As the revolt became generalized and bloody, U.S. troops landed in Oriente and Camagüey provinces. The status quo was reestablished and opposition newspapers and periodicals were shut. Enrique Díaz Quesada shot three features this year, *La careta social* (Social Masquerade), *La hija del policía o en poder de los Ñáñigos* (The Policeman's Daughter or in the Power of the Ñáñigos) and *El tabaquero de Cuba o el capital y el trabajo* (The Cuban Tobacco Worker or Capital and Labor), this last one starring the very popular actor Regino López. The second film, *La hija del policía*, tells the story of a young lover who delivers the object of his affection, a policeman's daughter, into the hands of a murderous secret religious organization of African origin. Díaz Quesada may have been catering to the prevailing tendencies of popular opinion: a few months before the release of the movie, many black Cubans had been lynched in Matanzas for having participated in the ritual murder of a white girl. The white mob had acted with the widespread approbation of an enraged white population, who was, for the most part, the film industry's most assiduous constituent, as it was white folks who could generally afford the ticket prices. *La careta social* dealt with a subject that would be broached many more times in Cuban culture: the runaway hypocrisy of the island's aristocracy. One of the year's most successful films was one distributed by Pathé whose title was *The Life of Our Lord Jesus Christ*, screened for the first time during the Holy Week celebrations. It became so popular that it turned into a tradition to show it at this same time every year. In spite of the innocuous nature of most films projected in Cuba, the outcry for censorship kept growing, fueled by the involvement of well-known figures like Fernando Llano, a Havana city politician. The Cuban Supreme Court, however, declared such censorship unconstitutional.

In 1918 a general strike virtually paralyzed the economy. The draft became law and all young Cuban men now were obliged to serve in the armed forces. As women demanded the right to vote and the divorce law was approved, the United States bought the year's sugar production in its entirety and famous composer Gonzalo Roig penned his haunting "Ojos brujos." The Association for the Defense of Cuban Cinematography was formed, bringing together producers, directors and distributors; Jesús Artigas was elected its first president. Julio Pomer shot a Chaplin imitation called *Quesitos de crema* (Cream Cheese) and Lastra and Cobos shot *Los Apaches cubanos* (Cuban Apaches).

By 1919 the workers were taking to the streets and staging violent clashes with the police. Gambling was approved and the sugar harvest surpassed the 4 million ton mark. As the artistic review *Carteles* and children's magazine *Pulgarcito* began publication, novelist Carlos Loveira wrote *Los inmortales* and Ernesto Lecuona composed "Siboney," one of the milestones of Cuban music. This is the year Díaz Quesada shot *La zafra o sangre y azúcar* (The Sugar Harvest or Blood and Sugar), a "poor boy falls in love with a rich girl" story starring Regino López, and *La brujería en acción* (Witchcraft in Action) focusing on African religious practices on the island. Díaz Quesada began to have significant competition, to judge by the number of films released in 1919: *Cuba en la guerra* (Cuba at War), *El soldado en Cuba* (The Cuban Soldier), *Las regatas de Varadero* (Varadero Beach Regattas), *La manifestación del honor en Estados Unidos* (How Honor is Expressed in the United States), *Acebal se saca el gordo* (Acebal Hits the Jackpot) and *Los matrimonios salvavidas* (Life-Saving Weddings). This last film dealt with the rash of weddings that were taking place for the wrong reason: married men were exempted from military service. By 1919 the main Hollywood film companies had opened offices in Havana.

Social and political problems multiplied in 1920. Strikes continued as bombs exploded in public places. In fact, an explosion damaged Havana's National Theater just before Enrico Caruso was to give his final performance there. As sugar prices began a free fall, banks failed and

President García Menocal was forced to decree a bank holiday. On a more positive note, the famed Sexteto Habanero musical group was formed this year, Moisés Simons composed his world famous ballad "Manisero," and Carlos Loveira published *Generales y doctores*, a novel that detailed the troubles Cuba was facing and would continue to face for some time. Havana's Municipal Library opened its doors for the first time. At the headquarters of the daily paper *La Noche*, Enrique Díaz Quesada directed a film he called *Cómo se hace un periódico* (How a Newspaper Is Made) and also shot, in ten episodes (one reel each), *El genio del mal* (The Spirit of Evil). Ramón Peón and Pedro Vázquez filmed *Dios existe* (God Exists), and Peón also directed *Realidad* (Reality) on his own this same year. The comedy *Entre flores* (Among the Flowers) was shot by Pedro Vázquez, *Inexperiencia* (Inexperience) by Jaime Gispert and *El soldado Juan* (Juan the Soldier) by Félix Callejas. This same year Juan Valdés began to shoot his *Suprem Films*, a series of shorts that deal with events of local interest as well as with the activities of high society types and commercials.

In 1921 Zayas was president and the outgoing García Menocal had left the country a $40 million debt. Cuban master Raúl Capablanca won the first of his several World Chess Championships and the First National City Bank of New York took control of 50 sugar refineries on the island. Enrique Díaz Quesada directed the features *Alto el fuego* (Cease Fire) and *Frente a la vida* (Face to Face with Life) while Ramón Peón directed *Aves de paso* (Rolling Stones), *Las cosas de mi mujer* (My Wife Is Like That) and *Mamá Zenobia*. Ramón Peón began to capture the prominent place once reserved for film pioneer Enrique Díaz Quesada. From this year until 1933, Peón would have the center stage, not only for the quality of his production, but for the number of films released. Other films released this year were *La maldita* (The Foresaken) by Alberto Román, *La perla del mar* (Pearl of the Seas) by Harry Haskins, *Los apuros de Guerito* (Guerito's Predicament) by Julio Powell, and *La insurrección de la carne* (Rebellion of the Flesh) by Matías Franco Varona. The film review *Cinelandia* was first printed in January of 1921.

The following year, the first congress of the Havana Federation of Workers prepared the grounds for a national federation to defend workers' rights. Julio Antonio Mella founded the Federation of University Students (FEU) and strikes paralyzed the docks and the railroads. At the Alhambra Theater, Adolfo Otero and Sergio Acebal played the gallego (the dim-witted Galician) and the negrito (the mischievous little black man), firmly establishing two of the best loved characters in the history of the Cuban stage. Enrique Díaz Quesada directed his last feature, *Arroyito* (Little Stream), and Ramón Peón shot *Casados de veras* (Truly Married). Julio

Powell directed *Entre col y col* (Between the Cabbages) and newcomer Ricardo Delgado shot *Desdichas y recompensas* (Misfortunes and Rewards) and *¿Por qué se casan las mujeres?* (Why Do Women Marry?).

In 1923 the "Protesta de los trece" (Protestation of the Thirteen) gathered intellectuals and artists against the growing corruption at all levels of government and industry; the first National Congress of Women met, and Julio Antonio Mella presided over the first National Congress of Students and helped found the José Martí University for workers. The "Minorista" group of intellectuals, formed by figures such as Alejo Carpentier, Juan Marinello, Emilio Roig de Leuchsenring, Jorge Mañach, Mariano Brull, Rubén Martínez Villena, Regino Pedroso, Eduardo Abela, José Zacarías Tallet, Conrado Massaguer and Max Henríquez Ureña, worked for a renovation of the political culture of the nation. While Amadeo Roldán composed his "Dos danzas cubanas" and Gonzalo Roig "Yo te amé," Federico Villoch and Jorge Anckermann staged the caustic political satire *La isla de las cotorras* (Parrot Island) at the Alhambra Theater. On May 14, 1923, the prolific Enrique Díaz Quesada died. He was 41. Shortly after his death, a fire destroyed all of his film negatives. Copies of his films were dispersed all over the country, and without proper control they all eventually disappeared without a trace. This is Cuban cinema's foremost tragedy. True to his calling, when he died he was preparing to film *El titán de bronce* (Bronze Titan), on the life of General Antonio Maceo, a national hero. Of this significant and consequential figure in Cuban culture the one surviving film is *El parque de Palatino*, a one-minute promotional short. Unfortunately, a significant portion of Cuba's film classics has been lost in this way.

Another insurgent revolt put Cuba on a war footing in 1924, staged by the veterans of the War of Independence, who hadn't fought against Spain to see an independent Cuba besieged by corruption and denied true democracy. In a climate of insecurity, General Gerardo Machado won the presidential elections. As the Havana Philharmonic Orchestra began its first season, Rodrigo Prats composed the ever-popular song "Una rosa de Francia." The legendary singer-composer Miguel Matamoros teamed up with Rafael Cueto to sing duets while Valentín Cané and Pablo Vásquez established the "Tuna Liberal," the future and world famous "Sonora Matancera." During the year Ramón Peón filmed his comedy *Al aire libre* (Out in the Open) and the influential paper *El Mundo* incorporated a section called "Cine-Carnet" dedicated to film review.

The Cuban Communist Party was founded in 1925, as was the National Confederation of Workers. Amid social turmoil, the government of President Gerardo Machado began a program of repression that would result in incarceration and even death for many of his detractors. Miguel Matamoros, Rafael Cueto and Siro Rodríguez created the "Trío Oriental," later to be called the "Trío Matamoros." The "Sexteto Habanero" became truly popular with their rendition of Antonio María Romeu's "Tres lindas cubanas" (Three Lovely Cuban Women), Evaristo Herrera directed his first film, *Entre dos amores* (Caught Between Two Lovers), and Ricardo García set up a film laboratory that would streamline movie production on the island.

The year 1926 brought a cyclone that killed over 200 people. Union leader Alfredo López was murdered and the sugar harvest reached the 5 million ton mark. The Spanish-Cuban Institute of Culture was founded and put under the direction of Fernando Ortiz, a well-known intellectual, and the Cuban Academy of Letters, analogous to the Royal Academy in Spain, was formed. Richard Harlan's Pan American Pictures Corporation produced five short-subject films: *La chica del gato* (The Girl with the Cat), *Amor y arena* (Love and Sand), *El inocente* (The Innocent), *Justicia mora* (Moorish Justice) and *El cobarde valeroso* (The Valiant Coward), this last one directed by Ramón Peón. American Lee de Forest, with the financial backing of General Machado's government, set up a lab that would eventually turn out films with sound using the "Phono Films" system.

With the support of the United States, General Machado paved the way for his reelection in 1927. Radical students form the "Directorio Estudiantil" prepared to actively oppose Machado. The "Minorista" group published a declaration against the prevalent corruption of values in Cuban society, in favor of a revamped national culture and in clear opposition to dictatorship, imperialism and economic dependence. At the Regina Theater, Ernesto Lecuona and Eliseo Grenet presented their musical operetta *Niña Rita*, with the lead part interpreted by the celebrated Rita Montaner, who sang a song that would become emblematic of the times, "Ay, mamá Inés." Carlos Loveira reached an apogee in his literary career with the publication of the novel *Juan Criollo*. The death of Enrique Díaz Quesada was acutely felt by the Cuban film industry: production plummeted as moviegoers settled for foreign movies such as *El crucero Potampkin* (The Cruiser Potampkin), the first Soviet production seen in Cuba.

In 1928, as Machado was reelected and the Panamerican Conference was held in Havana, Amadeo Roldán assembled his Afro-Cuban Ballet, "La Rebambaramba," and Joseíto Fernández wrote the most Cuban of all songs, "Guantanamera." This was a prolific year for music: Lecuona produced three musical operettas, *El cafetal*, *El batey* and *El maizal*, as Félix Caignet wrote his ballad "Te odio," and Miguel Matamoros composed the famous "El que siembra su maíz" and "La bomba lacrimógena." In one of the most profound sociological studies of the young Republic, Jorge Mañach delved into the causes and aspects of that particularly congenial yet defamatory sense of humor Cubans seem to be endowed with, in his groundbreaking *Indagación del choteo*. Federico Piñero played "El gallego," the stereotyped dimwit, in Leopoldo Fernández' troupe, while the popular drama *Alma guajira*, written by the anarchist Marcelo Salinas, was performed in the capital. On the big screen the only production for this year was *El traficante* (The Dealer) by Juan Díaz Quesada, Enrique's brother.

In 1929, with Machado firmly in power and actively decimating his opposition, Julio Antonio Mella was murdered in Mexico, where the dictator's long arm had reached him. The worldwide economic crisis hit Cuba hard, especially with the free-fall of sugar prices. Amidst the confusion, Aniceto Díaz composed the first "danzonete" style song, "Rompiendo la rutina," sung by Paulina Álvarez, while Nilo Menéndez composed the ballad "Aquellos ojos verdes" and Miguel Matamoros his picaresque melody "La mujer de Antonio." In literature, Regino Boti wrote *Kodak-Ensueño*, poems in prose, José Antonio Ramos the novel *Las impurezas de la realidad*, Carlos Montenegro the stories *El Renuevo y otros cuentos*, and intellectual Max Henríquez Ureña the essay *Tablas cronológicas de la literatura cubana*. Starting this year, José Manuel Valdés Rodríguez, film critic and enthusiast, began his fruitful collaboration with the daily *El Mundo*. His column would be a permanent fixture in that newspaper until 1965. Armed with an absurd plan to conquer the United States film market, Arturo "Mussie" del Barrio, Ramón Peón and Antonio Perdices set up the company BPP Pictures (after their surname initials), which actually produced films with Spanish *and* English subtitles. Their first effort, directed by Peón, was *El veneno de un beso* (The Poison of a Kiss), a film based on a novel by Guy de Pelletier in which Perdices (the "Cuban Rudolph Valentino") had the leading role. Mario Orts Ramos directed the film *Alma guajira* (Soul of a Farmer) based on Salinas' drama, and the Machado government created a Film Department that would, for the most part, make documentaries that gave the government's views on current events.

In 1930 a general strike lead by Rubén Martínez Villena against the Machado government intensified the repression. University students were at the forefront of the fight against the dictatorship and paid a heavy price: their leader, Rafael Trejo, was murdered and the army occupied the University. In spite of the social turmoil, Cuban enterprise moved steadily forward: by 1930 the island had 61 radio stations, ranking it fourth in the world in this sector behind the U.S., Canada and the Soviet Union. Ernesto Lecuona and Gustavo Sánchez Galarraga presented their musical *María la O* at the Payret Theater while Nicolás Guillén began a prolific literary career with the publication of his book of poems *Motivos de son*. As Ignacio Piñero composed *Suavecito* and Miguel Matamoros *El paralítico*, Ramón Peón directed *La Virgen de la Caridad* (The Virgin of Charity), the only Cuban feature-length silent film preserved in its entirety, and this thanks to the painstaking efforts of the Cinemateca de Cuba. This film is important not just because it is the only extant silent feature, but because it is the first that really delves into the life of rural Cuba and the psychology of its naïve inhabitants. BPP Pictures produced a series of current-event documentaries: *El baile de las naciones* (The Dance of Nations), *La última jornada del Titán de Bronce* (The Last Day of the Bronze Titan), and *Conozca a Cuba* (Come Get Acquainted with Cuba). *El caballero del mar* (The Knight from the Sea), by Jaime Sant Andrews, is partially endowed with sound using the Vitaphone system.

By 1931 even the conservatives were battling the Machado regime. Secret revolutionary societies like ABC proliferated as the government opened its "Model Prison" in the Isle of Pines, the second largest island in the Cuban Archipelago. In Brussels, an international agreement reduced the Cuban sugar production quota to 3 million tons a year. The Lecuona Cuban Boys Orchestra was formed, and the "Escuela Normal de Música de La Habana" and the "Escuela de Ballet Pro-Arte Musical" were inaugurated. Odilio Urfé formed his "Orquesta Ideal" and Julio Brito composed the song "Ilusión China." Cuban literature kept searching for originality of expression, as Nicolás Guillén published *Sóngoro cosongo, poemas mulatos*, making him, essentially, the poetic voice of the black population, while Eugenio Florit published his influential book of poems *Monólogo de Charles Chaplin en una esquina*. Félix O'Shea and Marcelo Agudo began their frolicsome and very popular radio program "Radiodifusión O'Shea." There is no record of any film being produced in 1931.

In 1932 the sugar production quotas were again reduced and the social turmoil and assassinations intensify. The town of Santa Cruz del Mar is razed by a tidal wave, adding to the ongoing national tragedy. At the Martí Theater Gonzalo Roig's musical *Cecilia Valdés* premieres; based on the novel by Cirilo Villaverde, the libretto is written by Agustín Rodríguez and José Sánchez Arcilla. Antonio Castell begins to write the radio sketches for the comedy team of Chicharito and Sopeira, a new version of the Galician and the Little Negro played by Enrique Arredondo and Federico Piñero (and somewhat later by Alberto Garrido and Piñero, who became the classic duo of Cuban comedy). At radio station CMBZ, Jorge Mañach began to conduct the cultural program "La Universidad del Aire." A short subject film called *Maracas y bongó* (Maracas and Bongo Drums), directed by Max Tosquella with music by Grenet, became the first Cuban film to have a sound track. Precursor to the type of quaint, superficial text that will characterize many Cuban films of the next two decades, *Maracas y bongó* is the story of a lovers' quarrel set in the typical "solar" or common dwelling where the poor live. Every typical character appears on screen: the mulatto woman, the pimp, the cop ... all interpreting the most popular tunes of the time. But by no means were all Cuban films now blessed with sound: the documentary *El terremoto de Santiago* (The Santiago Earthquake), filmed this same year, was silent.

Nineteen thirty-three was a tumultuous year. A general strike against Machado, again led by Rubén Martínez Villena, had international repercussions: under pressure from the United States, Machado quit and left the country. The popular uprising brought Ramón Grau San Martín to the presidency and an obscure sergeant-typist to the top of the military: Fulgencio Batista, the new Army Chief of Staff and perceived strong man. Liberal government minister Antonio Guiteras pushed for and obtained the passage of the 8-hour work week and minimum-salary laws. The University was proclaimed autonomous and beyond any government interference, and the farm workers began instituting Soviets, or Russian-style parliaments. Influential radio station CMQ began operations under the direction of Miguel Gabrial and Ángel Cambó. As political and social changes spawned a profusion of activity in the arts, novelist Alejo Carpentier published his *¡Ecue-Yamba-O! Afro-Cuban Story,* Lino Novás Calvo wrote *El negrero* and Jorge Mañach his biography of Cuba's national hero, *Martí, el apóstol.* A very popular character was introduced to radio listeners this year, detective Chan-Li-Po, played by Aníbal de Mar. Documentaries were still silent, as in the case of *La epopeya revolucionaria* (Revolutionary Epic) and *Una página de gloria* (A Glorious Event), but Ernesto Caparrós filmed the short subject *El frutero* (The Fruit Vendor) with an outstanding musical score by Ernesto Lecuona.

The next year, 1934, brought Cubans back to reality: Batista deposed President Grau San Martín and put Carlos Mendieta in his place. The Platt Amendment, which gave the U.S. the right to intervene in Cuban affairs, was repealed, but the Left began to be persecuted. Carlos Prío Socarrás and Ramón Grau San Martín founded the Cuban Revolutionary Party (Auténtico), an important political force for the next two decades. Nicolás Guillén published a new book of poems, *West Indies Ltd.,* and Ramón Guirao his *Bongo, poemas negros,* both with a strong African flavor. Caledonio Borbolla, Jr., began publishing his monthly magazine *La Revista del Cine,* dedicated entirely to the cinematic arts.

The following year, the few who still had hopes for a better future for Cuba lost it completely: A general strike was crushed in a particularly bloody manner by the army and the population was forced to go through a state of siege. The death penalty was instituted, a Batista puppet, José A. Barnet, made president and the patriotic statesman Guiteras assassinated. Enrique Perdices bankrolled the publication of the weekly magazine *Cinema*, which became the official organ of the film industry.

In 1936 Miguel Mariano Gómez was elected president, but through Batista's efforts he was replaced with Vice-President Federico Laredo Bru. Women got the right to vote and the University of Havana was reopened; the Spanish Civil War had profound repercussions in Cuba, still intimately connected to Spain by ties of blood and history. As Pirandello plays were staged in the theater La Cueva-Teatro de Arte de La Habana, at the Teatro Principal de la Comedia Ernesto Lecuona and Gustavo Sánchez Galarraga presented their musical *La rosa china* and painter Felipe Orlando exhibited at Havana's lyceum. Enrique Labrador Ruiz published *Cresival* as Spanish poet Juan Ramón Jiménez began his sojourn on the island and Lydia Cabrera put out the first edition of her groundbreaking *Cuentos negros de Cuba*. Ernesto Caparrós filmed the short *Como el arrullo de palmas* (Like the Whisper of the Palms), based on the homonym and haunting melody by Ernesto Lecuona, who is fast becoming one of the reliable icons of national culture. Spanish film star Imperio Argentina toured the island to promote her new films *Morena clara* (Light-Skinned Black Woman) and *Nobleza Baturra* (Southern Nobility); she was a guest at Havana's CMQ radio station for two weeks, and the toast of the town.

In 1937 celebrated writer José Lezama Lima published his poem *Muerte de Narciso*. Osvaldo Farrés composed the song "Mis cinco hijos" and Julio Brito "El amor de mi bohío," both compositions becoming musical icons for this generation of Cubans. Ernesto Caparrós directed the first full-length feature with a sound track in the history of Cuban cinema, *La serpiente roja* (The Red Snake), based on polemical radio episodes by Félix B. Caignet. The series had become eminently popular, to the point where movie house managers were installing radios and interrupting projections so that moviegoers could listen to *Serpiente Roja* episodes. They featured detective Chan-Li-Po and starred the ever-more-popular Aníbal de Mar. Ernesto Caparrós directed another musical short, *Tam Tam o el origen de la rumba* (Tam Tam or the Origin of Rumba), while Manuel Alonso put out his animated cartoon *Napoleón, el faraón de los sinsabores* (Napoleon, Pharaoh of Hatred). Film magazines *Cine Fans* and *Exhibidor* were first published during this year.

In 1938 the *Serpiente Roja* series was still going strong, with Chan-Li-Po now interpreted by Oscar Luis López and directed by Luis Manuel Martínez Casado on radio station COCO. Alejandro García Caturla's

"Obertura cubana" won First Prize in the National Music Contest while Gonzalo Roig founded the National Opera. Orestes López composed "Mambo, danzón," Bobby Collazo "Retornarás," and Abelardito Valdés "Almendra." Popular singer Paulina Álvarez, the "Empress of the danzonete," formed her own orchestra, while the bands "Orquesta Cosmopolita" and "Riverside" began to play the legendary rhythms that became emblematic of this epoch. This was a busy year for Cuban letters: Emilio Grenet published his *La música popular en Cuba*, José Lezama Lima his *Coloquio con Juan Ramón Jiménez*, Cintio Vitier his first poems, Ramiro Guerra his *Manual de historia de Cuba*, Herminio Portell Vilá his *Historia de Cuba en sus relaciones con los Estados Unidos y España*, Emilio Roig de Leuchsenring his *Martí en España* and Medardo Vitier his *Las ideas en Cuba*. Ramón Peón directed two popular musical features this year, both starring Rita Montaner: *Sucedió en La Habana* (It Happened in Havana) and *El romance del palmar* (Romance Under the Palms). This second one broke all attendance records.

The two films were produced by Peón's new company, PECUSA (Películas Cubanas, Sociedad Anónima), a production company intended to mass-produce films and whose studios were situated near the village of Punta Brava, on the property of an entrepreneur named Bustamante. The endeavor needed an investment of 300,000 pesos and was undertaken without any help from the state. By the time the studios closed in 1942, it had produced six films, but these first two were the most successful. The other recently completed studios, "Compañía Habana Industrial Cinematográfica" (CHIC), turned out *Ahora seremos felices* (Now We'll Be Happy), by American director William Nolte and starring Mexican singer Juan Arvizú and popular Puerto Rican vedette Mapy Cortés. The film featured the hit songs "Farolito" and "Ahora seremos felices," which are popular to this day. Max Tosquella proposed a well thought out project for creating a "Film City," which could eventually become a Caribbean Hollywood; it would incorporate within its perimeter the major studios turning out film in Cuba and would also receive government support. But not much came of it. "Cuba Sono Films" was created in 1938 by Cuban communists and was administered by Luis Álvarez Tabío and his cousin José Tabío. They produced "Noticiero Gráfico Sono Films," which turned out current event documentaries such as *Gran manifestación del 25 de septiembre de 1938 contra la ley de impuesto por el peaje y otras medidas arbitrarias* (Demonstration Against the New Toll Tax Law and Other Arbitrary Measures), *Toma de posesión del comité nacional del Partido Comunista* (Installation Ceremony for the Communist Party's National Committee), *Acto a Castelao* (Homage to Castelao), and *Llegada de los primeros combatientes internacionalistas de la guerra de España* (Arrival of the First International Brigades of the War in Spain). The magazine *Lente* began its monthly publication; it deals with film, theater, radio and music.

In 1939 celebrated Communist labor organizer Lázaro Peña founded the Confederation of Cuban Workers (CTC), social security laws were passed and the Tropicana nightclub opened its doors. Painter Wilfredo Lam's exhibition at the Pierre Gallery in Paris was a success, while Eduardo Zamacois prospered with his radio series *Traición, radio-novela*. Spaniard Jaime Salvador directed the last four films produced by PECUSA, *Mi tía de América* (My Aunt from America), *Estampas habaneras* (Images of Havana, also called *Chaflán en La Habana* because of the famous Mexican comic Chaflán's participation), *La última melodía* (The Last Melody) and *Cancionero cubano* (Cuban Songbook), these last three starring the duo of Garrido and Piñero. Ramón Peón directed *Una aventura peligrosa* (A Dangerous Adventure) with Aníbal de Mar, while the historical drama *Siboney* introduced Cuban moviegoers to Spanish director Juan Orol and "Rumba Queen" María Antonieta Pons. "Cuba Sono Films" produced a number of militant documentaries in 1939, including *Primero de mayo de 1939* (May Day Celebrations, 1939). Manuel Alonso began production of a sensationalist news series called *La noticia del día* (The Daily News), featuring items such as *El crimen de la descuartizada* (The Crime of the Torn and Quartered Woman), and Leo Aníbal Rubens directed *El caso de Margot García Maldonado* (The Case of Margot García Maldonado). Through their formal characteristics, films produced this decade reveal their origin in the popular theater plays and radio shows. First, the camera work is very static, as if the viewer were sitting in front of a stage where the action occurs. Second, their sets seem to be inspired by theater backdrops. Third, the characters are basically the same you would see in the theater or listen to on the radio: the "gallego," the "negrito," the mulatto woman, the Chinese vegetable vendor and the cop. Sometimes the whole cast unexpectedly broke into a song and dance routine, just like you would expect in most of Havana's playhouses.

By 1940 a new Constitution introduced many progressive social statutes. Supported by Left-wing parties, Fulgencio Batista won the elections and the Ministry of Education was created. Fernando Ortiz published *Contrapunteo cubano del tabaco y el azúcar*, a long essay that gives a social, economic and ethnographical history of the nation through the story of its two basic products: tobacco and sugar. Emilio Roig de Leuchsenring published *Habana, apuntes históricos*, a history of the capital city, and Félix Lizaso wrote his *Martí, místico del deber*, on the life and work of Cuba's national hero, José Martí. It was a busy year for music: Osvaldo

Farrés composed "Acércate más," Bobby Collazo wrote "Rumba matunga," Orlando de la Rosa wrote "Ya sé que es mentira" and Juan Bruno Tarraza "Penumbra." Chano Pozo built on his reputation as the best conga drum player in the land and legendary musician Arsenio Rodríguez first put together his band. Bandleader Machito and trumpet player Mario Bauzá introduced their Cuban sounds at several New York dance halls, where Cuban rhythms became *le dernier cri*. At CMQ radio station 1940 marked the golden age of the "controversias," a popular musical form where two opposing singers make up rhymed verses and hurl them against each other in an effort to outdo their rival in inventiveness, dexterity and artistry. Recognized "controversia" masters were two characters called "Clavelito" and "La Calandria."

In 1940 Ernesto Caparrós directed two feature films, *Prófugos* (The Fugitives), an adventure film starring Ramiro Gómez Kemp and Blanquita Amaro, and *Yo soy el héroe* (I'm the Hero), a comedy starring Federico Piñero. A beer company named "Polar" financed a short subject musical *Mis cinco hijos* (My Five Sons), also directed by Caparrós, while Jean Angelo directed another short titled *Embrujo del fandango* (The Charm of the Fandango), with Carmen Amaya. Max Tosquella and Sergio Miró directed the feature *La canción del regreso* (Song of Return), and the news documentary market became a battleground where Aurelio Lagunas Gómez's *Noticiario Nacional*, Manuel Alonso's *Noticiario CMQ–El Crisol* and the *Noticiario Royal News* vied for supremacy. "Cuba Sono Films" continued to produce documentaries; one of its films, *El desahucio* (The Eviction) obtained the contribution of several prestigious individuals in its production: directed by Luis Álvarez Tabío, the text was written by essayist Juan Marinello and the music by novelist-musicologist Alejo Carpentier. Its social theme is highly charged, and it employed the construction workers that at the time were building National Route 20.

On February 4, 1941, the Commander in Chief of the army, colonel Pedraza, attempted a coup d'état against Batista. The colonel gave Batista 24 hours to leave the Presidential Palace. Batista calmly drove to the Columbia barracks and ended the insurrection. When presented with a list of the rebels, the president, without reading the names, tore it in small pieces and left. Pedraza was reassigned to the army reserves and no one was punished. Mario García Menocal, who at 75 years old was being considered to run for the presidency, died on September 7th, throwing the political scene into confusion. War was declared on the Axis powers and the University Theater was founded and put under the direction of Austrian national Ludwig Schajowicz, who opened its doors with *Antigone*. Caridad Bravo Adams wrote *La novela del aire* episodes which aired daily under the direction of Luis Manuel Martínez Casado, while Rita Montaner starred in humorous sketches on the radio, portraying a character called "La chismosa" (the gossip-monger). José Lezama Lima published his book of poems *Enemigo rumor*, and Virgilio Piñera *Las furias*. The feature film *Manuel García, rey de los campos de Cuba* (Manuel García, King of the Cuban Countryside), a remake of the 1913 film that was subsequently serialized in radio episodes, was released this year but was immediately prohibited by the authorities. Several Soviet films were also proscribed, but Cuban communists distributed them through their own company, Blue Ribbon Films. The magazine *Cinema* organized a competition to choose the best directors, actors, producers and other participants in Cuban cinema, and grant them a Cuban "Oscar" of sorts, and Salvador Cancio directed *La Quinta columna* (The Fifth Column).

In 1942 Batista made a formal visit to the United States and *La tremenda corte*, a serialized comedy starring Leopoldo Fernández (Tres Patines), Mimi Cal, Aníbal de Mar and Adolfo Otero, thrived on the RHC–Cadena Azul radio waves. As Lino Novás Calvo published *La luna nona y otros cuentos*, Gonzalo Roig composed his "Fantasía cubana" and José Manuel Valdés Rodríguez began to teach a course at the University of Havana called "Cinematic Industry and Art in Our Times." Ernesto Caparrós directed the feature *Romance musical* (Musical Romance) and a short called *Ritmos de Cuba* (Cuban Rhythms) featuring the Casino de la Playa Orchestra. Enrique Bravo, Sr., filmed a documentary called *El caso de Oriente* (Oriente's Case).

In 1943 a national census gave Cuba a population of 4,778,583 inhabitants. Eduardo Chibás, a leader of the "Auténticos" (Cuban Revolutionary Party) began a series of radio shows that made him one of the most popular politicians in the country. Wilfredo Lam and René Portocarrero continued their successful exhibitions, as poets Cintio Vitier (*Sedienta cita*), Virgilio Piñera (*La isla en peso*) and Guillermo Villaronda (*Poemas a Walt Disney*) published significant works. In music, Osvaldo Farrés compuso "Toda una vida" and José Carbó Menéndez "Hablemos de los dos" while a young man named Benny Moré began to wander around Havana's seamy nightclubs and cafés trying to earn a living as a singer. He would soon become a national icon. This year Ernesto Caparrós directed the feature *Fantasmas del Caribe* (Caribbean Ghosts) with the collaboration of Alejo Carpentier, who wrote some of the dialogue. Another feature film, *La que se murió de amor: La niña de Guatemala o Martí en Guatemala* (Martí in Guatemala), directed by Jean Angelo, was banned by the censors because it did not proffer the appropriate reverence to Cuba's "Apostle." This exposition of Martí as a man of flesh and blood, as it were, doesn't seem unbefitting to the modern viewer. Such fetishization of national symbols calls to our attention the fabricated nature of symbols, particularly those that have become dependable icons of national heritage. Angelo also directed a musical short entitled *La flor de Yumurí* (Yumurí Flower), and Manuel Alonso, with the support of the Polar Beer Company, directed comic sketches performed by Garrido and Piñero that bore titles like *Cosas de Cuba* (Things Cuban), *Dos cubanos en la guerra* (Two Cubans in the War) and *Ratón de velorio* (Funeral Mouse). Alonso also directed the farcical full-length feature *Hitler soy yo* (I Am Hitler), with Adolfo Otero playing a buffoonesque Führer. Cuba Sono Films continued in its production of militant films, putting out *Azúcar amargo* (Bitter Sugar) and *La lucha del pueblo cubano contra el nazismo* (The Struggle of the Cuban People Against Nazism). The Photography Club of Cuba organized the first contest for amateur filmmakers. Among the competing entries were *La vida de los peces* (The Life of the Fish), *Varadero* (Varadero Beach) and the first-prize-winning *Desfile gimnástico femenino* (Feminine Gymnastics Pageant).

In 1944 the candidate for the "Auténtico" Party, Ramón Grau San Martín, won the election for president over Batista's handpicked candidate, Carlos Saladriga. Batista left for the United States, although his popularity among the armed forces was still significant. Cuban culture continued to flourish from every perspective: Juan José Arrom published *Historia de la literatura dramática cubana*, Jorge Mañach published *Historia y estilo*, while Dámaso Pérez Prado began seasoning Cuban music with jazz spices, a formula that would make him the original "Mambo King." Gonzalo Roig continued exploring Afro-Cuban rhythms with his composition "Fantasía sobre dos temas del cocuyé," and René Touzet wrote the popular ballad "Tu felicidad." On CMQ radio station, Carlos Badías and María Valero (a refugee from the Spanish Civil War) performed Félix B. Caignet's serialized radio-novel *El precio de una vida*, a must-listen for a large portion of the island's population. José Lezama Lima and José Rodríguez Feo began publication of *Orígenes*, one of the most important and influential cultural magazines in the history of Latin America, while Alejo Carpentier published his book of stories *Viaje a la semilla*, technically, a work profoundly influenced by Carpentier's experiences in the film industry. José Tabío, working with Cuba Sono Films, directed *Sur de Batabanó* (South of Batabanó), while Víctor Reyes directed the short *El diablo fugitivo* (Fugitive Devil).

Nineteen-forty-five brought havoc to the island. In the absence of a strong figure heading the government, Rolando Masferrer founded the Socialist Revolutionary Movement, Emilio Tro founded the Insurgent

Revolutionary Union, and they unleashed a veritable gang war in the streets of the cities. Harold Gramatges founded the Municipal Conservatory of Havana Orchestra. Rosendo Ruiz, Jr., one of the big names in the musical movement called "feeling," wrote the ballad "Hasta mañana vida mía," and Rita Montaner was proclaimed the "Queen of the Radio." It was a scanty film production year. Amateur filmmaker and medical doctor Roberto Machado filmed *Caleidoscopio* (Kaleidoscope), a film that was placed among the three best of the year by the critics. The other two were *La dama duende* (The Goblin) by Argentine director Luis Saslavsky and *María Candelaria* by Mexican director Emilio Fernández.

By 1946 chaos was generalized, gangs ruled the streets and corruption was rampant. One of Cuba's most revered items, the large diamond that was incrusted in Havana's capitol building, was stolen. Fernando Ortiz published his influential essay *El engaño de las razas*, Alejo Carpentier his sociological study *La música en Cuba*, and Lydia Cabrera spoke at Wilfredo Lam's exposition of his recent paintings in Havana. Amid the turmoil, Cuban composers flourished: Bobby Collazo wrote "La última noche," and César Portillo de la Luz wrote "Contigo en la distancia." Both were "feeling" ballads called "boleros," the likes of which made Olga Guillot famous this year with her special voice and dramatic singing style. Augustinians founded the Santo Tomás de Villanueva Catholic University in 1946. Cuban studios began to work with foreign producers and personnel. Juan Orol directed *El amor de mi bohío* (Love in a Country Home), starring Yadira Jiménez, and *Embrujo antillano* (Caribbean Enchantment) starring María Antonieta Pons and Blanquita Amaro. Both were co-produced with Mexico. Argentine director Roberto Ratti put out *Como tú ninguna* (There's No One Like You) with a cast of Spanish and Chilean actors. Another feature filmed this year was *Sed de amor* (Thirst for Love), directed by François Betancourt. A half-hour long pirate adventure by the title of *El tesoro sangriento* (Bloody Treasure) was directed by amateur filmmaker Plácido González Gómez, while in Santiago de Cuba, César and Mario Cruz Barrios founded the Productora Nacional de Películas dedicated to the making of animated cartoons. Cuba Sono Films continued production with films such as *Un héroe del pueblo español* (A Hero of the Spanish People) and a series of documentaries.

Gang war was teeming all over Havana in 1947, and the terror distinctively targeted the university. Chibás attacked the Grau San Martín government directly in his popular radio show, and an expedition led by radicals to invade the Dominican Republic failed before it got started. Sugar production hit 5.7 million tons. A new station, Radio Reloj, hit the airwaves; the concept was that of a talking clock with news flashes. The

University of Oriente, the easternmost region of the island, was founded, and Chano Pozo played with Dizzy Gillespie in New York, introducing Cuban rhythms into be-bop. Osvaldo Farrés composed another big hit, "Without You," and Isolina Carrillo joined the ranks of "feeling" composers with her "Dos gardenias." The magazine *Prometeo*, organized by Francisco Morín, was first published this year; it endeavored to develop a more sophisticated theater ambience in Cuba. Such sophistication was beginning to show, with plays like Carlos Felipe's *El Chino*. In film, co-productions were beginning to be the norm. Directed by Adolfo Fernández Bustamante, the film *María la O* was a Mexican co-production based on the homonym musical by Ernesto Lecuona, and Raúl Medina directed the feature film *Oye esta canción* (Listen to My Song). In 1947, a young film enthusiast named Tomás Gutiérrez Alea, the man who would later become Cuba's most celebrated director, put out two innocuous productions on 8 mm film: *La caperucita roja* (Little Red Riding Hood) and *Un fakir* (A Fakir). In Santiago de Cuba, Mario Cruz Barrios put together the first 35-mm color animated cartoon produced on the island, a film called *El hijo de la ciencia* (The Son of Science), while José Manuel Valdés Rodríguez directed *La guerra gaucha* (The Gauchos' War), a historical war epic.

The political scene heated up in 1948 as labor leader Jesús Menéndez was murdered and Carlos Prío Socarrás, the official candidate, took the presidential election from the very popular Edy Chibás. To some it seemed that everybody in Cuba was attentively listening on CMQ radio to Félix B. Caignet's serialized novel *El derecho de nacer*, starring María Valero and Carlos Badías. It was calculated that more than two million Cubans listened to all 314 episodes. Alicia Alonso founded the dance company that would eventually become the National Ballet of Cuba. Rafael Lay became the director of the ever more famous Orquesta Aragón, while César Portillo composed the ballad "Delirio," Eliseo Grenet "El sitierito," and Gonzalo Roig "Prisionera de mi amor," three of the island's all-time favorite songs. After apparently involving himself with criminal elements in New York, extraordinary trumpet player Chano Pozo was murdered in Harlem. Central University in Las Villas was inaugurated this year, while in film, *El ángel caído* was a new co-production with Mexico directed by Juan J. Ortega. *Los funerales de Jesús Menéndez* (Jesús Menéndez's Funeral), directed by José Tabío and Francisco Altuna, would be Cuba Sono Films' last production.

In 1949 more labor leaders were murdered and Chibás was ordered off the airwaves. While a tribunal investigated the embezzlement of monies committed during the Grau San Martín administration, the Senate approved a core of Constitutional guarantees. Alejo Carpentier published the groundbreaking novel *El reino de este mundo*, whose preface became one of the philosophical foundations of the new literary movement "Lo real maravilloso," and José Lezama Lima published *La fijeza*, an influential book of poems. Jaime Sant Andrews directed a film adaptation of Cirilo Villaverde's (1838–1882) novel *Cecilia Valdés* (1882) in which the practice of *blanqueamento,* or whitening the black slaves through the coupling of black slave women with white men, served as a framework for the story line. Luis Bayón Herrera directed the first Cuban-Argentine co-production, a film called *A La Habana me voy* (I'm Off to Havana), a comedy starring Blanquita Amaro and Tito Lusiardo; *We Were Strangers*, directed by John Huston, was an American film whose plot develops in Cuba. In this movie, China Valdez (Jennifer Jones) vows to avenge her brother's death (he's been murdered by Cuban authorities) and joins a resistance group with the ultimate plan to assassinate the Cuban president and his dignitaries. The University of Havana inaugurated its new Department of Film, under the direction of José Manuel Valdés Rodríguez. The 1950s opened with Sarumba, a feature filmed in Cuba by Marion Gering and starring Michael Whaling and Doris Dowling.

Speaking in general terms of the decade of the '50s, we can say that by this time Cuba's enthusiasm for film was at an apex. La Rampa Avenue, an elegant thoroughfare that descends from the hills of El Vedado to the clear waters of the Caribbean, had a good number of exclusive nightclubs where the beautiful (and not-so-beautiful) people gathered at night to flaunt their habits of conspicuous consumption. In 1947 a superb new movie theater was built in the upper part of La Rampa, where it intersects with "L" street, called Radio Centro (today its name has been changed to "Yara"). It shared its building with radio station CMQ's headquarters. Again on La Rampa but closer to the sea, the Arte y Cinema La Rampa was built in 1955, a state-of-the-art movie house. The posh El Vedado neighborhood had other classy cinemas, like the Cine Teatro on Línea Street (today it's called Mella), the Chaplin (today the headquarters of the Cinemateca de Cuba) and the Acapulco on 26th Street.

These were not your run-of-the-mill corner movie theaters. They were designed and built in the modern "International Style," which featured straight lines, pure volumes, large windowpanes, fluid interior spaces and sober ornamentation. In the '50s the architectural models gave preference to the screen, with the stage area losing prominence or being left out altogether.

One of the most innovative movie theaters in Havana was the Multicine, right in the middle of the exclusive San Rafael shopping district. Built in 1938 in the art deco style, it was reformed in 1948 to include two cinemas with a common vestibule under one roof.

All these movie theaters were air-conditioned and featured comfortable seats, excellent acoustics and delicate indirect lighting. Some of them became specialized, with the Rex Cinema, for example, offering only international newsreels, cartoons and documentaries. The Duplex offered musical and melodramatic features, favorites of the elegant ladies who had gone shopping at the well-stocked and trendy "Fin de Siglo" or "El Encanto" fashion stores on San Rafael Avenue.

Havana was also the home of three drive-ins, called auto-cines in Cuba. The first built was Autocine Vento, in 1955, and it was shortly followed by La Novia del Mediodía and Tarará, where suburban yuppies could go watch films without having to drive into downtown Havana, negotiate the heavy traffic and look for a parking spot.

There was also a proliferation of "neighborhood cinemas" in the '50s, buildings of large proportions that were less elegant, charged less for the ticket, and could accommodate large numbers of film enthusiasts from the more humble barrios of the city. Such halls went by names like Consulado, Egido, Neptuno, Rancho Boyeros and Marianao, and they were decorated, if not with the elegance and good taste of their classier counterparts, with ancient Egyptian or Mayan motifs that accentuated the myth and mystery of the moviegoing experience. And this experience was very different from the experience afforded by the more expensive venues. At neighborhood cinemas one could expect just about anything: once in the anonymous darkness, people would smoke, chew gum, talk, scream, and the stereotypical neighborhood punk would seek to add to the magic by simulating a lovemaking session in the back row.

The interior of the island offered a different perspective. Provincial capitals had older, converted theaters where movies were shown. These large, outdated buildings did not offer optimum conditions for the projection of film, and their viewing was often uncomfortable. In the interior of the provinces it was more difficult to watch a film, and when a film came along, it was often shown in locales intended for very different purposes, be they store houses or garages, where the locals would have to bring their own chairs with them.

But nothing could stop the progress of film throughout the island. By the end of the '50s, film had all but done away with native live theater. Let us now look at a year-by-year description of this important decade.

In 1950 President Carlos Prío Socarrás inaugurated Cuba's first television network, Canal 4, directed by Gaspar Pumarejo, while CMQ followed suit with Canal 6. Celia Cruz, a singer who would become legendary in and out of Cuba, recorded her first song with the Sonora Matancera Orchestra, "Cao cao maní picao," written by José Carbó Menéndez, and trumpet player Félix Chapotín became director of Arsenio Rodríguez's orchestra. Labrador Ruiz published his novel *La sangre hambrienta* this year, and Wilfredo Lam painted *Rumor de la tierra* and *Umbral*.

This was a record year for Cuban film, with fourteen feature length films shot. Manolo Alonso directed *Siete muertes a plazo fijo* (Seven Deaths on the Installment Plan), a suspense yarn starring Raquel Revuelta and Alejandro Lugo. José González Prieto shot *Cuando las mujeres mandan* (When Women Rule), a comedy starring Alberto Garrido and Federico Piñero and the two Mexican comedians Tin Tan and Marcelo. Raúl Medina directed *Rincón criollo* (Country Corner), which was based on a radio show directed by José Rodríguez Díaz and starred Paco Alfonso and Blanquita Amaro, and *Qué suerte tiene el cubano* (Cubans Are Very Lucky). Manuel de la Pedrosa directed four films: *Música, mujeres y piratas* (Music, Women and Pirates), *Cuba canta y baila* (Cuba Sings and Dances), *Hotel de muchachas* (Hotel for Girls) and *Príncipe de contrabando* (Contraband Prince). Jaime Sant Andrews remained active, directing *Ídolo de multitudes* (An Idol for the Multitudes) and *Paraíso robado* (Stolen Paradise). Other feature films included *Escuela de modelos* (School for Models), by José Fernández and starring Garrido and Piñero; *La rumba en televisión* (The Rumba on Television), by Evelia Joffre; *Una gitana en La Habana* (A Gypsy in Havana) by Juan José Martínez Casado, and *Sin otro apellido* (Without Another Surname) by Sergio Miró. Media mogul Manolo Alonso distributed toys to 32,000 children in front of his executive offices in Havana with the collaboration of the First Lady, while Tomás Gutiérrez Alea turned out another 8 mm film named *Una confusión cotidiana* (Daily Confusion).

In 1951, popular radio personality and politician Eduardo Chibás shot himself through the brain in front of the microphone during a live radio show. His funeral would turn into one of the most massive demonstrations ever witnessed in Cuba. As Fulgencio Batista prepared his coup d'état, Olga Guillot was proclaimed "The Queen of Radio." In 1951 René Portocarrero painted *Homenaje a Trinidad*, Pérez Prado scored his first big hit with the song "Rico mambo" and Enrique Jorrín composed the popular tune "Engañadora." In film, Ramón Peón directed the melodrama *La renegada* (The Renegade), starring Yadira Jiménez, Gina Cabrera and Rita Montaner. Zacarías Gómez Urquiza directed a film version of *El derecho de nacer* (The Right to Life), an adaptation of Félix B. Caignet's popular serialized novel for radio, and José Fernández released his film *Nudismo en el trópico; bajo el cielo habanero* (Nudism in the Tropics; Under the Havana Sun).

In 1952, as the Orthodox Party prepared to launch their candidate, Roberto Agramonte, for the presidential elections, Fulgencio Batista seized power in a coup d'état on March 10th. Sugar production surpassed the 7 million ton mark and diplomatic ties with the Soviet Union were severed. As Fernando Ortiz worked on the five volumes of his *Instrumentos de la música afro-cubana*, Cintio Vitier published the anthology *Cincuenta años de poesía cubana* and Aida Diestro put together a quartet made up of some of the best voices in contemporary Cuba: Elena Burke, Moraima Secada, Omara Portuondo and Haydée Portuondo. Ramón Peón directed two feature-length films this year: *La única* (The Only One) and *Honor y gloria, o la vida de Ramón Ortiz* (Honor and Glory: The Life of Ramón Ortiz). The Batista government organized its own executive commission for the film industry (CEPLIC) which would underwrite films such as *Misión al norte de Seúl, o cuando la tarde muere* (Mission to the North of Seoul), directed by Juan José Martínez Casado. Even the Ministry of Information became involved in filmmaking, releasing the short *Los zapaticos de rosa* (The Little Pink Shoes), directed by Jean Angelo. Other feature films include *San rifle, o ladrón en seda* (Saint Rifle, or The Thief in Silk) by Salvador Planells, *La mentira* (The Lie), a Mexican production of a Caridad Bravo Adams novel, directed by Juan J. Ortega, and *Bella, la salvaje* (Bella, the Savage), a Spanish co-production directed by Roberto Rey. Cuba then had 530 movie halls equipped with 35-mm projection apparatus and 164 movie halls with 16-mm equipment; 541 films were distributed in the country that year. In the small town of San Antonio de los Baños, in Havana Province, a group of amateur filmmakers shot *El invasor marciano* (The Martian Invader), and a group of courses dedicated to film was included in the curriculum at the University of Oriente.

In 1953, student demonstrations against the government caused the University of Havana to be shut. Fidel Castro attacked the Moncada Barracks on July 26. Alejo Carpentier added to his reputation as novelist with *Los pasos perdidos*, and José Lezama Lima published his essays *Analecta del reloj*. Benny Moré put together his legendary band, "Banda Gigante," and became the main attraction in Havana's night scene. In film, Manuel Alonso directed the bucolic melodrama *Casta de roble* (Caste of Oak), Juan J. Ortega directed *Piel canela* (Cinnamon Skin) starring Spanish actress Sarita Montiel, and Agustín Delgado directed *Ángeles de la calle* (Street Angels) based on Félix B. Caignet's serial novel for radio. Gilberto Martínez Solares shot *Mulata* (Mulato Woman) starring Ninón Sevilla and Pedro Armendáriz. Juan J. Ortega also shot *Me gustan todas*, or *Hotel tropical* (All Women Please Me), starring Mexican comedian Resortes and Cuban actress Rosita Fornés, while Tulio Demicheli directed *Más fuerte que el amor* (Stronger Than Love), starring Jorge Mistral and Miroslava. Juan Orol tested the waters with the off-color *Sandra, la mujer de fuego*

(Sandra, Woman of Fire), starring the spectacular Rosa Carmina, while the San Antonio de los Baños amateurs produced *La herencia maldita* (Bewitched Inheritance) with a minimal production budget.

In 1954, Catholic activist José Antonio Echeverría was elected president of the Federation of University Students (FEU) and promptly began accusing the government of rigging the elections. The only presidential candidate, Fulgencio Batista, was elected president to no one's surprise. Repression hardened, to the point where Antonio Núñez Jiménez's monumental work *Geografía de Cuba* was seized and destroyed to the last copy. Astoundingly, the government created a national institute of culture while at the same time it was destroying books. The Little Theater of Havana, under the auspices of the United States Embassy, began to offer shows in English, while Lydia Cabrera published her major work, *El monte*. In spite of the tribulations that the José Martí topic brought its makers, the film *La rosa blanca* (The White Rose), by Mexican director Emilio Fernández, managed to reach fifth place in the charts behind four Hollywood films. Mexican co-productions were the norm this year, with *La mujer que se vendió* (The Woman Who Sold Herself) by director Agustín P. Delgado and based on a Félix B. Caignet novel for radio, *El sindicato del crimen* or *La antesala de la muerte* (The Crime Syndicate) by Juan Orol, *Un extraño en la escalera* (A Stranger on the Staircase) by Tulio Demicheli, *Frente al pecado de ayer* (Face to Face with Yesterday's Sin) by Juan J. Ortega, and *Golpe de Suerte* (Stroke of Luck) by Spanish poet Manuel Altolaguirre.

By 1955, student demonstrations against the government were relentless. American Vice-President Richard Nixon visited Cuba and a general amnesty freed Fidel Castro and other revolutionaries. In literature, father Ángel Gaztelu published the poems *Gradual de laúdes*, while Dulce María Loynaz published her poems in *Obra lírica* and Lydia Cabrera her book of proverbs *Refranes de negros viejos*. In film, Manuel Pedrosa directed the comedy *Tres bárbaros en un Jeep* (Three Punks in a Jeep), while Vicente Oroná shot *El tesoro de la Isla de Pinos* (Treasure Island), based on another radio novel by Félix B. Caignet. Miguel Morayta shot *La fuerza de los humildes* (The Strength of the Humble), produced by Félix B. Caignet, Juan Orol shot *La mesera del café del Puerto* (The Waitress from the Docks), René Cardona shot *Una gallega en La Habana* (A Galician Woman in Havana) and Fred Zinnemann began filming *The Old Man and the Sea*, based on Hemingway's novel. José Antonio Sarol filmed a social documentary called *Jocuma o el Cabo de San Antonio* (Jocuma or Cape St. Anthony), and Julio García Espinosa and Tomás Gutiérrez Alea directed *El Mégano*, evocative of the harsh conditions coal workers endure in the Zapata swamps, billed as the first neo-realist film produced in Cuba. Two new movie theaters were opened in Havana, La Rampa and Cine-club Visión, and one in Camagüey, Cine Club Estudiantil. Of the 506 films distributed this year, 49 percent came from the U.S., while of the 130 titles in Spanish, 90 came from Mexico. The ten highest grossing films were all from Hollywood. This year, Manuel Alonso was made president of the Instituto Nacional de Fomento de la Industria Cinematográfica Cubana.

In a 1956 attack on the Goicuría Barracks in Matanzas, the army annihilated the attackers, members of the Directorio Estudiantil. Constitutional guarantees were suspended and the press censored. There was an attempt on the life of Colonel Antonio Blanco Rico, head of the Military Intelligence Service, and the police killed a number of political activists that had taken refuge at the Haitian embassy. Frank Pais led an insurrection in Santiago de Cuba to facilitate the arrival of Castro and a force from the 26th of July Movement. A number of avant-garde plays were performed in Havana, and Virgilio Piñera published *Cuentos fríos*, Alejo Carpentier *El acoso*, and Enrique Serpa *La trampa*. The magazine *Orígenes* ceased to publish as René Portocarrero painted his famous *Catedral* and the *Noticiero Oriental* news service was opened in the eastern part of the island. Gonzalo Roig composed his well-known "bolero" "Estás en mí," and famed singer Roberto Faz formed his own band. In film, as Mario Barral was directing *De espaldas* (With My Back Turned), several Mexican co-productions were put on the screens: the musical *Tropicana*, directed by Juan J. Ortega, the melodramas *No me olvides nunca* (Never Forget Me), also directed by Juan J. Ortega and starring Rosita Fornés, and *Y si ella volviera* (If Only She Returned), by Vicente Oroná. American productions in Cuba include *Affair in Havana* by Laslo Benedek, *The Sharkfighters* by Jerry Hopper and *The Big Boodle* by Richard Wilson. This year 521 films were shown in Cuba, 49 percent of which were from the U.S. and 16 percent from Mexico. Havana's influential Cardinal Arteaga recommended the continued development of the national film industry, as the Centro Católico de Orientación Cinematográfica edited the magazine *Guía cinematográfica*, Acción Católica Cubana published *Mundo cinematográfico* and 18 Catholic "cine-clubs" operated throughout the island.

By 1957 the war between the Batista government and the insurgents heated up. The rebels launched a successful attack on the La Plata barracks, while Herbert Matthews published proof that the rebel army was alive and well in the Sierra Maestra mountains. In an attack on the Presidential Palace staged by the Directorio Revolucionario, Antonio Echeverría was killed. An expeditionary rebel force sailing in the yacht *Corinthia* landed in Cuba and was obliterated by the army. At El Uvero a guerrilla force obtained a victory over the army; Frank Pais was murdered and a mutiny by the navy at the Cienfuegos naval base was put down by the army and the air force. In literature, José Lezama Lima published *La expresión americana*, Cintio Vitier *La luz del imposible*, and Lydia Cabrera *Anagó, Vocabulario lucumí*. At radio station CMQ the serialized novels still reigned. *Pobre juventud* by Félix B. Caignet and *Luis Dragón, conquistador del espacio* by Armando Couto were the most popular. There were two Mexican co-productions this year: *Yambaó*, directed by Alfredo Crevenna and starring Ninón Sevilla, and *Un farol en la ventana* (A Light in the Window). Manuel de la Pedrosa directed *Olé Cuba*, and another American production was filmed in Cuba, *Mr. Pharaoh and Cleopatra*. In an interesting publicity short, the Siboney Agency filmed *Una chica en apuros* (A Girl's Dilemma) starring Ricardo Montalbán and Zsa Zsa Gabor and intended for the American market. The authorities proscribed a radical documentary filmed by Antonio Sarol, *Cooperativa del hambre* (Hunger, Inc.). Of the 509 films shown throughout the island, 49 percent were American, 16 percent Mexican, 10 percent British, 9 percent Italian, 8 percent French and 4 percent Spanish.

By 1958 Batista was quickly losing his hold on the nation. Another armed group landed to join the fray, the March 13 Movement led by Faure Chomón. Radio Rebelde, Castro's voice in the mountains, began transmissions from the Sierra Maestra. In view of the rebels' hold on the eastern section of the island, Batista made one last great effort to defeat them, but the large force he sent against them was defeated at El Jigüe. Rebel forces advanced on Santiago, Cuba's second city, and came west towards Havana. When the central city of Santa Clara fell to the rebels after bitter fighting, Batista decided to abandon the island. In literature, one can point out *Teatro cubano contemporáneo* by Natividad González Freire, *Lo cubano en la poesía* by Cintio Vitier, *Tratados en La Habana* by José Lezama Lima, *Idea de la estilística* by Roberto Fernández Retamar, and the poems of Eliseo Diego, *Por los extraños pueblos*. This last year before the revolution was quite productive for the film industry. Manuel Samaniego Conde shot *La vuelta a Cuba en 80 minutos* (Around Cuba in 80 Minutes), Manuel Barral *Con el deseo en los dedos* (Desire at the Tip of My Fingers), and Manuel Mur Oti directed the Spanish co-production *Una chica de Chicago* or *¡Qué mujer!* (A Girl from Chicago, or What a Woman!). Other Mexican co-productions are *Thaimi, la hija del pescador* (Thaimi, the Fisherman's Daughter), risqué adventures by Juan Orol, *Santo contra el cerebro del mal* (Santo Versus the Evil Brain), and *Santo contra hombres infernales* (Santo Versus Infernal Men). Amateur filmmaker Antonio Cernuda shot the musical short *Ritmo en tránsito* (Rhythm in Transit) and Rita Montaner, "La única," died this year. On the first day of January of the following year, 1959, rebel forces rolled into Havana. Everything would change dramatically.

In total, there were some eighty full-length films produced in Cuba before the 1959 revolution, well-known films like *La Virgen de la Caridad* (The Virgin of Charity) and *Romance del palmar* (Romance under the Palms) by Ramón Peón. As we have seen, the Cuban film industry was periodically revitalized by the constant influx of foreign film producers who came to work in Havana; many Cuban actors also worked outside Cuba, mainly in Mexico and Argentina, contributing thus to the perennial regeneration. Well-known Cuban musicians like Ernesto Lecuona, Bola de Nieve and Rita Montaner made important contributions to the film industries of other countries.

In March of 1959, only three months after the triumph of the revolution, the state mandated the creation of the Instituto Cubano del Arte y la Industria Cinematográficos (ICAIC). (The army's film department, operating from January to March of 1959, was the precursor of what would become the ICAIC.) In 1960 the government expropriated the large film distribution and production concerns, a move that was completed in 1965 with the expropriation of the movie theaters themselves. By this year the ICAIC was the sole proprietor of every commercial and production aspect of the film industry on the island. Now the Instituto's objective was feasible: to create a new cinema ideology, starting from scratch, as well as to change and overhaul the character of the product. This included the transformation of the system of production, exploitation and consumption of film. The ICAIC's charge also included the formation of a film public that would be capable of appreciating and even demanding a new art form, one that reflected its condition and that was free from the colonizing imagery of the capitalist world. Alfredo Guevara, the first president of the ICAIC, has stated that the ICAIC had only one objective: authenticity; one enemy: conformity; and an ethics that was founded on the respect for the spectators' dignity and sensibility ("Habla Guevara," in *INRA*, vol. 1, year 1, Havana, 1960). Once these ideals are put into practice, the profit motive ceases to have validity, replaced by the film's social, political and artistic merits. True to the Marxist ideas that nurtured the revolution, Cuban artists, filmmakers included, were to create a new work of art for the spectator, and a new spectator for the work of art. Without this interaction it would be impossible to create the new culture advocated by the revolutionary authorities. This interface between film and its consumer is necessary not only to elevate the social and political awareness of the public, but also to make of film a medium for revolutionary mass education.

For the first time, the Cuban public would have access to an art form that reflected its social conflicts and its collective experience and in the very least attempted to capture its complex daily realities. The medium would no longer be a vehicle for evading reality, but one to recapture the true image of that reality and of a history lost among the romantic songs, the palm trees and soft breezes of 1940s and '50s productions. A daunting task indeed, to make films for all the people, not just one class, to place on screen the common objectives of the people of Cuba, and to construct an image of a whole nation, overcoming the separations of class and race that had divided it in the past. Documentary production was seen as the short path to achieving the above-mentioned goals. Already by the end of 1959 ICAIC was launching into a steady production of documentaries. Of these, the most accomplished is Julio García Espinosa's *Sexto aniversario* (Sixth Anniversary); it deals with the 400,000 guajiros (peasants) who showed up in Havana (July 26, 1959) to celebrate the sixth anniversary of the Moncada barracks attack. Another important documentary this year was Humberto Arenal's *Construcciones rurales* (Rural Constructions), which deals with the construction projects that the new government was undertaking in the rural areas of the country.

In this revolutionary spirit, the years 1961 and 1962 saw a genuine crusade of film education in the rural regions of the country. Using the "Cinemóvil" units, roving film projection corps reached every corner of the island. These units carried their own electricity generators and transported their 16 mm projectors and other equipment on trucks, though sometimes burro-drawn carts and boats were needed to reach the most remote places. Shows were held under large, circus-type tents when the weather was foul, under palm trees when it was not, and in the ten years that they operated, they brought film to thousands of people who had never seen a film before.

In general, there were bigger obstacles than the rivers and mountains: the public's tastes had to be changed. The magazine *Cine Cubano* began publication in 1960 with just such a task. The Cinemateca de Cuba, owner of one of the largest collections of Latin American films in the world, also had a key role in bringing the best of Latin American cinema to the provinces. In addition, several texts dealing with film theory were published and weekly television programs brought film criticism to the masses.

The creation of a true national cinema, in a country whose industry was in many ways dependent on foreign traditions, was complicated, to say the least. Other national cinematic industries were studied to see what elements could be extracted from them and critically assimilated into the fledgling Cuban industry, elements that could be integrated or grafted onto the Cuban project without clashing with its ideals of creating a faithful voice for the national discourse. Thus, independent U.S. filmmakers, the French Nouvelle Vague, Italian Neo-realism and the Soviet classics came under Cuban scrutiny.

The objectives were manifest, but the path to reach them was not. Some things were clear: ICAIC would do its best to steer clear of bureaucratic entanglements and work within a dynamic, creative atmosphere that would preclude personal clashes over procedure or ideology. Political and ideological coherence was, therefore, the requisite and the necessity. In a Cuban film, the moviegoer would see an image free from prejudices concerning the reality it aimed to capture, free from propaganda and the products of aesthetic virtuosity.

Some of the risks faced in ICAIC's project were of a human dimension. As with any industry in a socialist state, the Film Institute workers were paid by a state where employment is a right and thus were not subject to capitalist standards of production. Film production, then, was guaranteed without regard to commercial success, and as such, the perils of stagnation and inactivity were always a concern. But the human element was most important as well: ICAIC workers had to compensate for the lack of technical means with their creative imagination. The differences between the inspiration for a film and its actual production were disheartening at times and had to be overcome through last-minute improvisation. But the renowned Cuban resourcefulness and the help of foreign filmmakers like Theodor Christensen, Joris Ivens, Chris Marker, Roman Karmen and Cesare Zavattini facilitated ICAIC's success. By 1965, a coherent system of Marxist production and a new generation of filmmakers were making the dream of creating a national cinema a reality.

As was to be expected, the first directors to produce films in revolutionary Cuba were the ones who were working before 1959. Julio García Espinosa completed *Cuba baila* (Cuba Dances) in 1960, and this same year Tomás Gutiérrez Alea made *Historias de la Revolución* (Stories of the Revolution). The first one is a new type of musical; unlike those of the past, the humor and music function as a vehicle for social criticism directed at the lingering bourgeois attitudes in certain individuals. Because of its innovative approach to the musical tradition in Cuban cinema, *Cuba baila* marks the birth of a new type of film. The style of these two films is markedly Italian Neo-realist. Although it is true that both these directors studied at the Centro Sperimentale in Rome, and that this may be a contributing factor in the style, it is also true that Neo-realism was an ideal medium for what the Cubans were trying to do. Otello Martelli, cameraman for Rossellini in *Paisà*, participated in Gutiérrez Alea's film, undoubtedly contributing to its Neo-realist style. Cesare Zavattini's contributions to García Espinosa's second film, *El joven rebelde* (The Rebel Youth) reinforced this particular artistic direction in the early revolutionary cinema.

The Neo-realist influence on the first films of the revolution is also evident in the narrative structure of the films. This structure is episodic, with a number of apparently unrelated events woven together by their common theme. The employment of several foreign directors and technicians, as mentioned above, is of major importance in this regard. From 1961 to 1963 Cubans directed only two Cuban films. In addition, it may be said that in the early '60s only two films escape the amateurism inherent to inexperience: *Las doce sillas* (The Twelve Chairs) and *Cumbite*. On the other hand, the films turned out by foreign directors such as Uruguayan Ugo Ulive (*Crónica cubana*—Cuban Chronicles—1963), Frenchman Armand Gatti (*El otro Cristóbal*—The Other Christopher—1963) and Soviet Mikhail Kalatozov (*Soy Cuba*—I Am Cuba—1964) aimed to give a new perspective on Cuba through the psychological drama, through tragedies that endeavored to correct historical inaccuracies, and through fantastic satire and socialist epic. But their results were schematic at best, with a penchant for the exotic that reveals the foreign point of view behind the cameras.

On the ideological plane, 1961 was an important year. Amateur filmmaker Sabá Cabrera Infante requested ICAIC that his documentary, *P.M.*, be shown in movie theaters. The documentary was a short depiction of the nightlife around the Havana docks. ICAIC's Evaluation Commission rejected the request, claiming that it was devoid of revolutionary content, presenting reality without assessing or judging it. The decision filled many an intellectual with trepidation, proving to them what they suspected all along, that the revolution would become dogmatic, intolerant and repressive. The upshot was that Castro himself had to meet with writers and intellectuals, telling them that within the revolution everything was possible, outside of it nothing was possible. This fundamental principle in the cultural politics of the new regime clearly defined the creative space for the artist. Although it is true that some artists quit the revolution, most accepted or were amenable to its directives.

Following the first formative years, Cuban cinema began to tackle issues such as intimate psychological problems, the revolutionary struggle, the development of revolutionary conscience in the populace, and the condemnation of pre–1959 society. These later films still had some of the problems that come with inexperience. The most palpable of these were the stationary camera work and the uncomplicated, lineal story lines. Yet with time and the influence of the Nouvelle Vague and the Free Cinema schools, ICAIC would develop into a more dexterous and proficient filmmaking enterprise. The Nouvelle Vague influence is evident in the short fictions of noephite directors like Manuel Octavio Gómez, Humberto

Solás, Sergio Giral and Manuel Pérez. One example is Sergio Giral's *La jaula* (The Cage, 1964), the story of a woman who suffers from paranoid psychosis, a story told first from the husband's point of view and then, as a sort of counterpoint, from the woman's. Interestingly, the role of the psychiatrist is played by Tomás Gutiérrez Alea. Another is 20-year-old Humberto Solás and Oscar Valdés' *Minerva traduce el mar* (Minerva Translates the Sea, 1962), a film that enjoyed the unique collaboration of internationally acclaimed poet José Lezama Lima. In it, two dancers perform next to the sea, hovering around a bust of the goddess Minerva as Lezama Lima's impenetrable verses are heard in the background. Another collaboration by Solás and Valdés is *El retrato* (The Portrait, 1963), the story of a painter who discovers the image of a woman in an abandoned house. He decides to pursue her in an attempt to find inspiration through her, but his efforts are fruitless. A more skillful production is *El acoso* (The Pursuit), by Solás without Valdés, the story of one of the invaders from the Bay of Pigs who manages to escape the militias seeking such survivors. He kills a man, steals his clothes, rapes a woman, and walks off into the sunset, without direction and without a future.

Help from socialist countries was important during the first half of the '60s decade. Three co-productions with the Eastern Bloc are *Preludio 11* (Prelude 11), *Para quién baila La Habana* (For Whom Havana Dances) and *Soy Cuba* (I Am Cuba). *Preludio 11* features an East German director (Kurt Maetzig) with a script by Wolfgang Schreyer and José Soler Puig. It tells the story of the military preparations for the counterrevolutionary invasion of the Bay of Pigs. *Para quién baila La Habana* was made by Czechs, with Vladimir Cech directing and a script by Jan Prochazka and Onelio Jorge Cardoso. It is the story of two friends who had fought Batista and now must come to grips with the new state of affairs they've helped to bring into being. One seems at ease with the new society, while the other was not anticipating the extent to which things were changing. *Soy Cuba* is a four-part story showing diverse aspects of pre-revolutionary Cuban society. It has a Russian director (Mikhail Kalatozov) and the script is by Yevgeni Yevtushenko and Enrique Pineda Barnet. More than anything, these films give us the foreigner's conception of what Cuba was all about, and they did not prosper.

A first glimpse into what Cuban cinema might be able to offer in the future came with Humberto Solás' film *Manuela* (1966). On the face of it, the film doesn't offer anything we might call extraordinary: it is the story of a disillusioned young woman who joins the rebel army and falls for a guerrilla fighter. But with the untamed mountainous region as its setting and the wild, unobstructed, unrehearsed Cubanness of the protagonist

(Adela Legrá) as its focal point, the astounded moviegoer saw what a truly Cuban cinema could be like. Here we had an art form that could overcome restrictions imposed by foreign penchants and express itself in its own language. In short, this was the start of an aesthetics rooted in the soil of the land and the soul of the people.

Yet not everything was success in this second wave of ICAIC productions. The two other films produced in 1966 were not as accomplished. *Papeles son papeles* (It's Only Paper) by Fausto Canel promised much due to its interesting concept. It is the story of people who are somehow or other affected by the sudden change of currency operated by the Castro government in 1961. The disjointed story line, however, prevented the success of what could have been an interesting tale. On the other hand, *La muerte de un burócrata* (Death of a Bureaucrat), by Tomás Gutiérrez Alea, became an instant classic of the Cuban cinema.

The most successful Cuban film of all time (up to that point) was produced the following year, 1967. This is Julio García Espinosa's *Las aventuras de Juan Quin Quin* (The Adventures of Juan Quin Quin), a film that attracted 3.2 million viewers. It is the picaresque story of a young man who has to do many things in order to survive, from singer to bullfighter to guerrilla fighter and everything in between. Because of its wide-ranging story, it has had widespread appeal, addressing the tastes of an extensive public while at the same time achieving a high degree of self-parody. In other words, the public is constantly reminded that this is fiction: "The elaborate inappropriateness of the parodies in *Juan Quin Quin*, succeeds in effectively calling attention to the artificiality and formulaic quality of the cinematic codes at work in each case ... the viewer [is] constantly aware of cinematic illusion as patterned convention" (Anna Marie Taylor, "Imperfect Cinema, Brecht and the *Adventures of Juan Quin Quin*," in *Jump Cut*, #20).

So the period after 1959 brought a marked change of perspectives to Cuban film. Perhaps the genre with which Cubans have had the most success is the documentary. Under the military's auspices, early documentaries such as Tomás Gutiérrez Alea's *Esta tierra nuestra* (This Is Our Land) and Julio García Espinosa's *La vivienda* (The House) were produced. And the main thrust of the ICAIC, as mentioned above, became the search for a mode of expression that was genuinely Cuban: Cuban film had to be a symptom of national aspirations and ideals, not an imitation of what was being done in other larger, more influential countries. Thus, the ICAIC produced and promoted an industry that not only yielded full-length feature films, documentaries and cartoons, but also expedited the general population's access to foreign films, supported the Film Archives of Cuba

(Cinemateca de Cuba), brought film to rural communities through the "Cinemóviles" (film on wheels) and sponsored international film festivals. ICAIC has also been the reference point for artists at the vanguard of Cuban culture, such as the Grupo de Experimentación Sonora — precursor of the Nueva Trova — and musicians like Leo Brower, Silvio Rodríguez and Pablo Milanés.

The 1960s are what is called the Golden Age of Cuban cinema, a period characterized by the search for that genuine expression of "Cubanness," by the sense of exploration and discovery and the recovery of the national past. Films like *La primera carga al machete* (The First Machete Charge) by Manuel Octavio Gómez (1969) are initial attempts at this recovery. But the zenith of Cuban film production in this decade is unquestionably Gutiérrez Alea's *Memorias del subdesarrollo* (Memories of Underdevelopment), completed in 1968, the same year Humberto Solás released his *Lucía*, an incisive look at the Cuban woman throughout history. This period was also marked by the curiosity expressed by many well-known film producers around the world with regards to Cuba, to the extent that a good number of them traveled to the island to become acquainted with the new directions the industry was taking there: people like Cesare Zavattini, Joris Ivens, Roman Karmen, Chris Marker, Jerzy Hoffman and many more.

In the 1970s the Cuban film industry had to cope with the increasing disillusionment of sectors of the population with the direction the revolution was taking. The growing economic problems and the regime's increased ideological intolerance put a damper on the energies that had characterized the 1960s. In spite of the advancing difficulties, the industry remained loyal to its perceived mission, and in 1978 it released the controversial *Un día de noviembre* (A Day in November), by Humberto Solás, a film that illustrated the languishing stagnation of the protagonist in an environment of want and hardship. Gutiérrez Alea's 1978 *Los sobrevivientes* (The Survivors) is a description of the adversities suffered by people who refuse to accept the changes brought forth by the Communist regime, while his *La última cena* (The Last Supper) (1976), falls back on a historical theme of slavery. Pastor Vega's 1979 production *Retrato de Teresa* (Portrait of Teresa) explores the issue of the changing roles of men and women and the institution of marriage, while Manuel Octavio Gómez's *Ustedes tienen la palabra* (It's Up to You) (1973) deals with the new judicial system. Other films that had a considerable impact in the 1970s are *Los días del agua* (Days of Water) (1971) by Manuel Octavio Gómez, an exploration of the myths and superstitions that account for much of the Cuban psychological makeup, and Manuel Pérez's 1973 film *El hombre de Maisinicú* (The Man from Maisinicú), dealing with the government's war against counter revolutionaries.

Humberto Solás' polemical *Cecilia* (1981) ushered in the 1980s. This film represents a profound questioning of the national identity and the role played in it by racial mixing. Solás' 1985 production *Un hombre de éxito* (A Successful Man) and the 1989 features *Papeles secundarios* (Secondary Roles) by Orlando Rojas, *La bella del Alhambra* (The Alhambra Beauty) by Enrique Pineda Barnet, and *¡Plaff!, o demasiado miedo a la vida* (Plaff! or Too Afraid of Life) by Juan Carlos Tabío round out the most successful films of the '80s.

Se permuta (For Trade) (1983), a description of the vicissitudes suffered by people who want to change their place of residence in contemporary Havana, was Juan Carlos Tabío's first production; in *Lejanía* (Parting of the Ways) (1985), Jesús Gómez tackles the thorny theme of exile. With clear references to the present, Humberto Solás' *Amada* (1984) presents a negative past whose elements parallel the contemporary state of affairs in Cuba. There is a marked shift towards psychological introspection in the '80s, with films like *Clandestinos* (Living Dangerously), *La vida en rosa* (La vie en rose), *Otra mujer* (Another Woman) and *Venir al mundo* (Coming to the World).

The '80s also produced several outstanding documentaries, like Enrique Colina's *Vecinos* (Neighbors) and *Estética* (Aesthetics), while in animation the work of Juan Padrón shows outstanding quality. The International School for Film and Television, located in San Antonio de los Baños, began to produce an increasing number of films, many of which were put out by amateur directors.

The '90s opened with a looming uncertainty for the future occasioned by the collapse of the Soviet bloc, Cuban Communism's safety net. Cuban film production plummeted, and ICAIC is forced to seek financing elsewhere: the government cannot pay. The quality remained in spite of the difficulties, and a new and sometimes thorny relationship with the ideologues of the revolution began. Daniel Díaz Torres' *Alicia en el pueblo de las maravillas* (Alice in Wondertown) (1991) is a scathing criticism of contemporary Cuban society that was banned from theaters soon after its debut, while Julio García Espinosa's *Reina y Rey* (Queen and King) (1994) explores the ideological and in many ways artificial divide that separates Cubans. Perhaps the best known and most successful of Cuban films, *Fresa y chocolate,* (1993) by Gutiérrez Alea and Juan Carlos Tabío, portrays the many difficulties attending the life of a homosexual in the new, intolerant, revolutionary society. Other important films of the '90s are *Hello, Hemingway* (1990, Fernando Pérez), *María Antonia* (1990, Sergio Giral), *Mascaró* (1992, Constante Diego), and *El siglo de las luces* (The Enlightenment, 1992, Solás). Gerardo Chijona's *Adorables mentiras* (Adorable Lies,

1992) deals with the ethical ramifications of having to survive by any means necessary in the new Cuba, and *El encanto del regreso* (Joyful Return, 1991), by Oscar Alcalde, explores the psychological subtleties of exile and return. In 1995 the fruitful cooperation between Gutiérrez Alea and Tabío gave us *Guantanamera*, a funny look at the bizarre vicissitudes of bureaucracy in the "Special Period" of post–Soviet poverty on the island.

In general terms, Cuban film in the '90s was characterized by a new independence from government officialdom, a new perspective that produced a fresh and disquieting look at Cuban society and the results of its revolutionary program. The decade was also characterized by an exploration of the poetical potential inherent to films: this would result in a drive to adapt existing literary texts (novels, short stories, theater) in order to facilitate this inquiry. The first few years of the new millennium brought films that looked much like those of the past decade. But the future of Cuban cinema, like the future of the nation itself, is keeping its directions veiled in secret.

Many film experts would most likely agree that Cuban film, under the guidance of the Revolutionary establishment, has become the preferred technology through which Cubans and foreigners alike can imagine an improved nation and a better revolution. Two major innovations must be emphasized when speaking of post–1959 film: the use of a popular discourse that reaches the masses straightforwardly, and the setting of its narratives within the urgent historical context of the nation. This appeal to the masses has not only permitted a wide dissemination of film to the people, but also allowed the shifting social, economic and historical configuration of society to be understood by the great majority of viewers. The film medium, as technology, does not by itself produce mechanisms for imagination or change, yet content is undoubtedly the most important element in it. In Cuban film, the underlying premise of content is political consciousness. It was the resultant shift in social and economic affinities after 1959 that eventually produced the particularly Cuban grid for imagining a community and determined content in national film. Revolutionary cinema, then, must be thought of as a conscious political project because it supports the state as it seeks to actualize the transformation of political, social and economic structures. But Cuban film also surprises for its individual appeal. It becomes evident that revolutionary cinema also contains a political "unconscious" component, that is to say, it is in many ways emotive and constituted on the individual level, conforming to a project of identity formation. Socialist, revolutionary unconscious may be thought of as the individual's everyday practice of socialism in an anonymous, quiet, automatic way. For the revolutionary government, film is vital in this regard, as it aims to create an image of Cuban society, of the socialist community to be consumed and appropriated by the masses, an image that underscores and stimulates the constitution of the revolutionary community. This image is critical, as societies, especially those on utopian missions, are distinguished by the manner in which they are imagined.

The particular style of Cuban film, then, as formed in the last 40 years, has been configured in the culturally and historically specific context of the Revolution. On the other hand, an in-depth assessment of the political theories on which the Cuban revolution is based must take into account the ways these have been inscribed in the cinema through codes and symbols.

The Films

A veces miro mi vida (Sometimes I Look Back on My Life) Orlando Rojas / ICAIC, 1981, color, 79 min.

A documentary biography of Harry Belafonte, narrated by Belafonte himself. From the beginning it is clear that it is a romanticized story of a man portrayed as an artistic freedom-fighter of sorts, one who placed his life and career magnanimously at the service of his race's progress. Unfortunately, after viewing this film many a Cuban moviegoer might have come out of the theater believing this ordinary singer to be another Martin Luther King.

El abuelo Cheno y otras historias (Grandpa Chano and Other Stories) Juan Carlos Rulfo / Centro de Captación Cinematográfica (CCC) de México–Escuela Internacional de Cine y T.V. de San Antonio de los Baños de Cuba–Instituto Mexicano de Cinematografía–Secretaría de Cultura del Gobierno del Estado de Jalisco–Universidad de Guadalajara, Mexico, 1995, color, 30 min. *Music:* Gerardo Tamez. *Cast:* Juan Cobián, Cirilo Gallardo, Juan Gallardo, Ramón García, Mariano Michel, José Nava Palacios, Octavio Nava, Doña Esperanza Paz, Don Jesús Ramírez "El Molitón," Doña Consuelo Reyes and Pablo G. Zamora (all playing themselves).

This documentary follows a young man as he sets off for a small town where his grandfather had lived; he wants to know the circumstances of the old man's death. He gets more than he bargained for, as the town elders not only reveal how his grandfather died, but tell the story of the town and its inhabitants; in short, they reveal how it all "used to be" and how much life has changed in the present.

Acerca de un personaje que unos llaman San Lázaro y otros llaman Babalú (All About a Character Some Call Saint Lazarus and Others Call Babalú) Octavio Cortázar / ICAIC, 1968, B&W, 18 min. *Music:* Raúl Gómez.

This documentary shows scenes that were shot on December 17, the date of the San Lázaro festivities. Because many Cubans of African descent regard the saint as their divinity "Babalú Ayé," the thrust of this short film is to show how religious syncretism has produced unique forms of worship on the island. The camera follows worshippers as they trek up to "El rincón," site of a popular congregation of Babalú believers.

Adorables mentiras (Adorable Lies) Gerardo Chijona / ICAIC-TVE (Televisión Española), 1992, color, 108 min. *Music:* Edesio Alejandro. *Cast:* Mirta Ibarra, Luis Alberto García, Jr., Isabel Santos, Thais Valdés.

Adorables mentiras

Top: Mirta Ibarra (*left*), Luis Alberto García, Jr. (*center*) and Isabel Santos (*right*) try to sort out the confusing roles they are supposed to be playing in Gerard Chijona's directorial debut *Adorables mentiras*. *Bottom left:* Flora (Thais Valdés) shows her husband Jorge Luis (Luis Alberto García) one of the many reasons why he doesn't have to look elsewhere for love. (ICAIC) *Bottom right:* Sissy (Isabel Santos) and Jorge Luis (Luis Alberto García) make the audience believe that they are husband and wife. We later learn that they are only role playing. (ICAIC)

A promising young screenwriter begins an affair with a woman who dreams of becoming the star of his next film. As the two become absorbed in their affair, their lives become a sort of fantasy film that in the end will never be made. This film is the story of two unsuccessful individuals who create fictional personae for themselves in order to escape the sadness and pessimism of their daily lives. They weave a web of charming little lies to brighten their otherwise dreary existence, thus crafting an intricate and uncertain love story that straddles that fine line between fiction and reality.

Affair in Havana Laslo Benedek / Allied Artists–Dudley Pictures International Corporation of Cuba, 1957, B&W, 71 min. *Writing credits:* from a story by Janet Green. *Music:* Ernest Gold. *Cast:* John Cassavetes, Raymond Burr, Sara Shane, Lilia Lazo, Sergio Peta, Celia Cruz, José Antonio Rivero and Miguel Ángel Blanco.

The very attractive wife of a crippled plantation owner has a lover who styles himself a songwriter and works in a piano bar in Havana. The two lovebirds make plans to elope together, and all would have gone right for them, except that greed gets in the way. As she is getting ready to leave him, her husband announces that he has only a few months to live, and that when he dies he will leave his wife a $20 million inheritance. Unable to resist the cash, the unfaithful wife decides to hang around until the old man's demise, but as the months come and go and the poor cripple is still hanging on to dear life, the restless chick decides to act. At the first chance she pushes her husband into the swimming pool, wheelchair and all, and after feigning much grief and sorrow she gets her hands on the dough. But wait, a household servant is very suspicious, and is not wise enough to hide his suspicions from the rich and unscrupulous widow. So she disposes of the servant also. But it seems that there is a surplus of suspicious servants still hanging around, so another of the deceased's servants, unable to stand for this crime against his master, avenges him by killing the faithless wife. The lover returns to his piano bar to mull over what could have been. The shots of a beautiful and affluent pre–Castro Havana and a young Celia Cruz are worth the price of the ticket.

Algo más que una medalla (Something More Than Just a Medal) Rogelio París / ICAIC, 1982, color, 96 min. *Music:* Leo Brouwer.

A panoramic overview of the most important events that took place during the XIV Central American and Caribbean Games, celebrated in Havana. The focus is on the athlete as a full person, human beings giving the best of themselves in the struggle to gain victory.

Director Rogelio París Ramírez was born in Havana in 1936. He studied law and advertising, and he has worked on television for many years. He began his film career with the feature *Nosotros la música* (q.v.) in 1964.

Alicia en el pueblo de las maravillas (Alice in Wondertown) Daniel Díaz Torres / ICAIC, 1991, color, 90 min. *Music:* Frank Delgado. *Cast:* Thais Valdés, Carlos Cruz, Idalmis Del Risco, Reinaldo Miravalles, Raúl Pomares, Alberto Pujols and Alina Rodríguez.

In this landmark, scathingly satirical film about the society created by Castro's revolution, the most outrageous situations are seen as normal by most of the inhabitants of Wondertown (Maravillas), a sarcastic proxy for Cuba. But one citizen, Alicia, makes a great effort to make sense of what is happening around her from the moment she enters the scene. This film by Daniel Díaz Torres combines irrationality, humor and terror in order to reflect the indoctrination, intimidation, and sundry absolutisms that are the daily bread in Cuban society. Labeled as counterrevolutionary trash financed by spies and traitors, it was banned by the authorities after the first showing in Havana.

Director Daniel Díaz Torres was born in Havana in 1948. He participated as a volunteer in the revolutionary government's campaign to wipe out illiteracy in the Escambray region in 1961, and in 1968 he joined ICAIC. He was mostly a film critic, publishing his columns in *Cine Cubano* and other publications such as *Granma* and *Bohemia*. He graduated from Havana University in 1978 with a degree in political science, and he is still active in film criticism.

El alma trémula y sola (The Lonely and Quivering Soul) Tulio Raggi / ICAIC, 1983, color, 7 min. 30 sec. *Animation:* Pepín Rodríguez and Alfredo Rodríguez. *Music:* Juan Márquez.

A short cartoon that focuses on an episode in the life of national hero José Martí. During his sojourn in New York, Martí had occasion to see the Spanish dancer "La Bella Otero" perform. Martí was the son of Spaniards (his mother from the Canary Islands, his father from Valencia), so his beef was not against Spain per se, but with the unjust system imposed by Spain on his native Cuba. Being also a great admirer of women, the presence of the beautiful Spanish dancer in New York brought him thoughts of anguish and loneliness. He was alone in a cold, gray and hostile environment while life proceeded in a normal fashion all around him. The dancer reminded him of better times and better days, of loved ones left behind in the struggle to free his nation.

Alsino y el cóndor (Alsino and the Condor) Miguel Littín / ICAIC–CRFC–Latinamerican Film–NFI, 1982, color, 89 min. *Music:* Leo Brouwer. *Cast:* Dean Stockwell, Alan Esquivel, Carmen Bunster, Alejandro Parodi, Delia Casanova, Marta Lorena Pérez, Reinaldo Miravalles, Marcelo Gaete, Jan Kees De Roy and Luz Amparo Gutiérrez.

The Alsino in question is a boy of about 11 who lives in a remote area of Central America at the height of the civil war. When a U.S. military advisor arrives at his village and sets up shop with a contingent of troops, Alsino's life begins to change. He tries as best he can to be a child in spite of the circumstances surrounding him, climbing trees, looking through his grandfather's belongings for clues to the past, and trying to fly like a condor. But it becomes increasingly difficult, especially after hurting himself subsequent to an attempt at flight. Alsino is introduced to the "American way of life," taking his first alcoholic drink, going to a brothel, and being taken on a helicopter ride by the American. After getting a firsthand taste of the soldiers' cruelties, Alsino and his community side firmly with the leftist forces. A very badly made, fragmentary film, superficial and outwardly political, unscrupulous in its depictions of events and in its toeing the party line. Many parts just don't make sense, and the others make one feel one is being preached at.

Amada Humberto Solás and Nelson Rodríguez / ICAIC, 1984, color, 105 min. *Writing credits:* based on the novel *La esfinge* by Miguel de Carrión. *Music:* Leo Brouwer. *Cast:* Eslinda Núñez, César Évora, Silvia Planas, Andrés Hernández, Gerardo Riverón, Mónica Guffanti, Georgina Almanza, Elio Mesa and Fela Jar.

The movie is set in Havana in 1914, the early years of the republic. Amada is a young woman belonging to the bourgeois class who falls in love with her cousin Marcial. Marcial is a rebel who attempts to take Amada away from that insincere and artificial social milieu, characterized by unfaithful husbands, treacherous liaisons and profitable political connections (her own father is in politics and has a extra-marital affair). He will not succeed, though, in pulling her away from her world. At the end of the film a glimmer of hope for the future appears, as people take to the streets in the anti-hunger demonstrations of 28 August 1928.

Amor en campo minado (Love in a Minefield) Pastor Vega / ICAIC, 1987, color, 100 min. *Cast:* Daisy Granados, Adolfo Llauradó, Omar Valdés and Lillian Rentería.

A leftist writer finds himself in quite a bit of trouble after the president of his country is deposed and a military dictatorship is set up. He suspects it's only a matter of time before they come to pick him up in a military Jeep and make him disappear. He seeks refuge in a friend's house, where his wife comes to visit him. He and his wife have a terrible argument there, and the quarrel adds to the writer's sense of frustration and insecurity. The film attempts to show the human side of political tragedy, it stresses the emotional price that committed individuals have to pay for their courageous stance against injustice.

Amor vertical (*Vertical Love*) Arturo Sotto Díaz / ICAIC–Pandora Cinema, 1997, color, 100 min. *Music:* Hernán López Nusa. *Cast:* Jorge Perugorria, Silvia Águila, Susana Pérez, Manuel Porto, Aramis Delgado, Vicente Revuelta, Paula Ali, Ileana Wilson, Rolando Brito, Ildefonso Tamayo, Rubén Pérez, Adriana Sánchez Estupiñán.

French producer Pandora cooperated with ICAIC in this sex comedy about the amazing difficulties that Cuban couples have when they want to consummate their love. This difficulty has to do with the stifling housing shortage suffered in Havana, a problem for which young architecture student Estela, played by Silvia Águila, thinks she has a solution. With her plan utterly rejected by the bureaucracy, a dejected Estela bungles a suicide attempt and ends up in a hospital where she meets male nurse Ernesto. In spite of the hilarious cynicism with which Ernesto faces reality, Estela takes a liking to him and brings him home for dinner, where he outrages everyone present.

There comes a time when the physical attraction they feel for each other needs to be fulfilled, but where? In their explorations of Havana they find a room in a crumbling structure that, incredibly, is free from squatters. As they begin to make love, the intensity of their passion brings down the house — literally — as the ceiling collapses on them. The search next takes them to an elevator, where they attempt lovemaking in a standing position (vertical love). Then they try their luck in the outskirts, next to a river under a bridge. This approach doesn't work out either, as local bureaucrats arrive with a summons: their hastily-constructed shack (love nest) under the bridge lacks the proper government permit. As was perhaps expected from the beginning, Estela and Ernesto ultimately fall in love.

Adult humor and sexual situations apart, the filmmaker has delved into the psychology of his main characters with a skill that is excitingly fertile, intuitive, and very subtle. A crisply graphic background of real places in Havana leads one to expect the exploitation of humorous situations at the expense of depth of characterization. Yet he has subtly superimposed and intruded a subjective account of the interior boredom, loneliness and emotional exhaustion of two dejected young people trying to survive in their psychologically stultifying milieu.

Aquella larga noche (That Long Night) Enrique Pineda Barnet / ICAIC, 1979, color, 102 min. *Cast:* Raquel Revuelta, María Eugenia García, Roberto Bertrand, José R. Marcos, Juan Palacios, Patricio Wood, Salvador Wood, Armando Bianchi and Enrique Almirante.

Lidia Doce and Cloromida Acosta joined Castro's guerrilla army as secret messengers for Fidel and Che Guevara. They were captured and tortured by a Batista commander named Ventura. The long night of torture they endured gives the movie its title.

Arte del pueblo (Art of the People) Oscar L. Valdés / ICAIC, 1974, color, 17 min. *Music:* Juan Márquez.

This documentary is set on a block in Havana's Juanelo neighborhood. The members of the local Committee for the Defense of the Revolution and the neighbors, led by painter Antonia Eiriz, make papier-mâché objects. The film not only shows that typical Havana residents are endowed with much artistic talent, but also that the feared watchdogs of the neighborhood Committees are just lovable art providers.

Asalto al amanecer (Dawn Assault) Miguel Torres / ICAIC, 1988, color, 60 min. *Cast:* Julio Alberto Casanova, Manuel Porto, Raúl Pomares, Rolando Brito, Rudy Mora, Ángel Toraño.

A one-hour reconstruction of the period between the historic battles of "La Plata" and "El Uvero," which took place respectively in January and May of 1957, during the civil war that would eventually bring Castro to power in 1959.

La ausencia (Absence) Alberto Roldán / ICAIC, 1968, B&W, 70 min. *Music:* Fabio Landa. *Cast:* Eduardo Moure, Miguel Navarro, Sergio Corrieri, Helmo Hernández, Irma Alfonso, Florencio Escudero, Carlos Gili, Isabel Moreno and Luis Alberto García.

During a delicate surgical operation, a man remembers the past: rebels attacked the army's Moncada Barracks on 26 July 1953 and the students began a series of acts of civil disobedience. This further reminds him of his love affair with a young woman who happened to be a rebel fighter with the Algerian National Liberation Front (FLN). He remembers suffering from amnesia, being wounded, and indirectly contributing to the death of a comrade.

Director Alberto Roldán was born in Havana in 1933. He studied theater, music, advertising and television, and before joining ICAIC he had worked on the radio and television. He has gone into exile.

Una aventura de Elpidio Valdés (An Elpidio Valdés Adventure) Juan Padrón / ICAIC, 1974, color, 6 min. 40 sec. *Music:* Lucas de la Guardia.

Juan Padrón had been a successful comic-strip artist before starting his collaboration with ICAIC in 1972. He brought with him his most successful character, one who had fascinated his young readers since 1970 in the magazine *Pionero*, Elpidio Valdés. This is the first in a series of cartoons starring the popular character, and although in general it lacks fluidity, this flaw is more than made up by the vigor and charisma of the character, which has captivated audiences young and old since its inception.

In this story, Spanish forces capture Elpidio's horse Palmiche. The courageous Elpidio manages to rescue his steed in spite of Spanish general Resóplez's efforts to prevent it. The cartoon places Elpidio in the historical context of the Cuban War of Independence, helping kids understand certain details of their nation's past.

Juan Padrón was born in Cárdenas, Matanzas, Cuba, in 1947. He is the most accomplished cartoonist in the history of the island. Before his success with Elpidio Valdés, he had worked as a comic-strip artist in the magazine supplements *El sable*, *La chicharra* and *DDT*.

Las aventuras de Juan Quin Quin (*The Adventures of Juan Quin Quin*) Julio García Espinosa / ICAIC, 1967, B&W, 113 min. *Writing credits:* Samuel Feijoo (from his novel *Juan Quin Quin en el pueblo Mocho*), Julio García Espinosa. *Music:* Leo Brouwer, Luis Gómez, Manuel Castillo. *Cast:* Julio Martínez: Juan Quin Quin. Erdwin Fernández: Jachero. Adelaida Raymat: Teresa. *Supporting cast:* Enrique Santiesteban, Agustín Campos, Blanca Contreras.

Set in pre-revolutionary Cuba and based on the novel *Juan Quin Quin en el Pueblo Mocho* by Samuel Feijoo, *The Adventures of Juan Quin Quin* is a comedy-adventure film that is a virtual directory of the classic film genres and styles. Part comedy, part western, war film, musical, gangster movie, slapstick, part Buñuel-style anti-clerical satire and Soviet social-realist tract, this hodgepodge tells the story of a Cuban "guajiro" (farmer) who wants to "make it" in the world. Together with girlfriend Teresa and buddy Jachero, our hero Juan goes through a series of adventures in which he is, alternately, a bullfighter, an altar boy, a circus hand and a revolutionary. In recounting the hero's adventures, García Espinosa forges a travesty of the traditional film genres, using their own conventions in order to undermine them from within. Do not look for memorable acting or profound social statements here: this is a film about film, with the main characters moving through cinematic genres more so than through physical time and space. The movie features Leo Brouwer as musical director.

Director Julio García Espinosa Romero was born in Havana in 1926. He studied cinematography at the Centro Sperimentale di Cinematografia in Rome, and before 1959 worked on several features as an assistant. He formed the Revolutionary Army's film section and was later one of the founders of the ICAIC, becoming its president in 1982; on the national level, he was named Vice-Minister of Culture in 1978.

Az én XX. Századom (My Twentieth Century) Ildikó Enyedi / ICAIC– Budapest Filmstúdió– Friedlander – Hamburger Filmbüro, 1989, B&W, 104 min. *Music:* Lázló Vidovszky. *Cast:* Péter Andorai, Gyula Kéry, Paulus Manker, Gábor Máté, Andrej Schwartz, Dorota Segda, Sándor Téri and Oleg Yankovsky.

This film was done by ICAIC in cooperation with Hungary and Germany. It is the story of Lili and Dora, twin sisters born late in the nineteenth century and separated at a very early age. They'll take very different paths in life: while one becomes an upper-class adventuress, the other becomes a revolutionary. In the lives and vital outlook of these two girls, the director seems to be aiming to represent every dichotomy possible the twentieth century has to offer, from capitalism vs. communism, individualism vs. socialism, to future vs. past and everything in between. Even Thomas Edison shows up on screen, the ultimate symbol of the 20th century, trying to prove to the world that his inventions are not foolish but will improve the lives of people in a very significant manner.

Another character is a psychologist who is trying to unravel the mysteries of the human mind through the observation of animals. He'll get involved with the twins to his regret and his own unraveling. In the end the psychologist will appear in a space full of mirrors where he can see the two girls ... sort of, and a voice, perhaps his alter-ego or an alien presence, talks to him (has Enyedi been reading Borges?).

The black and white photography and the mono sound (Buñuel redux?) give the film an aura of 1930s charm, while the camera work achieves the political / fairy-tale story texture that the director goes to pains to build. The film has all the bizarre elements needed to result in a dud, like the bomb in one of the twins' hands that never goes off.

As Hal Hinson sees it, "Enyedi tells her story in a rush of lamebrain enthusiasm; it gushes out in a disorderly torrent of metaphors, half-chewed feminist notions, dream fragments and historical allusions that sometimes make sense, sometimes not. Initially this heady mix of encyclopedic wit and magical surrealism is fascinating, even if it is something of a muddle" (Hal Hinson, *The Washington Post*, 4 Jan. 1991).

Tibor Mahe's camerawork gives the images a dreamlike quality, especially at the beginning of the film when we are taken (1880) to Menlo Park to see a display of Edison's inventions, or when the girls visit their dead mother riding on a donkey. Later on the girls (who are named for Lillian and Dorothy Gish) will be kidnapped and raised separately. As the new century dawns, one sister's life revolves around high society escapades while the other has become a revolutionary. The storyline, in spite of the inventive concept and haunting imagery, becomes a predictable jumble of exotic metaphors. Logical organization is sacrificed for the sake of inventiveness, a schema that doesn't work out in the end.

Azúcar amarga (Bitter Sugar) León Ichaso / Azúcar Films–First Look Pictures, 1996, B&W, 120 min. *Writing credits:* from a story by Pelayo García and León Ichaso. *Music:* José Ferro, Jr., and Víctor Víctor. *Cast:* René Laván, Mayte Vilán, Miguel Gutiérrez, Larry Villanueva, Luis Celeiro, Teresa Rojas, Orestes Matacena, Caridad Ravelo, Jorge Pupo, Víctor Checo, Augusto Feria and Félix Germán.

This is perhaps the most accomplished film made by Cubans outside of Cuba. "Set in contemporary Havana, 'Bitter Sugar' is a stark, revealing look at contemporary Cuba through the eyes of a fiercely pro–Castro youth (René Laván) suddenly disillusioned with the government in which he has invested his faith. The wonderful performances, the clever direction, and the energizing cinematography and editing maximize the limitations of this low-budget black-and-white film" (Jon Silberg, Boxoffice Online Reviews, Oct. 1996).

The diverse tragedies that color the film are made possible by the calamitous situation in which the country finds itself after the fall of the Soviet bloc. The complete devaluation of the Cuban peso has made possession of dollars or other "hard currencies" a must. Foreigners now effectively own the island and its inhabitants. Cubans, no matter what their education or background, dream of one day getting a job at a foreigners-only hotel; women who prostitute themselves to foreigners can make more in one night than their husbands can in one year. Scarcity is everywhere, and the only other option left the islanders is to flee to Miami. "Hope" and "future" are words in a dictionary that nobody understands. In this moral moonscape, Gustavo, an ardently pro–Castro youth, becomes involved with a beautiful young woman (Mayte Vilán) who ends up sleeping with a wealthy Italian investor, a man who can treat her to good meals and pretty jewelry. Gustavo's father, a prominent psychiatrist, is lucky to obtain a job playing the piano at a tourist-only bar, a situation whose tragically humorous nature does not escape the elder gentleman. The most problematic character is Gustavo's brother, who hangs out with a group of rock and roll–loving youths that is constantly being harassed by the police. As the ultimate act of defiance, the brother and his friends inject themselves with AIDS-tainted blood, a piece of melodrama that would seem a bit overdone, except that it is based on a true incident. Every situation presented in the film is emblematic of a national problem. The scarcity of every product needed to lead an endurable existence, the intolerance of anything that does not conform to the party line, the dissatisfaction of the general population, the dreams of escaping the island, everything gets exposure in this story, filmed in the Dominican Republic with exiled Cuban actors. The one scene that leaves one in consternation for its unexpected abruptness is the final one, where a distraught Gustavo attempts to assassinate Castro himself.

"Seething with bitterness toward Castro, viewed as a betrayer of his people, Ichaso calls for nothing less than the dictator's overthrow.... It doesn't hurt that 'Bitter Sugar's' stars are talented and spectacular-looking" (Kevin Thomas, *L.A. Times*, 22 Nov. 1996).

Bajo presión (Under Pressure) Víctor Casaus / ICAIC, 1989, color, 100 min. *Cast:* René de la Cruz, Isabel Moreno, José A. Rodríguez, Broselianda Hernández, Orlando Casín and Alberto Pujols.

A worker is injured at his job in a factory in a suburb of Havana in 1974. The incident brings to the fore a number of blunders and mistakes on the part of the factory managers as well as errors in judgement on the part of the worker.

Barroco (Baroque) Paul Leduc / ICAIC–Sociedad Estatal Quinto Centenario–Ópalo Films, 1992, color, 111 min. *Writing credits:* Alejo Carpentier, adapted from his novel by the same name. *Cast:* Dominique Abel, María Luisa Alcalá, Brígida Alexander, Natividad Andreu, Norma Angélica, Viviana Barnatan, Maria Blancoa, Eva Cano, Isabel Casado, Paloma Casado, Raquel Casali, Lina Cruz, Olga Dicuasa, Lorena Díaz Núñez, Yalitza García, Anastasia González, Josefina González, Patricia Guerrero, Anastasia Guzmán, Ernesto Gómez Cruz, Leticia Huijara, Nina Johanson, Ziwta Kerlow, Del Carmen Madrid, Cristina Marsillach, Isabelle Martinez, Irene Martínez, Francisca Miranda, Ángela Molina, Teresa Nieves, Alberto Pedro, Dolores Pedro, Ottavia Piccolo, Francisco Rabal, Adela Riguer, Manuela Rodríguez, Kala Ruiz, Isabel Sobrino, Roberto Sosa, Ana Sáez, Margarita Sánchez, Marisa Tejada, Tania Texidor, Ana María Tomé, Julia Torres, Alicia Téllez, Elvira Valdés, Carmen Varela and Luisa Ávila.

A Cuban–Spanish–Mexican co-production, this film presents a series of images, music and sounds which convey us through the musical history of Latin America without any narrative sequence. The film persistently asks the question, ¿De dónde son los cantantes? (Where are the singers from?), the title of a popular Cuban song. The film is, then, a sonorous journey through Cuba, Spain and Mexico from pre–Columbian times to the present. It was produced for the occasion of the 500th anniversary of the Spanish discovery and conquest of America.

El bautizo (The Baptism) Roberto Fandiño / ICAIC, 1967, B&W, 101 min. *Cast:* Dulce Velazco and Eloísa Álvarez Guedes.

On the Isle of Youth (formerly Isle of Pines, the Cuban archipelago's second-largest island) lives Pablo, an old lobster fisherman. Pablo gets the news that his grandson Rolandito is sick, and that a physician must be called immediately. The family goes forth in search of the doctor, eventually found by Pablo. But Rosa, the grandmother, is adamant that the illness is due to the fact that little Rolandito was never baptized. In order to cure him, she insists, a priest must be found and the baptism carried out as soon as possible. The film speaks to a very curious social phenomenon: as fewer and fewer Cuban families baptized their newly born children after the triumph of the Revolution, many people began to attribute all types of diseases and bad luck to this detachment from the Church.

Before Night Falls Julian Schnabel / El Mar Pictures–Grandview Pictures, 2000, color, 125 min. *Writing Credits:* Reynaldo Arenas (from his memoirs), Cunningham O'Keefe, Lázaro Gómez Carriles and Julian Schnabel. *Music:* Laurie Anderson, Carter Burwell and Lou Reed. *Cast:* Javier Bardem, Olivier Martínez, Andrea Di Stefano, Johnny Depp, Sean Penn, Michael Wincott, Olatz López Garmendia, Vito Maria Schnabel, Najwa Nimri, Héctor Babenco, Jerzy Skolimowski, Sebastián Silva, Maurice Compte and Robert Downey, Jr.

Although technically not a "Cuban" film (made in the U.S. by Americans), its Cuban theme merits its inclusion in this book. In many respects, this film is remarkable. It traces the life of Cuban writer Reynaldo Arenas from childhood in Cuba to his early death in New York in 1990.

As a young boy up in Oriente province in the 1940s, he is brought up by his mother, grandmother and aunts, with an occasional intervention by the authoritarian grandfather. The scene is one of extreme poverty, as we see the young Reynaldo playing with an empty bottle in what looks like an empty grave. Although the details of his birth are not given, one scene has his mother returning to the paternal home with baby Reynaldo in her arms, "living proof of her failure." The brief appearance by his father, a cigar-smoking man who hands little Reynaldo two pesos, is punctuated by his mother's violent, stone-throwing rejection of her former lover, suggesting a less-than-amiable breakup between them.

From the beginning we see that the boy's talent will bring him much pain. When his grade-school teacher visits the home to inform the family of Reynaldo's beautiful poetry, the grandfather becomes enraged, pounds on the table and goes to the back yard to cut down trees where the boy had carved some of his verses.

Reynaldo decides to leave this abusive environment and joins the revolutionaries who in 1959 toppled the Batista dictatorship. This move seems to be the best at first, as he is able to indulge his appetites in relative freedom, even with soldiers who join them at a nighttime seaside sex-fest. But things change quickly in a revolution, and Reynaldo soon finds himself in prison. Escaping the island during the Mariel boatlift of 1980, he ends up in New York, where he seems disconnected and completely alone save for his companion, the doorman Lázaro. It is Lázaro who in the end suffocates the AIDS-stricken Reynaldo with a plastic bag and stops his suffering.

In spite of the chaotic and energetic world that surrounds him, in spite of the political repression that hounds him in Cuba and the dynamic city (New York) where he eventually ends up, we get a strong sense that Arenas is alone, absolutely alone in a world that doesn't understand him and that will always seem incomprehensible to him. As we begin to see the world through Arenas' eyes, we tend to put aside the political context in which his life evolves and interpret his surroundings through the emotions they evoke. This seems to be the director's purpose, as he accompanies key scenes with poetical language and melancholic music.

The images contribute as well to the emotional impact of the film (we must remember that Schnabel is a painter). A garish party in a dilapidated convent church contains sex, music, dance, alcohol, and a hot air balloon that rises through where the roof used to be on its way to Florida. In a visual depiction of the futility of expecting anything better from life, Arenas lies dying of AIDS while scenes of a decaying Havana interplay with scenes from New York City as he repeats the word "cerrado, cerrado," closed, everything is closed to him. Scenes like that of a hot air balloon rising from a hole in a church roof would suggest that Schnabel has been influenced by "Magical Realism" writers such as Cuban poet-novelist José Lezama Lima (who, by the way, is one of the characters in the film). On another note, the actors' English is quite awkward, making intelligibility a tedious procedure.

For all the film's achievements, the inner mystery of the man remains lodged behind the splendid figure and the wistful dark eyes of señor Bardem. But if the film has the power to encourage people to read Arenas' work, it will have accomplished an important tangential objective, for it is in his work that the face of Arenas, the man, becomes very clear.

La bella del Alhambra (The Beauty of the Alhambra) Enrique Pineda Barnet / ICAIC-TVE (Televisión Española), 1989, color, 108 min. *Writing credits:* Miguel Barnet, from his novel *La canción de Rachel*. *Music:* Gonzalo Romeu and Mario Romeu. *Cast:* Carlos Cruz, Verónica Lynn, Jorge Martínez, Isabel Moreno, Beatriz Valdés, Omar Valdés and César Évora.

A period musical, loosely based on the novel *La canción de Rachel* (The Song of Rachel) by Miguel Barnet. Full of melancholy music and inspired backdrops, the film tells the story of a woman who exploits everyone in sight to achieve her dream of being a singer and dancer at Havana's famous Alhambra, Cuba's top burlesque theatre in the early years of the twentieth century. The story is told as a series of flashbacks by an aging showgirl who, for the most part, appears on her bed surrounded by objects of her past.

The Big Boodle (a.k.a. A Night in Havana) Richard Wilson / Monteflor, 1957, B&W, 84 min. *Writing credits:* from a novel by Robert Sylvester. *Music:* Raúl Lavista. *Cast:* Errol Flynn, Pedro Armendáriz, Rosanna Rory, Francisco Carrero, Luis Oquendo, Charles Todd, Enrique Cruz Álvarez, Rogelio Hernández, Carlos Mas, Jacques Aubuchon, Guillermo Álvarez Guedes, Aurora Pita, Velia Martínez, Gia Scala, Sandro Giglio, Sonya Rudy, Josefina Enríquez, Jerónimo Rente and Carlos Rivas.

An unsuspecting casino dealer in pre-revolutionary Havana is handed 500 pesos by an attractive woman who then disappears into the woodwork. As we all feared, a couple of tough guys pummel the dealer in an effort to recover the cash. The dealer can't call the police, for they suspect him of being linked to a ring of counterfeiters that produced the 500 pesos in the first place. As if he didn't have enough problems, the real counterfeiter shows up believing the dealer has the plates that have gone missing. But these are not real problems: the dilemma is that someone else is trying to kill the dealer, so to save himself he has to become a detective of sorts and try to get to the bottom of the quandary.

The film features the historic phrase, uttered by a colonel to the casino dealer Ned Sherwood, "A man is not a man until he's caught at least one bullet." To which Ned replies, "Catch it in the right place and a man isn't a man ... period."

It is also interesting to see a young Guillermo Álvarez Guedes (a Cuban comic icon) cast as a casino dealer.

El bohío (The Hut) Mario Rivas / ICAIC, 1984, color, 9 min. 40 sec. *Animation:* Mario García-Montes. *Music:* Daniel Longres.

Cuban history unfolds around a rustic hut. Colonizing Spaniards replace the natives and bring in the slaves from Africa. The wars for independence rage around the hut, and Yankee intervention prevents the nation from fulfilling its destiny. At last, the Revolution changes things around the small shack.

El brigadista (The Rural Teacher) Octavio Cortázar / ICAIC, 1977, color, 113 min. *Music:* Sergio Vitier. *Cast:* Salvador Wood, Patricio Wood, René de la Cruz, Luis Alberto Ramírez, Mario Balmaseda, Luis Rielo, Elier Amat, Maribel Rodríguez, Adela Legrá, Javier González and Miriam Learra.

During the alphabetization campaign of 1961, a young volunteer named Mario arrives at the village of Maniadero Chiquito, on the southern coast of what was then Las Villas province (where the famous film *El Mégano* was made 22 years earlier) and proceeds to work. Gonzalo, an elder in the village, feels that Mario is too young to teach him, that it is beneath him to sit in a class taught by a youngster. One day at a time, Mario gains Gonzalo's confidence and in turn is helped by the old man to overcome his own doubts and misgivings.

The Bay of Pigs invasion hits close to Maniadero Chiquito and the outraged villagers form a people's militia to hunt down the invaders, who of course turn out to be the old, evil landowners and their bloodthirsty, wicked, malevolent minions. Mario's parents arrive to take him home, but he stands fast and they have to return to Havana empty-handed. To spotlight the true nature of the invaders, one of Mario's companions is brutally lynched by these counterrevolutionaries using barbed wire.

The final part of the film turns into a Mark Twain life-on-the-Mississippi yarn, with Mario learning how to hunt wild boar and indispose alligators. Other scenes show the manhunt to trap the evil capitalist landowner who is on the loose in the marshes with his CIA-supported cutthroats. Mario finally leaves, but promises to return after finishing medical school.

This is the typical good-guy vs. bad-guys epic you would expect in a country that has just been invaded, or in a John Wayne western. The characters are truly superficial and every outcome is predictable.

Camilo Fernando Pérez / ICAIC, 1982, color, 24 min.

A documentary biography of Camilo Cienfuegos. Cienfuegos was a student revolutionary who was instrumental in the rebels' victory over the

Batista government and protagonist of some of the best-known events in that struggle. In January 1956, for example, he was one of the three people wounded when the police strafed a group of students in Havana's San Lázaro and San Francisco streets. He was Castro's constant companion until he was killed under mysterious circumstances.

The documentary follows Camilo's life, emphasizing the process that made him a revolutionary. Through a reading of his letters we gain a better understanding of the man and his intimate feelings; he comes through as a simple man driven to greatness by the circumstances and by the power of his convictions.

Cantata de Chile (Chile's Song) Humberto Solás / ICAIC, 1975, color, 119 min. *Music:* Leo Brouwer. *Cast:* Nelson Villagra, Shenda Román, Eric Heresmann, Alfredo Tornquist, Leonardo Perucci, Peggi Cordero, Flavia Ugalde, Roberto Contreras, Alejandro Pérez and Pedro Chaskel.

In 1907, saltpeter workers of northern Chile go on strike in an attempt to improve their working conditions. The miners and their families are being exploited by foreign companies and their living conditions are very poor, so they decide to march on the town of Iquique to make their demands known. The government's response to the strike is what has become known in history as the Iquique Massacre. The film evokes Chile's historical fight for freedoms, from the Araucano Indians' struggles against the Spanish conquerors to the war for independence and the resistance against the Pinochet regime.

"The film employs a potpourri of styles to unfold its solidarity-party line. Stressed is the propaganda regarding the Spanish takeover of Latin America, British imperialism and the slaughter of Chileans by the military, all events interspersed with music, poems, myths—a blend that has been described as 'Bertolt Brecht combined with Diego Rivera.' *Cantata* is a highly stylized film, full of theatrical tableaux, shifting back and forth in time, utilizing the same performers in all epochs of Chilean history, underlining the links between Chile's past and present. Music and dance and the recitation of Pablo Neruda's poem "Cantata de Chile" are used to effect the transitions between realism and surrealism; the techniques and striking styles of Latin American painters, especially the Mexican muralists, bring the film to vibrant heights. A prize-winning film, *Cantata de Chile* is a worthwhile experience if the viewer can separate the propaganda from the artistic merits of this sometimes overlong, overdidactic film work" (Ronald Schwartz, *Latin American Films, 1932–1994*, p. 56).

Director Humberto Solás Borrego was born in Havana in 1941. As a

14-year-old, Solás joined Castro's 26th of July Movement, and in 1960 he joined ICAIC. He has a degree in History from the University of Havana.

Capablanca Manuel Herrera / ICAIC–Gorky Film Studios, 1986, color, 96 min. *Writing credits:* Eliseo Alberto, Manuel Herrera and Darl Orlof. *Music:* Sergio Vitier. *Cast:* César Évora, Galina Belyayeva, Eslinda Núñez, Adolfo Llauradó, Boris Nevzorov, Javier Ávila, Marina Yakovleva, Beatriz Valdés, Ramón Veloz, Alejandro Lugo and Rogelio Meneses.

José Raúl Capablanca y Graupera was born in Havana, Cuba, on the 19th of November 1888. He learned chess at the age of four by watching his father play and in 1901, at the age of 12, he beat Juan Corzo, the Cuban champion. Capablanca was considered the most naturally gifted chess player anyone had ever seen. He was educated in the United States, studied engineering at Columbia University and spent much of his free time playing masters at the Manhattan Chess Club in New York City, where, in 1909, he achieved a sensational win against U.S. Champion Frank Marshall, crushing him by 8 wins to 1 with 14 draws. Capablanca was only 20 years old.

In 1911, on the insistence of Marshall, Capablanca played in San Sebastian, Spain, at one of the strongest tournaments in the world at that time. He astounded everyone by taking first place with a score of 6 wins, 7 draws and 1 loss.

In 1914 at a tournament in St. Petersburg, Capablanca met reigning world chess champion Lasker over the chessboard for the first time. Capablanca took the lead by one and a half points in the preliminaries but eventually lost to Lasker in the finals. Capablanca finished second to Lasker with a score of 13 points to Lasker's 13.5. In the ten years after this tournament (from 1914 to 1924) he lost only one game and the chess world was beginning to think he was invincible. However, Capablanca had to wait another seven years until he could prove he was the world champion. It was in Havana in 1921 when he met Lasker again, beating him handily. The acknowledged best player in the world was now, finally, world champion. He was world champion of chess from 1921–1927 but was the strongest from c.1919 till 1927, when he lost to Alexander Alekhine, a player against whom he had winning record. He suffered a mild stroke in 1938, yet in spite of his condition he only lost 3 games that year. He holds a record that has yet to be beaten: in 248 games, he lost 19. The 19 only covers 7.7 percent of his matches. This is the best record in the history of chess: only Anatoly Karpov and Gary Kasparov have come close to Capablanca, with a 9 percent losing ratio. As a result of his prowess in chess, José Raúl Capablanca became a national hero of sorts.

As a chess player, it was only natural that he travel to Russia, a mecca for the game. This feature co-production with the Soviet Union is the story of his love affair with a Russian woman named Sasha, a beautiful ballet dancer who captured his heart in spite of the many cultural differences that separated them.

Caravana (Convoy) Rogelio París and Julio César Rodríguez / ICAIC, 1992, color, 100 min. *Cast:* Manuel Porto, Omar Moynello, Patricio Wood and Samuel Claxton.

The film is set in Angola, during the Cuban army's intervention in that country's civil war on the side of the Marxist government. Cuban troops are guarding a strategic bridge in the interior of the country, but they are quickly running out of supplies. A caravan is sent to the outpost with stores, equipment and men, but the South Africans and the anti-government UNITA fighters have sent a special forces COBRA unit to intercept. It is a well-made and moderately absorbing story.

Cartas del parque (Letters from the Park) Tomás Gutiérrez Alea / ICAIC–International Network Group–Televisión Española, 1988, color, 85 min. *Writing credits:* Gabriel García Márquez, from his story. *Cast:* Víctor Laplace, Ivonne López, Miguel Paneque, Mirta Ibarra, Adolfo Llauradó, Elio Mesa, Paula Ali, Amelita Pita, Dagoberto Gainza and José Pelayo.

Pedro is a professional letter writer who lives in Cuba in 1913. He puts into words the feelings and emotions that other people cannot articulate. A hot air balloon enthusiast by the name of Juan wants Pedro to write love letters to his sweetheart. Pedro obliges, but he finds himself slowly falling in love with the girl and his letters become increasingly intimate. This is a nice version of the well-known Cyrano de Bergerac story.

Casta de roble (Hearts of Oak) Manolo Alonso / San Miguel S.A., 1954, B&W, 81 min. *Music:* Félix Guerrero. *Cast:* Xonia Benguría, David Silva, Ricardo Dantés, Rosendo Rosell, Laila Fraga, Antonia Valdés, Santiago Ríos, Ángel Espasande, Álvaro Suárez and Paco Alfonso.

A country girl is seduced by a rich landowner and gives birth to his child. The landowner takes the child away from her to be reared in luxury and wealth. Years later the country girl marries a farmer and has another child, but she scorns both her husband and her second child, reserving her affection for her firstborn. The firstborn has become a successful man, and she follows his exploits from afar; her second child becomes a farmer like his father. The two brothers eventually clash over a woman.

Much of this film was shot in the world-famous Viñales Valley. Spanish cameraman Alfredo Fraile, in response to the style of the times, used filters on his camera, taking away much of the rich luminosity and vibrant light-shade contrasts this part of Cuba is known for. The excessive sentimentality inherent in the plot reveals the great influence that the made-for-radio soap operas had on the screenwriter.

Cayita, una leyenda (Cayita, a Legend) Luis Felipe Bernaza / ICAIC, 1980, color, 29 min.

Cayita Araujo is a teacher who has been working Cuban classrooms for most of the twentieth century. This documentary follows the high points in her life and work, and interviews with Cayita help the audience get a good glimpse at the character of this extraordinary, generous woman.

Cecilia Humberto Solás / ICAIC–Impala (Spain), 1981, color, 147 min. (first part); 100 min. (second part). *Writing credits:* Cirilo Villaverde, from his novel *Cecilia Valdés. Music:* Leo Brouwer. *Cast:* Daisy Granados, Imanol Arias, Raquel Revuelta, Gerardo Riverón, Miguel Benavides, Eslinda Núñez, Nelson Villagra, José Antonio Rodríguez, Linda Mirabal, Antonia Valdés, Alicia Bustamante, Omara Portuondo, César Évora, María Regla

Daisy Granados and Imanol Arias talk of love and evoke the bygone era of colonial Cuba in Humberto Solás' *Cecilia*.

Social climber Cecilia (Daisy Granados) entices Havana's high-class gentlemen at a dance. The actress's partner in this still is her real-life hairdresser, Felo Márquez. (ICAIC)

Gutiérrez, Alejandro Lugo, Alfredo Mayo, Enrique Almirante, Mayda Limonta, Ángel Toraño and Hilda Oates.

Set in Havana in the first half of the nineteenth century, the film tells the story of a beautiful mulatto girl (Daisy Granados) who seeks entry into white upper-class society. To accomplish this feat, she sets her sights on young Leonardo Gamboa, a nihilistic white man (played by Spaniard Imanol Arias) who falls for her charms. Leonardo's mother disapproves of her son's interest in the African temptress and has her heart set on his marriage to the rich heiress Isabel. Cecilia burns with jealousy when she learns of the marriage plans. To further alienate her son from the mulatto, the mother unleashes a violent repression of a rebellion that was brewing among the blacks. In the night, one of the conspirators, a devotee of Cecilia, kills Leonardo.

Like *El otro Francisco*, this story is set in an epoch in which whites were a minority in Cuba, a nervous minority that viewed the fate of Haitian whites with trepidation. This slave-owning minority had been recently massacred in the slave revolt that led to Haiti's independence. Cecilia and Leonardo's complicated passion serves to bring to light many of the injustices and contradictions of Cuban society.

It may be surmised that credit for this poignant story cannot be localized. Certainly, the idea is generated by Villaverde's novel, but the film goes beyond that romanticized original version. Director, producer, scenarist and cast have managed to transfer convincingly the muscularity of a brutal society, the poignance and futility of inter-racial love as well as its indictment by those opposed to change. This powerful story gives us people trapped in a world they made and one that defeats them; above all, it is a portrait etched in historical truth.

The Christian Herald's Relief Station, Havana American Mutoscope and Biograph, 1898, B&W, 41.45 meters long.

Released in March of 1898, this early silent shows a throng of people who've been put into a concentration camp by the Spanish colonial government in the outskirts of Havana. The camera moves around the group, which is milling around the relief station that has been set up there by New York's *Christian Herald*.

Clandestinos (Living Dangerously) Fernando Pérez / ICAIC, 1987, color, 88 min. *Music:* Edesio Alejandro. *Cast:* Luis Alberto García, Isabel Santos, Susana Pérez and Miguel Gutiérrez.

Ernesto is a young revolutionary who has been caught by the dictator's police and put in jail. In jail he receives the visit of a complete stranger, an attractive but odd young woman named Nereida. Ernesto is instantly suspicious of the young woman and has misgivings as to her reasons for having visited him. Once Ernesto is freed, he gets the chance to become more intimately acquainted with Nereida and, slowly but surely, his misgivings dissipate. They fall madly in love and together they battle the evil forces of the dictator. Eventually, only heroic death will break up this strange and unlikely couple.

This film is spectacularly disappointing. These seem harsh words for a film which promises very much and which, even for all its disappointments, has a couple of flashes of brilliance in it. But the ultimate banality of the story and its juvenile slobbering over the good revolutionaries versus evil dictator premise compels their use. Reduced to its bare essentials and cleared of the clutter of clichés worn thin in a hundred previous Cuban films, *Clandestinos* seems indeed to offer very little which one might remotely presume to be original.

Coffea Arábiga Nicolás Guillén Landrián / ICAIC, 1968, B&W, 18 min. *Music:* Armando Guerra.

At the end of the 1960s coffee plants were cultivated in a cordon that surrounded the city of Havana. The idea was to provide for Havana's enormous thirst for coffee while cutting down on transportation and other ancillary costs. This documentary explains the characteristics of this fickle plant, the ways to grow it and the maladies that affect it. Opinions and the testimony of agricultural technicians mix with a musical background that includes tunes by the Beatles.

Como la vida misma (As Life Itself) Víctor Casáus Sánchez / ICAIC, 1986, color, 107 min. *Writing credits:* from the play *Molinos de viento* by Rafael González. *Music:* Silvio Rodríguez. *Cast:* Fernando Echevarría, Beatriz Valdés, Pedro Rentería, Sergio Corrieri, Flora Lauten, Carlos Pérez Peña, Israel Martínez, Jorge Félix Alí, Jorge L. López, Gilda Hernández, Elio Martín, Concepción Aus, Roberto Jiménez and the Grupo Teatro Escambray.

This is the story of a high school theater group that is getting ready to stage a play while awaiting the inspection of academic authorities. A problem of academic dishonesty upsets the normally cordial relations between students and teachers. This situation especially upsets a young woman who was hoping for a career in comedy.

Con el corazón en la tierra (With the Heart on the Land) Constante Diego / ICAIC, 1982, color, 18 min. *Music:* José María Vitier.

This documentary gives the life story of Carlos Almenares, president of a rural agricultural cooperative. It shows us how a cooperative works and the problems faced daily by its workers. The theme seems too important to tackle in an 18 minute documentary, and we are left to speculate as to the many workings of a typical Cuban cooperative farm.

Director Constante Diego García-Marruz was born in Havana in 1949, the son of poet Gerardo Diego.

Confesión a Laura (Confessing to Laura) Jaime Osorio Gómez / ICAIC, 1991, color, 90 min. *Music:* Gonzalito Rubalcaba. *Cast:* María Cristina Gálvez, Vicky Hernández, Gustavo Londoño and Walter Rojas.

A Cuban-Colombian-Spanish co-production. The story is set in one of the most momentous days in the history of Colombia. On April 9, 1948, a very popular politician and candidate for the presidency, Jorge Eliécer Gaitán, is assassinated. An ensuing popular uprising then throws Bogotá and other cities in Colombia into turmoil. In the midst of it all, a man is forced to spend the day in the house of an older schoolteacher. What develops is an attractive and poignant story of love, memories, and hope in the midst of chaos.

El corazón sobre la tierra (The Heart on the Land) Constante Diego / ICAIC, 1985, color, 102 min. *Music:* José María Vitier. *Cast:* Reinaldo

Miravalles, Nelson Villagra, Annia Linares, Tito Junco, Argelio Sosa, René de la Cruz, Luis Alberto García, Samuel Claxton, José Ramón Marcos, Oneida Hernández, Lilian Llerena, Alejandro Lugo and Raúl Eguren.

Juan Manuel Aguilera, a hardy mountain man, wants to make his son's dream come true. His son has been killed during one of Cuba's "internationalist missions" to Africa, and the father wants to create a cooperative farm in his mountain region just like the one his son would have wanted. The mountainous region is not the best place for such a farm. He must also contend with the skepticism of those like El Gallego, an old revolutionary army soldier, who puts much stock on individualism and dislikes collective enterprises. After much effort, he is successful in his endeavor.

Corresponsales de guerra (War Correspondents) Belkis Vega / ICAIC, 1986, color, 27 min.

This documentary is part of a larger, feature-length documentary that focuses on Cuban war correspondents. It attempts to put a human face of woe and suffering on the cold figures that tally the casualties in various conflicts around the world.

La cosa (The Thing) Harry Reade / ICAIC, 1962, B&W, 5 min. *Animation:* Hernán Henríquez. *Music:* Natalio Galán.

Very simple stick figures tell the story of an object, resembling a stone, that passes from hand to hand although nobody knows its purpose. A peasant boy plants it and, lo and behold, a beautiful tree grows from the site.

Cosas que dejé en La Habana (Things I Left in Havana) Manuel Gutiérrez Aragón / Alta Films (Spain)–Argentina Video Home–Primer Plano Film Group (Argentina) Dist., 1998, color, 110 min. *Cast:* Jorge Perugorría, Violeta Rodríguez, Kiti Manver, Daisy Granados, Broselianda Hernández and Pepón Nieto.

This is the story of three Cuban sisters who arrive in Madrid, having left the island in search of freedom and a better life. There they find an old aunt who had migrated to Spain many years ago and a testosterone-laden Cuban exile (Jorge Perugorría) who feigns an interest in their plight hoping to take them to bed. The comedy of errors that ensues has its funny and entertaining moments while portraying, with candid compassion, the trials and tribulations suffered by many Cuban émigrés to Spain.

An interesting side note: well-known Spanish director Manuel Gutiérrez Aragón is in part descended from Cuban émigrés to Spain.

Crónica cubana (Cuban Chronicles) Ugo Ulive / ICAIC, 1964, B&W, 123 min. 0*Music:* Piloto and Vera, Félix Guerrero. *Cast:* Carmen Delgado, Miguel Benavides, Pedro Álvarez, Juan Cañas, Adela Escartín, Violeta Jiménez and Sindo Triana.

Several characters are opposed to the radical turn the 1959 Revolution is taking, but after the failure of the Bay of Pigs invasion (1961) they come to terms with the new system. A union official that had become a political prisoner is finally freed. He now advocates the social project initiated by the Revolution and heads the negotiations that lead to the nationalization of foreign enterprises. His daughter becomes romantically involved with a mulatto who eventually joins the militia. At the university, students and professors are divided in their opinions of the new system being put in place: some of them will end up leaving the country.

Crónica de una infamia (Chronicles of Infamy) Miguel Torres / ICAIC, 1982, B&W, 16 min.

This documentary portrays the events surrounding the profanation of the José Martí monument in Havana by U.S. sailors in 1949. Their ship docked in Havana, they took advantage of their shore leave to become drunk, go out on the town, climb the statue, sit on its head, and generally vandalize the most respected symbol of Cuban nationhood. The director goes out of his way to portray the Cuban government's efforts to avoid a major international incident as proof of its subservience to the U.S. The Cuban student protests that ensued are rendered as the only dignified response given to the Americans' insolence.

Cuando las mujeres mandan (When Women Rule) José González Prieto / Victoria Films, 1951, B&W, 93 min. *Music:* Humberto Rodríguez Silva and Osvaldo Estivil. *Cast:* Federico Piñero, Alberto Garrido, Zulema Casals, Jorge Montalván, Emilita Dago, Olga Uz, Xonia Benguría, Aidita Artigas, Tin Tan and Marcelo, Fela Jar, Alberto P. Arrechavaleta, Carmen Varela, Rafaela Correa, Sandra, and Armando Oréfiche with the "Habana-Cuban Boys" Band.

This comedy has women taking power on an island and making the men follow all their rules; men will now do all the housework and general chores previously reserved for the women. But the men are hatching a plan, with the complicity of some women, to bring things back to "normal." This role-reversal story has its moments, and Garrido and Piñero are at their best.

Cuarteto de la Habana (Havana Quartet) Fernando Colomo / Aurum Producciones–El Paso, 1999, color, 105 min. *Music:* Mariano Marín, José María Vitier. *Cast:* Ernesto Alterio, Mirta Ibarra, Javier Cámara, Laura Ramos, Daisy Granados and María Esteve.

A young Spanish jazz musician learns from a woman in Cuba that she is his mother. Elated by the expectation of meeting Lita, his mother, he hops on the first plane to Havana. There he meets Diana, a beautiful young woman who is about to marry a fellow named Segis. He is instantly taken by the young woman, but there's catch: she is Lita's daughter, and therefore his half-sister. The many complications and snags keep the action moving well, to the point that one exonerates the screenwriter for the predictable ending.

Cuba Richard Lester / Holmby Pictures–United Artists, 1979, color, 122 min. *Music:* Patrick Williams. *Cast:* Sean Connery, Brooke Adams, Jack Weston, Héctor Elizondo, Denholm Elliot, Martin Balsam, Chris Sarandon, Danny De La Paz, Lonette McKee, Alejandro Rey, Louisa Moritz, Dave King, Walter Gotell, David Rappaport, Wolfe Morris, Michael Lees, Tony Matthews, Roger Lloyd-Pack, Leticia Garrido, María Charles, Pauline Pert, Anna Nicholas, Earl Cameron, John Morton, Anthony Pullen Shaw, Stefan Kalipha, Raúl Newney, Ram John Holder and James Turner.

A U.S. production filmed in Spain, *Cuba* tells a story set in 1959 during the final days of Fulgencio Batista's dictatorial regime. Sean Connery plays a British soldier-for-hire who comes to Cuba at the insistence of one of Batista's generals (Martin Balsam) to help defeat Castro and his army. Once in Cuba, Connery happens upon a past love, Brooke Adams, who now manages a tobacco factory. A sexy re-acquaintance has them sleeping together while the social and political mayhem around them intensifies. This mayhem is but a stage set for the Connery-Adams affair, a relationship that tangles their lives with the other major characters. Jack Weston is an opportunistic American entrepreneur, Denholm Elliott is a drunken pilot, Chris Sarandon is Adams' womanizing husband (she must have an excuse to slip into bed with Connery), and Héctor Elizondo is a military man. Drama and comedy mix freely in this satire of the parties at war, although the more disquieting elements, such as the brutality in which both sides engage, remain at the forefront of the story. There are no bad guys here. Every individual is treated with sympathy by the director, who avoids taking sides in this conflict. Connery is at his usual, superior level, while Adams provides a less-than-memorable performance.

Cuba 15 Elizabeth Schub / Sueño Azul Productions, 1998, color, 12 min.

This short documentary shows how small-town Cubans still spend more than they can afford in order to give their daughters the most elaborate "coming out" party. It's very work-intensive and costly to obtain the dress, the shoes and the cake, and select the boy who will escort her and dance the traditional waltz. With the thousands of minutiae involved, it's almost impossible to ensure that everything will come out right. A nicely done short, it won several international prizes.

Cuba 58 José Miguel García Ascot (episodes I & II); Jorge Fraga (episode III) / ICAIC, 1962, B&W, 78 min. *Music:* Bebo Valdés and Félix Guerrero (episode I), Natalio Galán (episode II) and Félix Guerrero (episode III). *Cast:* episode I: Sergio Peña, Luis Alberto Ramírez, Ricardo Lima; episode II: Sergio Corrieri, Yolanda Arenas and Helena Huerta; episode III: José A. Rodríguez, Jorge Martínez, Raúl Xiqués and Adolfo Llauradó.

These three stories are set in the chaotic last year of the Batista government. The first one is called *Un día de trabajo* (A Day of Work), and it deals with the routine of a Havana policeman, an overweight and apparently inoffensive character that is more wayward than his external demeanor would indicate. The second, *Los novios* (The Sweethearts), tells of a radical trying to make his way to the Sierra Maestra Mountains to join the rebel fighters. To better his chances of success, he brings a woman who passes as his fiancée, and as the audience may expect, they end up falling in love. The third episode, *Año Nuevo* (New Year's), shows the last day of the old order, the chaos and disintegration of the old system and the spectacle provided by the panic-stricken minions of the previous administration. Three of the government's torturers were practicing their trade on a young revolutionary in a basement when they learn of the triumph of the Revolution. They, of course, are panic-stricken, so they try to revive the tortured revolutionary to use him as a hostage. Then they begin to accuse each other, and at last they have a brilliant idea: find the brother of one of them, who is a revolutionary fighter, and plead for mercy. They subsequently find that this brother has died in a police basement not unlike the one where they worked. Finally they are captured by the masses, who take their terrible revenge.

Cuba baila (Cuba Dances) Julio García Espinosa / ICAIC, 1961, B&W, 81 min. *Cast:* Raquel Revuelta, Alfredo Perojo, Vivian Gude, Humberto García Espinosa, Eric Romay, Luciano de Pazos, Wilfredo Fernández, Elena Bernal and Enrique de la Torre.

A middle class couple discusses the pros and cons of having the traditionally lavish "coming out" party for their fifteen year old daughter. The mother is willing to spend all they have and more to make an impression on the guests, and the father, an office worker, gets involved in political rallies and schemes which render him unable to pay for his daughter's party. The one person willing to lend him a hand is a black neighbor whom the wife had refused to consider inviting to the party because of his skin color. As it turns out, financial problems dictate that the party will not be an exclusive affair after all, but given in a public garden where everyone is invited and will dance to the sounds of Cuban popular music.

Cuba baila was not begun by ICAIC, but it is the first film to be completed by them. Although its pre–Revolutionary subject of society parties seems out of tune with the continuing struggles the nation is experiencing, there is a didactic element aimed mainly at the urban bourgeois and their class- and race-centered mentality. In a way, the film takes the conventions of the typical Cuban melodrama and turns them upside down.

García Espinosa takes his audience on a tour they are familiar with, showing them how the melodrama's superficial images have served to cover social ills. Yet he does not put his audience in a classroom in order to accomplish his goals: following his concept of "cine imperfecto" (imperfect cinema), he knows that films must entertain if there is any hope of getting the message across. One of the best tools for entertainment is music. In this film the music does not function as a vehicle for evasion, but rather as a tool that will help the filmmaker analyze Cuba's class and race consciousness. This analysis begins with the mother character, who dreams of having a Viennese waltz orchestra for her daughter's party, one that will impress her class-conscious guests. The girl and her friends, of course, prefer Cuban music, but the mother will not hear of it. Yet Cuban music lurks everywhere under the surface, as we hear when passengers on a bus spontaneously begin to whistle a popular tune. Music, then, symbolizes not only the patriotic nature of the popular classes, but also portrays their social cohesion. Finally, when the party takes place in the public garden, the bourgeois guests dance awkwardly to popular Cuban tunes, while the girl and her boyfriend — representatives of the future — dance unhindered by the weight of bourgeois etiquette.

Cuba feliz (Happy Cuba) Karim Dridi / ADR Productions, France–Centre national de la Cinématographie CNC, France–Movimiento Nacional de Video de Cuba–Le Studio Canal +, France, 2000, color, 90 min. *Cast:* Miguel del Morales, Pepín Vaillant, Mirta González, Aníbal Ávila, Alberto Pablo, Armandito Machado, Mario Sánchez Martínez, Zaida Reyte,

Gilberto Méndez, Alejandro Almenares, Alisan Mallet, Eulises Sánchez, Carlo Boromeo Planches and Cándido Fabré.

This is one of those documentaries (one is reminded of *Buena Vista Social Club* and *Lágrimas negras*) where the spotlight shines on Cuban music. In this case there doesn't seem to be a connecting tissue of personal stories, as one is led from one jam session to another in a dizzying array of tunes and rhythms. The music is always improvised and acoustic. It tells mournful stories of broken hearts, palm trees, soft breezes and treacherous women. It swings in a square with a municipal brass band and in much more intimate environments. The camera is hand-held and very fast moving: it seems to capture everything that is going on.

There is one main character called "El Gallo" (The Cock) who takes us around to all those places where conga drums are beating and the sweet and satisfying progressions of boleros and guarachas fill the air. But there are no sophisticated studios or music halls, it's all improvised: from a session in a fat woman's kitchen through a living room to the street. In Cuba, the film seems to imply, music has no boundaries.

This is a swinging, charming and uninhibited look at music in Cuba, without pretensions to great documentary status.

Cuban Ambush William "Daddy" Paley / Edison Manufacturing Company, 1898, B&W, 15.24 meters in length.

A silent short that documents a firefight between Cuban insurgents firing from the windows of a ruined mill and a Spanish patrol. Released in August of 1898, its commercial value was great, as it was playing on the most current of events at the time, the Spanish American War. We can tell many shots are being fired from the amount of smoke that chokes the screen.

Cuban Fireball William Beaudine / Republic, 1951, B&W, 78 min. *Cast:* Estelita Rodríguez, Warren Douglas, Mimi Aguglia, León Belasco, Donald MacBride, Rosa Turich, John Litel, Russ Vincent, Edward Gargan, Victoria Horne, Jack Kruschen, Pedro de Córdoba, Olan Soule, Tony Barr, Luther Crockett and Timothy Ryan.

Protagonist Estelita Rodríguez, it was hoped, was going to be Republic's answer to 20th Century–Fox's Carmen Miranda. A pretty, bubbly brunette born in Guanajay, Cuba, in 1913, she made her American film debut in 1945 in *Mexicana*, and from then on she appeared in features such as *The Gay Ranchero* (1948), *Hit Parade of 1951* (1950), *Havana Rose* (1951) and *Rio Bravo* (1959). Frequently billed simply as Estelita, she typically played a Latin American firecracker with a proclivity to break out into song every chance she got. Although she retired after playing an important role in *Rio Bravo*, she returned in 1966 to play a major role in the memorable *Jesse James Meets Frankenstein's Daughter*. Her death of influenza this same year at the age of 52, in Van Nuys, California, was unexpected. In *Cuban Fireball*, Estelita is cast as "herself," an attractive Cuban artist gone to Los Angeles to claim a hefty inheritance. Once there, she must disguise herself as a little old lady to ward off interested parties and con men. She gets plenty of opportunities, of course, to display her musical talents as she overcomes the diverse obstacles she finds along the way.

The Cuban Love Song W.S. Van Dyke / M.G.M., 1931, B&W, 80 min. *Writing credits:* from a story by Bess Meredyth and C. Gardner Sullivan. *Music:* Charles Maxwell and Herbert Stothart. *Cast:* Lawrence Tibbet, Lupe Vélez, Ernest Torrence, Jimmy Durante, Karen Morley, Louise Fazenda, Hale Hamilton, Mathilde Comont, Philip Cooper, George Davis and Harry Strang.

An entertaining film in which an American G.I. (Lawrence Tibbet) goes down Havana way with his buddies (Ernest Torrence and Jimmy Durante) and meets up with a sexy, fiery, hot tempered Cuban peanut vendor named Nanita (Lupe Vélez) with whom he begins a love affair. But the true star of the film is the song "Manisero" (The Peanut Vendor). As it happens, the actress playing the fiery Cuban wasn't Cuban at all: Lupe Vélez (nee María Guadalupe Villalobos Vélez) was born on 18 July 1908 in San Luis Potosí, Mexico. The "Mexican Spitfire" was barely 5 feet tall and was the daughter of a prostitute. She was discovered by Hal Roach in 1927 and was cast in a comedy with Laurel and Hardy. She became so popular that a number of films were tailored for her, such as *Mexican Spitfire* (1939), *The Mexican Spitfire Out West* (1940), *Mexican Spitfire's Baby* (1941), and *Mexican Spitfire's Blessed Event* (1943). She was married for five years to Johnny Weissmuller and later had a romantic liaison with Gary Cooper. True to her name, she had a number of love affairs as her career steadily waned. She became pregnant by Harold Raymond and, abandoned by him, she committed suicide with an overdose of Seconal. She was 36.

The film's title, *Cuban Love Song*, derives from Antonio Lugo Machín's "El manisero," one of the first Cuban songs to become a hit in the U.S. In 1929 Machín had toured the U.S. with the Casino Nacional orchestra, and on April 26 of that year he sang "El manisero" at New York's Palace Theater, becoming an instant hit. Such was the song's popularity that two years later this film was released with a story tailored to fit its title.

Cuban Patriots American Mutoscope, 1898, B&W, 46.94 meters in length.

This is an early silent documentary filmed in Tampa as part of the anti–Spanish frenzy being roused in the U.S. population. *Cuban Patriots* shows a large number of Florida Cubans marching, loaded with military equipment. They're off to help their compatriots fighting against the Spanish colonial army in their War of Independence. It was released in the U.S. in May of 1898.

Cuban Pete Jean Yarbrough / Universal, 1946, B&W, 61 min. *Music:* Milton Rosen. *Cast:* Desi Arnaz, Beverly Simmons, Don Porter, Jacqueline De Wit, Ethel Smith, Pedro de Córdoba, Eddie Parks, Shirley O'Hara, Ellen Corby, Peter Seal, Joan Shawlee, Rico de Montez, The King Sisters, Ann Lawrence, Charles Jordan, Robert E. O'Connor, Roseanne Murray, Ruth Lee and Peggy León.

A young woman is intent on persuading a good-looking Havana bandleader (Desi Arnaz) to leave his city and fly to New York to perform on the radio. The show, as it were, will not go on unless this bandleader in particular comes to N.Y. But Cuba has always been difficult to leave behind, and in Desi's case it is no exception. He thinks it over, and over; he procrastinates, not giving the young woman the answer she wants. Only after being convinced by his niece, the musician decides to try his luck in the Big Apple. The skeletal storyline is of no consequence, for one is entranced by the music that harks back to that particular 1940s naïve romanticism that found fertile ground in Cuba. Some of the tunes are "The Breeze and I," "After Tonight," "El Cumbanchero," "Lullaby," "Cielito Lindo," and "Rhumba Matumba."

Cuban Rebel Girls (a.k.a. Assault of the Rebel Girls and Attack of the Rebel Girls) Barry Mahon / Exploit Films, 1959, B&W, 68 min. *Cast:* Errol Flynn, Beverly Aadland, Jackie Jackler, Marie Edmund, John Mackay, Ben Ostrowsky, Allen Baron, Tod Scott Brody, Andrés Fernández, Clelle Mahon, Esther Oliva, Ramón Ramírez and Reynerio Sánchez.

This is Errol Flynn's last film, one for which he helped write the screenplay. Filmed with Castro's help on location in Cuba, it is the story of a group of teenaged girls that help Fidel Castro as he battles Batista's forces. Flynn plays himself as an American correspondent gone to Cuba to report on the progress of the war. Flynn was able to procure a spot on the cast for his latest girlfriend, 16-year-old Beverly Aadland. Flynn died of a heart attack in Vancouver this same year (1959); he was thus spared the enduring embarrassment this flick would most certainly have caused him. Director Barry Mahon (d. 4 Dec. 1999) also got a spot on the cast for his wife Clelle. Barry Mahon was a prisoner of war during World War II, and the film *The Great Escape* (1963) is partly based on his exploits.

Flynn's girlfriend Aadland looked much older than she was: we might remember her as the nurse in the Thanksgiving show in the movie *South Pacific* (1958).

Cuban Reconcentrados American Mutoscope and Biograph, 1898, B&W, 41.76 meters long.

As a last-ditch effort to win the war against the Cuban insurgents, Spanish colonial authorities in Cuba concentrated large portions of the island's population around Havana and other sites. They were attempting to stop the population of the island from helping the rebels. A crowd of these unfortunate "reconcentrados" is shown milling around a free soup kitchen. This is a very powerful image of a very inhumane practice. It was released in March of 1898.

Cuban Refugees Waiting for Rations Edison Manufacturing Company, 1898, B&W, 15.24 meters in length.

Filmed in Tampa in 1898 by the Edison Company, this early silent shows a group of escapees from Spanish "reconcentration" camps in Cuba as they stand in line holding tin plates waiting for food. Interestingly, some fine ladies can be seen to the side of the refugees; they seem to be on a pleasant outing, taking in the spectacle afforded by those much less fortunate than they are.

Cuban Volunteers American Mutoscope Company, 1898, B&W, 88.09 meters long.

This early silent documentary shows us a battalion of Cubans that was raised in Florida, marching with all its weaponry on its way to the war. Released in July of 1898, it was filmed in Tampa, main embarkation point for soldiers going to fight against Spain in Cuba.

Cubans Sharpening their Machetes American Mutoscope Company, 1898, B&W, 44.81 meters in length.

A large group of Cubans from Florida has volunteered to go fight in Cuba. In this film some of them are shown sharpening their machetes, an indispensable item in every Cuban soldier's accouterments. This film was released in July of 1898 and was filmed in Tampa.

Culpa (Fault) Jorge Molina / EICTV (Cuba)–La Tiñosa Autista (Cuba), 1993, B&W, 20 min. *Music:* Edesio Alejandro. *Cast:* Luis Enrique, Idalmis Del Risco, Jorge Molina, Claudio MacDowell, Edesio Alejandro, Edgar

Soberón Torchia, Fernando Pérez, Arturo Sotto Díaz, Walter Cruz, Ernesto Leyva, Raúl Fidel Capote, Conceição Senna, Marcelino Pérez and Adolfo Llauradó.

The object of this 20-minute film seems to be to show the two poles of Cuban sexual life. Or maybe not. A town is beleaguered by a lunatic (the Killer of the Seven Leathers) who is sending residents to a better world in the afterlife. In this chilling environment, a religious youth is beset by hoodlums and is saved by a prostitute. When they both go back to his place (a dirty hovel full of Christian objects), the inevitable struggle ensues: he wants to remain pure, she does her best to break down his heroic resistance to her womanly charms. This is an unsurprising yet alluring story.

Cumbite Tomás Gutiérrez Alea / ICAIC, 1964, B&W, 82 min. *Writing credits:* based on Jacques Roumain's novel *Les Gouverneurs de la Rosée*. *Music:* Papito Hernández, Tata Güines, Oscar Valdés and Enrique Simón. *Cast:* Teté Vergara, Lorenzo Louiz, Marta Evans, Luis Valera, Rafael Sosa, Polinise Jean, Ambroise Macombe, Elvira Cervera, Victoria Nápoles, Leonardo Morales, Ti-Bombon, Chatti and Emilio O'Farrill.

An accomplished neorealist flick made with the participation of Haitian Cubans, it is remarkable in every aspect. The black and white photography captures that astonishing contrast between sun and shade so characteristic of the Caribbean, while the slow pace of the action allows for the patient observation of the events in this historical period (early 1940s).

Manuel, a Haitian laborer in Cuba, returns to his native country after fifteen years. Manuel's Cuban sojourn has changed him: he now sees the defects inherent to the villagers' way of life and patterns of thought. As it happens, he has returned home in the middle of a drought, and the stoic villagers complain that if it doesn't rain, that's just the way it is and nobody can do anything about it. When Manuel tries to explain to them that irrigation systems can be built, that they can change their lot, his words are resented and his interference is unwelcome. In a subplot, Manuel begins a liaison with a local girl, Analaisa, an affair that only adds to the villagers' resentment of him and will lead to his demise.

In order to proceed with his scheme to obtain water for the village, Manuel needs to call a *cumbite* or assembly of villagers, where he will propose that they all work together and make the water a communal property. Some doubt the legality of his plan, others call him subversive, and he is eventually killed by his rival for Analaisa. As he dies in his mother's arms, he tells her that Analaisa knows where the water source is; the village, shocked by the violence, now begins to realize the value of Manuel's ideas. His death will not be in vain.

Cinéma vérité is woven into Sara Gómez's love story *De cierta manera.*

De cierta manera (In a Certain Way) Sara Gómez Yera / ICAIC, 1974, B&W, 79 min. *Music:* Sergio Vitier. *Cast:* Mario Balmaseda, Yolanda Cuéllar, Mario Limonta, Isaura Mendoza, Bobby Carcasés, Sarita Reyes and the neighbors of the Miraflores district.

The Miraflores neighborhood, one of the Revolution's first projects intended to eradicate marginal barrios around Havana, is the set for this love story. A mulatto named Mario and former middle class damsel Yolanda meet in a bus assembly plant and fall in love. In the course of their conversations they discover class prejudices that have been inherited from capitalist society and whose effects they still feel. The conflicts between the old value system and the new ideas brought in by the new society turn out to be the real subject. Mario yearns for the old days of the shantytown, when men lounged around and were served by their women, while Yolanda believes that women should work and that everyone should obtain an education. As expected, pre-revolutionary Cuba is represented by the backwards Mario, while enlightened Yolanda serves to defend the revolutionary ideas. As the film ends and they are still arguing, one is left with the feeling that Cuba's problems are going to be resolved by a patient discussion between people who hold antagonistic ideas.

Director Sara Gómez died of an asthma attack in 1974 shortly after the film's release. Black and female in a formerly white male world, much was expected of this talented pioneer. She was born in Havana in 1943 and studied piano. She became assistant to Tomás Gutiérrez Alea, Jorge Fraga and Agnès Varda and then went on to direct a number of shorts that deal with practical matters such as work hours and the tobacco industry.

De tal Pedro, tal astilla (Apples Don't Fall Far from the Tree) Luis Felipe Bernaza / ICAIC, 1986, color, 90 min. *Writing credits:* adapted from a musical comedy by Luis Felipe Bernaza. *Music:* Toni Taño and Aneiro Taño. *Cast:* Reinaldo Miravalles, Ana Viña, Nancy González, Gilberto Reyes, Thais Valdés, Néstor Rivero, Hilario Peña, Orlando Casín, Tito Junco and Tania Pérez James.

Two cowboys, encouraged by the socialist fervor evident all around them, vie for first place on the production lists. Their kids and families pick up on their rivalry and, like a Romeo and Juliet saga, begin a feud that reaches the point of violence. You must have much patience to sit through this one.

Director Luis Felipe Bernaza was born in Santiago de Cuba in 1940. He joined the 26th of July Movement in 1956 and studied cinema arts in Moscow. He is also the author of the novel *Buscavidas* (1987).

La decisión (The Decision) José Massip / ICAIC, 1965, B&W, 86 min. *Music:* Leo Brouwer. *Cast:* Mario Limonta, Daisy Granados, Miguel Benavides, Adela Escartín, Alfredo Perojo, Lidia Lavallet, Julio Martínez, Pastor Vega, René de la Cruz, Vivian Gude, Juan Carlos Romero, Rafael Sosa, Melchor Casals, Miguel Gutiérrez, Yolanda Zamora and Omar Valdés.

This is the story of two mulatto brothers during the years of clandestine war against the Batista regime. The movie opens in a classroom at the University of Santiago de Cuba during a lecture on Greek classical society, a subject cleverly analogous with the social and political differences among the students in attendance. The first brother (Pablo) is a brilliant student at the university who falls in love with María, a white, middle class girl (Daisy Granados in her first screen appearance). But her family rejects him because of his race. The second brother, who works in a factory managed by María's father, is a revolutionary who scorns Pablo for having harbored outlandish illusions: a person of color will never be considered equal until society is changed to its roots. Pablo crashes a bourgeois party in disguise, but he is found out and forced to leave. Pablo's brother incites him to join Fidel Castro's 26th of July

Movement, but the young man is too docile to consider revolutionary violence.

Director José Massip was born in Havana in 1928. He studied Philosophy at the University of Havana and Sociology at Harvard. He was a member of the association "Nuestro Tiempo," a group opposed to the Batista government. A militant in the Socialist Party, he was one of the founders of the ICAIC and worked as assistant to Joris Ivens.

The Defence of the Flag American Mutoscope Company, 1898, B&W, 47.81 meters in length.

This is a reenactment of a battle in the Spanish American War in Cuba. Filmed at Camp Meade, Pennsylvania, using the Charleston Cadets of Boston, *The Defence of the Flag* shows us a number of soldiers rushing up a hill, firing as they come up, and finally planting the flag at the top. It was released in September of 1898.

Derecho de asilo (The Right to Asylum) Octavio Cortázar / ICAIC, 1994, color, 96 min. *Cast:* Jorge Perugorria, Enrique Molina, Luisa Pérez Nieto, Jorge Cao, Manuel Porto and Carlos Padrón.

In an imaginary country of Latin America lives Felipe, right-hand-man of the dictator, ladies' man and man-around-town. He is so close to the dictator that he even knows the number of his secret bank account. Ambitious Felipe has many dreams for the future; one of them is to become, when the right time comes, the dictator. But his dreams will never come true: a military uprising topples the government and Felipe is forced to flee to the Gaetanian embassy (another imaginary country), where he claims his right to asylum.

Desperate Peter Markle / Toots Productions–Warner Bros. TV, 1987, color, 96 min. *Cast:* Liane Langland, Andrew Robinson, John Savage, Chris Burke, Meg Foster and George Dickerson.

In spite of his wealthy family's expectations for him, a young man decides to live the life he dreams of, so he heads down to Florida and becomes the captain of an excursion boat. But when things get tough and a storm threatens to sink his ship, the young captain abandons ship and passengers, leaving his customers behind to fend for themselves. He returns to the business some years later in Key West, but he is a changed man, having picked up a sense of ethics along the way. He is able to display ethical behavior as he foils the plans of some gun-running bad guys operating in southern Florida and Cuba. This was supposed to be the pilot for a T.V.

series. Good performances by Meg Foster as lead man John Savage's girlfriend, and by Chris Burke, the star of the television series *Life Goes On*.

Un día de noviembre (A Day in November) Humberto Solás / ICAIC, 1978, B&W, 110 min. *Music:* Leo Brouwer. *Cast:* Gildo Torres, Raquel Revuelta, Eslinda Núñez, Silvia Planas, Alicia Bustamante, Miguel Benavides, Omar Valdés, Miriam Learra, Luis Otaño, Rogelio Blain, Jorge Fraga and Delia Aragón.

A man is diagnosed with an incurable disease and becomes despondent, not even speaking with his close relatives. He searches for comfort among his good friends and old comrades from the rebel army that toppled the Batista regime, but to no avail. The society that surrounds him makes him more miserable still. To compound his troubles, he bitterly disputes with his brother and his brother's wife after he learns that they want to leave Cuba and search for a better life overseas. He meets a young woman and begins a love affair with her, but that relationship doesn't make him happy or relieve his despair. Only when he meets a war veteran that has lost his arm, but not his will to live happily, does the despondent young man begin to look at life in a more positive manner.

This film was shot in 1972 and was not released until 1978. The early '70s were years when artists and filmmakers had misgivings as to the reception that Castro's authorities would give to innovative works of art. Writer Heberto Padilla had recently been jailed, showing that the censors were not disposed to indulging artistic deviations from the official line. A film that discusses the existential despair of a young man and the dreams of a family to escape Cuba to end a life of misery and penury could have caused problems for many at the particular moment in which it was shot.

Un día en el solar (A Day in the Tenement) Eduardo Manet / ICAIC, 1965, Color, 86 min. *Music:* Tony Taño. *Cast:* Sonia Calero, Tomás Morales, Roberto Rodríguez, Asenneh Rodríguez, Regla Becerra, Alicia Bustamante, Olivia Belizaire, José M. Rodríguez, Rogelio Rodríguez, Prudencia Valencia, Andrée González Manet, Juana Albuquerque.

The first color feature produced by ICAIC, this musical comedy is based on the ballet composition *El solar*, by Cuba's leading choreographer Alberto Alonso, with added dialogue and songs. The film aims to capture a day in the life of Havana poor, with marital disputes, sentimental frolic and varied incidents, all aired out in the patio of the tenement with song and dance. Old values and prejudices meet new values brought in by the Revolution. Eduardo Manet has certainly studied Stanley Donen musical comedies, which he seems to be imitating here with limited success.

Los días del agua

Unsavory characters plot to take advantage of Antoñica Izquierdo's miraculous powers in Manuel Octavio Gómez's *Los días del agua*.

Director Eduardo Manet was born in Havana in 1927. A writer and theater worker, he lived for many years in Europe before the revolution. At the ICAIC, he served as assistant to Armand Gatti and Chris Marker. He subsequently left Cuba and went into exile.

Los días del agua (Days of Water) Manuel Octavio Gómez / ICAIC, 1971, color, 110 min. *Music:* Leo Brouwer. *Cast:* Idalia Anreus, Raúl Pomares, Adolfo Llauradó, Mario Balmaseda, Omar Valdés, Raúl Eguren, Teté Vergara, Ángel Toraño, Luis Manuel Martínez Casado and Eugenio Domínguez.

The Cuban Image described the film as "a story of the political manipulation of religious hysteria in the 1930s, based on real events in the province of Pinar del Río in 1936." The central character is Antoñica Izquierdo, a woman whose miraculous healing powers draw crowds of the sick to her door. Among the crowds one day are a journalist seeking to write about Antoñica, and a businessman who smells opportunity — all these people need to eat, after all, and so he sets up food stalls nearby. Amid the resulting half-church, half-carnival atmosphere, the local physicians, pharmacies and priests see a challenge to their hold on the public. They plot to get rid of Antoñica. When one of the sick visitors dies, Antoñica faces a charge of murder. She is successfully defended by a lawyer, who then rides his popularity to a governorship. Once elected, however, he too feels threatened by Antoñica and sends his army against her. The sick followers respond violently in a doomed rebellion. As the cynical journalist has declared, "What a waste of power! What a stupid woman! People believe in her and she doesn't know how to lead them!"

"On the one level," writes Chanan, "the film is about who pays the costs of sickness in a sick society. Antoñica declares her powers a free gift, an act of social rebellion against the cartel of the priests and medics. But she also declares that there are diseases that cannot be seen. Like *Una pelea cubana*..., this narrative is offered not in the form of a cold and considered historical reconstruction, but in the form of an hallucinatory allegory. The story is told inside out, as it were, and from a series of different angles, like a written narrative which shifts the point of view of the narration between the different characters..." (Michael Chanan, *The Cuban Image*, Bloomington: Indiana Univ. Press, 1985, p. 261).

Author Ronald Schwartz adds this appraisal: "By basing his story on real events and by trying to recapture the dialogue and feeling of the era by using actual testimony from the case, our director has created a bold production. The film is exuberant, with a flamboyant visual and narrative style that illustrates the social origins and distorted uses of popular culture. It also offers a trenchant critique of Cubans exploited by both religious fanaticism and political opportunism. Idalia Anreus as Antoñia [*sic*] gives a remarkable, sympathetic performance, a 'saint' overwhelmed by forces she does not understand. The director also shows himself to be a master of the crowd scene. Hysterical and fanatical mobs are beautifully controlled by the director's will..." (*Latin American Films, 1932–1994*, Jefferson, NC: McFarland, 1997, p. 80).

El dirigible (The Blimp) Pablo Dotta / ICAIC–CICV France–Centro de Captación Cinematográfica Mexico–Channel Four Films U.K.–Fondazione Montecinemaveritá, Italy–Instituto Nacional de Audiovisual, Uruguay– Nubes Producciones, Uruguay–Rockefeller Foundation, 1994, B&W and color, 80 min. *Music:* Fernando Cabrera. *Cast:* Ricardo Espalter, Laura Schneider, Marcelo Buquet, Gonzalo Cardozo and Eduardo Maglionico.

Many countries (Cuba, Uruguay, U.S.A., France, Italy, the U.K. and

Las doce sillas

Mexico) collaborated in this feature. The surreal atmosphere is the most salient feature of this film, the story of several odd characters that seem to be attempting to solve a mystery. Essentially, they aim to link the suicide of an ex-president of Uruguay with the recent death of a famous poet. Among the myriad of characters is a juvenile antisocial named Moco (Snot), a French newspaperwoman and a translator, all looking for the last interview the poet gave before his death. This is a rather strange film with a very artsy, attractive ambiance.

Las doce sillas (The Twelve Chairs) Tomás Gutiérrez Alea / ICAIC, 1962, B&W, 97 min. *Writing credits:* Based on a play by Ilya Ilf and Eugene Petrov. *Music:* Juan Blanco. *Cast:* Max Beltrán, Idalberto Delgado, Humberto García Espinosa, María Granados, Gilda Hernández, Julio Matas, Reinaldo Miravalles, María Pardo, Manuel Pereiro, Pedro Martín Planas, Silvia Planas, Enrique Santiesteban, René Sánchez, Pilín Vallejo, Ana Viña, Raúl Xiqués and Yolanda Zamora.

This comedy by Gutiérrez Alea has a long history indeed. The play on which it is based has been used on many occasions. Film savants may remember Monty Banks' (a.k.a. Mario Bianchi) *Keep Your Seats, Please* (1936), a musical comedy where the popular English comedian George Formby plays George, an heir trying to discover in which of six chairs his peculiar late aunt has hidden his inheritance. It's not an easy task, for the chairs have been sold at auction, compelling George to track them down.

Fans of Mel Brooks will also recognize the plot from his own *The Twelve Chairs* (1970). This is a sort of treasure hunt where an aging ex-nobleman from Czarist times, now trying to adjust to the Communist regime, finds out that his family jewels were hidden in a chair, one of a set of twelve. He therefore returns to Moscow to find the hidden fortune. One of the brightest spots here is Dom DeLuise playing Father Fyodor, a Russian priest who disregards his priestly condition to join in the pursuit of the treasure. Ron Moody as nobleman (now file clerk) I.M. Vorobyaninov is memorable as well, refusing to let go of his pre–Revolutionary mind-set.

The plot was also used by Richard Wallace in his *It's in the Bag* (1945) starring Fred Allen, Don Ameche, Jack Benny and William Bendix. Here, wealthy Frederick Trumble makes an eccentric new will, hides most of his wealth in a chair, and is murdered a few moments later. The new heir, flea circus director Fred Floogle, is disgusted by his inheritance of five chairs and sells them. He then discovers that $12 million was hidden in one of them, and the hunt begins.

Gutiérrez Alea's version is set in a nursing home that used to be a mansion before the Revolution. The mansion's old owner had hidden her jewels in one of the mansion's chairs before she died, and three men now set off in their search: the priest who took her last confession, the heir and her ex-employee, the gardener. The problem is that the chairs have been dispersed throughout Havana and even beyond, so the hunt is far-reaching and will involve many people in many humorous situations.

Dolman 2000 Adrián García Bogliano, Ramiro García Bogliano and Jorge Molina / EICTV–La Tiñosa Autista, Cuba–Roman Porno Eiga, 2000, B&W and color, 35 min. *Cast:* Yaima Fernández, Carmen Morales, Tamara Melián, Jorge Molina, Jesús Rosabal, Edgar Soberón, Torchia, Alexis Álvarez, Leopoldo Pinzón, Mirtha Licea, Elián Golpeador, Máximo Hernández, José Borrás and Patricia Bisbé Tapia.

This film is divided into three very different parts of roughly ten minutes each. In the first episode, "Yo soy Godzilla" (I Am Godzilla), an irritable writer, at odds with his abusive editor, meets a prostitute who shows much interest in literature. The second episode, "Estupro" (Rape), an underworld tough is astounded to meet a truly depraved teenage girl. In the third episode, "Fría Jennie" (Cold Jennie), a man who has been dumped by his lover gets the chance to get closer to his strange but beautiful next door neighbor.

Ecos (Echoes) Tomás Piard / Ciné-clubs Sigma–Prisma–René David Osés, 1987, B&W, 87 min. *Music:* Carl Orff, Juan Marcos Blanco, Stravinsky. *Cast:* César Évora, Gisela Rangel, Josefina Izquierdo, Rebeca Rodríguez, José Antonio Roche, Berardo Forbes, Francisco Parra, Héctor Eduardo Suárez, Javier Medina, Osmar Vázquez, Terence Piard, Igor Díaz and Arturo Soto.

This is the story of three women, of very different epochs, whose lives are strangely parallel. The first story, during colonial times, has a man brutalizing both his wife and a female black servant. Parallel with this story is that of a modern couple who perpetuate the stereotyped role of the woman as subservient. Director Tomás Piard González was born in Cárdenas, Matanzas, Cuba, in 1948. He obtained a degree in Art History, and subsequently studied film and television in Havana's "Instituto Superior del Arte." Basically an amateur filmmaker producing films for Havana's "cineclubs," he crosses over into professional filmmaking with *Ecos*.

¡Eh, taxi! (Hey, Taxi!) Miguel González Betancourt / ICAIC, 1980, color, 5 min. *Animation:* José Reyes Rodríguez. *Music:* Lucas de la Guardia.

An endearing cartoon character is having numerous problems hailing a taxi in the city. He misses some taxis because of his bad luck, but others just refuse to stop for him. Eventually, and after much trying, he has a nervous breakdown; the ambulance that comes to pick him up is mistaken by him for a taxi.

1868-1968 Bernabé Hernández / ICAIC, 1970, B&W, 30 min.

In 1968 Cuba celebrated the beginning of its first war of independence, one that ended in a draw with the Spanish army. A succeeding war gave Cuba independence, but a powerful neighbor was going to make things difficult for some time to come. This documentary follows the first hundred years after that first war, a period fraught with struggle and toil, all leading to the "Promised Land" of freedom and sovereignty represented by Castro's revolution.

El elefante y la bicicleta (The Elephant and the Bicycle) Juan Carlos Tabío / ICAIC, 1995, color, 85 min. *Music:* José María Vitier. *Cast:* Martha Farré, Luis Alberto García, Daisy Granados, Raúl Pomares, Lilian Vega.

As the film opens, a group of children contemplate a large, puffy cloud that floats lazily over their little island. Some of the children claim that the cloud is an elephant, while another group sees a bicycle. This simple fable reminds the viewer that what we may perceive as absolute truth is but an individual interpretation of reality. It aims to show that we as human beings assign value and meaning to what we see according to our own makeup; consequently, we must not begrudge others their interpretations, as they are just as valid as our own.

The story begins when an ex-convict returns to the island bringing a spectacular invention: an old movie projector and a single silent film, *Robin Hood*. The simple folk on the island marvel at the contraption to the point where they can't get enough of the film, which they view again and again. After a while a strange thing begins to occur: the island folk see the Robin Hood story as an allegory for their own situation of subservience to an unscrupulous landowner and as a guide for successful struggle against oppression. In the end they naively begin revolutionary action against the landowner.

In spite of the simple storyline, the film demands a measure of sophistication and sensitivity in its audience. Whether one finds it intellectually stimulating or a redundant bore will depend, I feel, upon the subtle attunement of one's sensibilities.

Director Juan Carlos Tabío Rey was born in Havana in 1943. He was a member of one of the first groups of young volunteers that went to rural areas in the early years of the revolution and virtually wiped out illiteracy. He began to work for ICAIC in 1961.

Elpidio Valdés Juan Padrón / ICAIC, 1979, color, 70 min. *Animation:* Erasmo Juliachs, Leonardo Piñero and and José Reyes. *Music:* Lucas de la Guardia and the National Symphony of Cuba.

Taking advantage of this character's popularity (see *Una aventura de Elpidio Valdés*), Juan Padrón decided to make a longer cartoon giving Elpidio Valdés' life story. Elpidio is born and grows up in the countryside next to the independence fighters that are struggling against Spanish colonial power. An informer gives them away, and Elpidio and his girlfriend María Silva are imprisoned. She is sent to a convent by the Spaniards, but they both manage to escape their captors and rejoin the Cuban fighters. The Spanish forces then attack the Cuban camp, but in spite of their superior numbers the Spanish are defeated.

Elpidio Valdés contra dólar y cañón (Elpidio Valdés Against Dollar and Cannon) Juan Padrón / ICAIC, 1983, color, 80 min. *Animation:* Mario García Montes and José Reyes. *Music:* Daniel Longres.

This is the second feature film with the cartoon hero Elpidio Valdés. Elpidio, a fighter in the Cuban Army of Liberation, is sent on an important and sensitive mission to Florida: he must insure that an arms shipment originating there gets to the insurgent Cubans. Once there, Elpidio must outwit Spanish agents, a greedy American sheriff, and the owner of a tobacco factory who not only exploits Cuban workers but dreams of getting the profits from the arms trafficking. In spite of all these obstacles, Elpidio gets the job done with the help of a Puerto Rican boat captain and an inventor.

Elpidio Valdés contra el tren militar (Elpidio Valdés Against the Military Train) Juan Padrón and José Reyes / ICAIC, 1974, color, 8 min. 10 sec. *Animation:* José Reyes and Erasmo Juliachs. *Music:* Lucas de la Guardia.

Popular cartoon character Elpidio Valdés has blown up a bridge in order to prevent Spanish reinforcements, traveling on a train, from reaching strong positions. The "bad guy," a Spanish general named Resóplez, ignores that the bridge has collapsed and falls with all his men into the ravine.

Elpidio Valdés contra la policía de New York (Elpidio Valdés Against the New York Police) Juan Padrón / ICAIC, 1976, color, 7 min. 6 sec. *Animation:* Erasmo Juliachs. *Music:* Lucas de la Guardia.

In the late 1800s, Cuban rebels have bought guns and ammunition to New York in order to bring them to the insurgents fighting the Spanish on the island. As the ship carrying them gets ready to sail, the expedition is denounced to the authorities. A contingent of police is sent to the docks, but the Cubans are able to outwit the dimwit "Yankees" and sail home with their cache.

En 3 y 2 (Three and Two Count) Rolando Díaz / ICAIC, 1985, color, 102 min. *Cast:* Samuel Claxton, Mario Balmaseda, Alejandro Lugo, Irela Bravo and Luis Alberto García, Jr.

The title refers to the terminal pitch count of three balls and two strikes in baseball. This is the story of one Mario "Truco" López, a famous ballplayer who must come to terms with his imminent retirement. As it happens with so many athletes, López still believes that he can play with the best of them, and it won't be easy for him to accept reality: time passes, our bodies decline, and life must continue through different paths.

En días como éstos (On Days Like These) Jorge Fraga / ICAIC, 1965, B&W, 83 min. *Writing credits:* Daura Olema, from her novel *La maestra rural*. *Music:* Juan Blanco and Ela O'Farrill. *Cast:* Mequi Herrera, Rebeca Morales, Carmen Delgado, Emérita Gerardo, Rosendo Lamadriz, Julia Menéndez, Marilys Ríos, Mirta Medina, Magaly Boix and Agustín Blásquez.

A young middle class woman living in the city, Elena goes off to the countryside as a volunteer worker to teach the peasants, but she has many misgivings about the radical (i.e. socialist) turn that the Revolution has taken. This causes a strain in her relationship with the other volunteers, who are more radical and committed than she is. Love relationships also come into the problematic mix, and as the alarm is given that an anti–Castro brigade has begun the invasion of the island, Elena flees while her new friend Miriam is left behind and tries to cover for her.

En la otra isla (On the Other Island) Sara Gómez / ICAIC, 1968, B&W, 41 min. *Music:* Tomás González Pérez.

The second largest island in the Cuban archipelago is the Isle of Pines, renamed Isle of Youth by the revolutionary authorities. It enjoys the dubious notoriety of being the "Siberia" of Cuba, the place where the major prison was built and where, after the triumph of the Revolution, young workers dreaded to be sent. This documentary follows the experiences of young people who actually chose to do their revolutionary work on that forsaken island. There they find interesting characters, like the black comedian whose career was stifled by racial prejudice. The director interviews some of the girls, asking them about sexual relations and other moral concerns. It is an interesting look at the Cuban youth of the '60s.

En tierra de Sandino (In the Land of Sandino) Jesús Díaz / ICAIC, 1980, color, 81 min. *Music:* Leo Brouwer.

This is a documentary that intrudes in the life of simple folk in Nicaragua at the time of the Sandinista revolution, filmed between August and October of 1979. It is a time of hope and hard work to build a new nation, and the documentary captures the spirit of the people of Nicaragua in times of great changes.

El enanito sucio (The Dirty Dwarf) Juan Padrón / ICAIC, 1975, color, 5 min. 15 sec. *Animation:* Erasmo Juliachs. *Music:* Lucas de la Guardia.

This cartoon is set in a camping ground where a young student tells the story of a dwarf. The dwarf in question enters a garden and dirties it with mud. An outraged girl, her toys and a dog give chase and capture the dwarf using a hose. They wash him, he likes himself clean, and he decides to stay in the garden, caring for the flowers and plants and painting them in pretty colors. This is a charming way to get kids to shower every day.

Escenas de los muelles (Scenes from the Port) Oscar Valdés / ICAIC, 1970, B&W, 29 min. *Music:* Roberto Valera. *Cast:* Humberto Molina, Ramón Ponce, Lupe Ramírez, Marta Cataya, Edwin Moore, Elsa Llangert and Lázaro Elliot (all non-professional actors).

This film is dedicated to Theodor Christensen, master of the documentary. A cross between fiction and the documentary, it follows the lives of Havana dock workers, their toil at the docks and the heated discussions among them. At a bar, surrounded by women, they argue and come close to blows. The atmosphere of drunken disputes and prostitution brings us back to a pre-revolutionary epoch, while the raging syndicalist struggle pits two friends against each other and reminds us of the many battles fought by Cuban labor during the life of the Republic.

Estampas habaneras (Postcards from Havana) Jaime Salvador / PECUSA–Antonio Perdices, 1939, B&W, 92 min. *Music:* Gilberto Valdés. *Cast:* Carlos López (Chaflán), Blanquita Amaro, Tony Bartolomé, Federico Piñero, Alberto Garrido, Julio Gallo, Julito Díaz, Alicia Rico, Margot Alvariño, María de los Ángeles Santana, José M. Linares Rivas, Alfredito Valdés, Wilfredo Grenier, Antonio Rodríguez and María Regina Rivero.

A young man kills a drunkard and has to flee to Mexico, leaving his sweetheart behind to be hounded by numerous suitors. Several misadventures take place in a boardinghouse which involve the guests, employees and owners, and in the end, as a result of young Caridad's prayers to the Virgin, her sweetheart is returned from Mexico. *Estampas habaneras* is at times teasing and amusing, but it simply does not come together well. It does not find a sufficiently firm line on which to hang, and the characters are much too shallow and vagrant for substantiality.

El extraño caso de Rachel K. (The Strange Case of Rachel K.) Oscar L. Valdés / ICAIC, 1973, color, 90 min. *Music:* Leo Brouwer. *Cast:* Mario Balmaseda, Norberto Blanco and Carlos Gili.

In the early years of the republic, Havana attracted the best nightclub dancers and most notorious prostitutes from around the world. They would often show up at orgies financed and attended by powerful politicians and prominent leaders who, the next morning, would resume their outwardly respectable family and social lives and nobody would be the wiser. When a French dancer turned up dead after one of these affairs, many a respectable leader became very nervous about what the ensuing investigation might turn up. Using all the resources available to them, they undertook to perplex the police and lead them down the garden path, making this case one of the strangest in the history of the Havana police.

El extraño caso de Rachel K. is a fictional though plausible recreation of that historical scandal.

Facciamo fiesta (Let's Have a Party) Angelo Longoni / ICAIC–Cecchi Gori Group Tiger Cinematografica (Italy)–Thunder Films (Italy), 1997, color, 96 min. *Music:* Paolo Vivaldi. *Cast:* Blas Roca-Rey, Yoandra Suárez Borrego, Carlos Miguel Caballero, Lorena Forteza, Alessandro Gassman and Gianmarco Tognazzi.

This is a Cuban-Italian co-production. Capitalizing on the wave of Italian tourists (mostly young males) who travel to Cuba to partake of forbidden pleasures (not-so-forbidden in Cuba if you have foreign currency), Angelo Longoni tells the story of two Italian fellows (Alessandro Gassman and Gianmarco Tognazzi) who go to Cuba to film a documentary. Once there, they meet the inevitable voluptuous vixens, get ripped off by local picaresque characters, and basically hang around Havana having a good time with the happy-go-lucky, devil-may-care Cubans. Yes, these Cubans may be mired in indigent penury, may be childishly amoral, devious and futureless, but give them a conga drum and they'll be unconsciously happy in their hovels and deteriorating streets, unlike the superior, well-fed, cheerless, neurotic Europeans who've lost their ability to get the spice out of life.

This flick reminds one of the worst stereotyping ever generated by United States imperialist visions of the island. It could serve the purpose of documenting European attitudes towards Cuba and as an example of movies to avoid. *Let's Have a Party* indeed.

55 hermanos (55 brothers) Jesús Díaz / ICAIC, 1978, color, 77 min., *Music:* Sergio Vitier.

A group of children who left Cuba after the Revolution now return to the island as members of the "Antonio Maceo Brigade." This documentary follows them as they are shown around the island and participate in diverse activities. Having the children of exiles return to have a look was a political coup for the Cuban government.

Director Jesús Díaz Rodríguez was born in Havana in 1941. He is primarily a writer, having won the prize "Casa de las Américas" with his collection *Los años duros* (1966). He is also the author of *Cantos de amor y de Guerra* (1978), *De la patria y el exilio* (1979) and his best known work is *Las iniciales de la tierra* (1987), a novel of the Revolution.

The Fighting Fifth Cuban Mascot Selig Polyscope Company, 1898, B&W, 15.24 meters long.

U.S. soldiers have come back from Cuba to Fort Sheridan with a little burro that became attached to them on the island. The young men wrestle with the animal and play around with it like children.

Filminuto 1 (Film Minute # 1) Juan Padrón / ICAIC, 1980, color, 6 min. 13 sec. *Animation:* Erasmo Juliachs. *Music:* Daniel Longres.

This cartoon short cramps much into its six-minute frame: the misadventures of a vampire that becomes drunk, a public execution in which the executioner becomes the executed, and the disillusionment of a vampire dad with his underachieving son. G-string wearing female victims of the vampires and the racy nature of the jokes gives us the strong impression that this cartoon is intended for an adult audience.

Filminuto 2 (Film Minute # 2) Juan Padrón / ICAIC, 1980, color, 6 min. *Animation:* Erasmo Juliachs. *Music:* Daniel Longres.

A series of jokes told through animation: a strange discovery at a planet's pole, all about door knockers, the cruelty of the desert, why a letter "T" is rejected, a hot vampire, the soul of a mercenary and a surprise in the shower.

Filminuto 3 (Film Minute # 3) Juan Padrón / ICAIC, 1981, color, 6 min. *Animation:* Erasmo Juliachs. *Music:* Daniel Longres.

In this third edition of the Filminuto series, the issues tackled are inflexibility of character, bureaucratic bungling, the dangers of the U.S.–caused armaments race, and machismo. Jokes involve the predicament of a vampire in a restaurant and of elves in contemporary society.

(Filminuto 4 was not finished.)

Filminuto 5 (Film Minute # 5) Tulio Raggi / ICAIC, 1982, color, 5 min. 18 sec. *Animation:* José Reyes. *Music:* Daniel Longres.

This fifth "Filminuto" cartoon offers a different take on the William Tell story: this time his arrow misses the apple. It also has Little Red Riding Hood's wolf committing suicide after the girl falls in love with another wolf; torture in the eighteenth century; and a musical escapade down the Nile River.

Filminuto 6 (Film Minute # 6) Mario Rivas / ICAIC, 1982, color, 5 min. 15 sec. *Animation:* Noel Lima. *Music:* Daniel Longres.

Four jokes told through animation. In the first, Dracula returns to terrify some children; the second has a prehistoric circus where a lion tamer practices his trade with a dinosaur; the third illustrates the consequences of sedentarism, and the fourth presents a musical brain.

Filminuto 7 (Film Minute # 7) Mario Rivas / ICAIC, 1982, color, 4 min. 54 sec. *Animation:* Noel Lima. *Music:* Daniel Longres.

This cartoon tells four more jokes in the "Filminuto" series. The Wolfman story gets a new ending, a woman is about to give birth with her significant other hovering nervously around her, a chess player takes his time to make his next move, and a samurai bestows a present.

Fires Within (Little Havana) Gillian Armstrong / United International Pictures (Spain), 1991, color, 86 min. *Music:* Maurice Jarre. *Cast:* Jimmy Smits, Greta Scacchi, Vincent D'Onofrio, Luis Ávalos, Bertila Damas, Raúl Dávila, Daniel Fern, Earl Hindman, Kevin Duffis, Victor Rivers, Lázaro Pérez, Angelina Estrada, Julia Rodríguez Elliot, María Vidal, Daniel Ades, Oswaldo Calvo, Rubén Rabasa, Michael McCleery, Raimundo Rey, Peppin Valera, Marie Curie, Mia Gurri, Juan Albert Aynat, Willy Areu, Carlos Gómez, Luis Malespín, Humberto "Nenque" Hernández, Ángel Figueroa, Jorge Raúl Guerrero, Raoul San, Christina Paige, Robert Escobar, Manny Rodríguez, Mario Ernesto Sánchez, Carmen López, Sergio Doré, Jr., Robert Marrero, Rose Trujillo, Sal Mares and Celia Cruz (as herself).

"Isabel and Néstor Barón lived a dangerous life. In 1982 she escaped from Cuba ... her husband was not so lucky. Eight years away from her past, she found another love in Little Havana. But now, the man she thought she'd lost forever is coming back into her life. Nothing burns as deeply as choosing between two passions..." (Trailer).

For Love or Country: The Arturo Sandoval Story Joseph Sargent / CineSon Productions–Jellybean Productions, 2000, color, 120 min. *Music:* Arturo Sandoval. *Cast:* Andy García, Mía Maestro, Gloria Estefan, David Paymer, Charles Dutton, Tomás Milián, Freddy Rodríguez, Andy Méndez, Félix David Manrique, José Zúñiga, William Márquez, Steven Bauer, Fionnula Flanagan, Michael O'Hagan, Miguel Sandoval, Nicky Farrell, Robert Wisdom, Oswaldo Calvo, Víctor Trujillo, Miriam Colón, Mario Ernesto Sánchez, Julio Óscar Mechoso, Mercedes Enríquez, Deborah Magdalena, Alfredo Álvarez Calderón, Tyler Cravens, Harrison A. Biswas and Britt George.

An HBO made-for-television production, the film tells the story of jazz trumpet great Arturo Sandoval. Andy García gives a masterful performance as Sandoval, as this role suits him perfectly: he loves Cuba and he loves Cuban music. Sandoval is torn between his love for his native Cuba and his love for music. The two loves come into conflict because in his native land he feels he cannot express himself freely or give free flight to his talents. So it comes to a point where he must choose one (Cuba) or the other (music). He chooses music only after a protracted struggle with himself and with his wife, who, along with his son, he does not want to leave behind when he goes. Another problem is that his wife (played by Mía Maestro) is a Castro supporter; she is, in fact, a government employee. But as events play out, she also goes through much soul-searching and eventually decides that the best course of action is to leave Cuba with her husband and son. Charles Dutton gives a good performance as Dizzy Gillespie, who, as it turns out, had a hand in the way the real story developed.

This is a story whose poignancy is enhanced by the knowledge that the events and characters portrayed are all real. The story, told as a series of flashbacks, is enhanced by the accomplished musical score and is made more engaging by the concomitant love story. It was filmed in Miami and Puerto Rico.

Fresa y chocolate (Strawberry and Chocolate) Tomás Gutiérrez Alea and Juan Carlos Tabío / ICAIC–Instituto Mexicano de Cinematografia–Miramax Films U.S.–Tabasco Films–Telemadrid, 1994, color, 111 min. *Writing credits:* from the novel *El lobo, el bosque y el hombre nuevo* by Senel

Fresa y chocolate

Under the stern gaze of national hero José Marti, David (Vladimir Cruz, left) and Diego (Jorge Perugorria, right) begin to break down traditional barriers that in the Cuban past have prevented straight men from befriending gays in the film *Fresa y chocolate*. Here they find they have much in common. (ICAIC)

Paz. *Music:* José María Vitier. *Cast:* Jorge Perugorria, Vladimir Cruz, Mirta Ibarra, Francisco Gattorno, Jorge Angelino and Marilyn Solaya.

David is a Communist student whose personal life is in somewhat of a shambles. His girlfriend has left him to marry a man of means and he is left drifting. He stops at Havana's Copelia park for a bit of ice cream; there he meets the flamboyant Diego. As if Diego's demeanor weren't enough to mark him as a homosexual, his choice of ice cream flavor (strawberry, on a rare day when chocolate was available) definitely marks him as such in David's mind. In their conversation, David is stunned to hear Diego overtly criticize the Castro regime, especially in its treatment of gays. In spite of the ideological and gender preference differences that separate them, David accepts Diego's invitation to visit his apartment. He is lured there by the expectation that he will find illicit delights such as American records, *Time* magazine and Scotch whiskey, in spite of knowing that Diego aims to seduce him. Miguel, a Communist Party faithful, encourages David to spy on Diego, whose sexual preference most likely makes him a dangerous dissident. Miguel can then pass the information on to the government. But the more time David spends with Diego, the more intrigued he is with this interesting, intelligent individual. He also starts fancying Diego's neighbor Nancy, with whom he will eventually make love.

David and Diego will in time develop a friendship that overcomes ideology and shatters the prejudices that are prevalent in their society.

All things considered, this is a sensational representation of certain aspects of life in contemporary Cuba, a brilliant graphic estimation of a repressed society and a withering commentary upon the tragedy of a nation adrift. Señores Gutiérrez Alea and Tabío are nothing if not fertile, fierce and urbane in calculating the social scene around them and packing it into the screen. They have, too, a splendid sense of balance and a sardonic wit that guided the cameras and the script. As a consequence there are scores of piercing ideas that pop out in the picture's nigh two hours and leave one shocked, amused, revolted and possibly stunned and bewildered at the end.

This comes through with devastating impact in an episode wherein one of Diego's gay friends, an artist, is prevented from participating in an art exposition overseas because of his sexual orientation. He throws a fit where he destroys his work and, devastated, has a nervous breakdown.

In sum, it is an awesome picture, perhaps a bit licentious in content but moral in its attitude and what it says. Also, an excellent cast gives a memorable performance.

Gallego (The Man from Galicia) Manuel Octavio Gómez / ICAIC–Televisión de Galicia, 1988, color, 128 min. *Writing credits:* based on a homonym novel by Miguel Barnet. *Music:* Pablo Milanés. *Cast:* Sancho Gracia, Manuel Galiana, Jorge Sanz, Linda Mirabal, Alberto Pedro, Álvaro de Luna, Leticia Herrera, Rosalía Daus, César Diéguez, Lorenzo Castillo, Antonio Ferrandis, Fiorella Faltoyano, Francisco Rabal, Conrado San Martín, Omar Valdés and Raúl Eguren.

Miguel Barnet is one of the first writers in Cuba to practice the "novela testimonio," a type of novel written after tape-recording certain subjects who tell their story. That story is incorporated as faithfully as possible, changing only those elements that clash with the flow of the story or the author's particular aesthetic and ideological needs. This film is based on his story of a Galician immigrant to Cuba. He goes to the island from his native Galicia as an adolescent in 1916, does a number of menial jobs in Havana, and watches Cuban history unfold before his eyes. The story ends during the first years of the Castro revolution; the youngster has grown old and wise.

Gay Cuba Sonja De Vries / Félix Varela Center (Cuba), 1995, color, 57 min. *Music:* Pablo Milanés and Silvio Rodríguez. *Cast:* Jennifer Maytorena Taylor (narrator).

Some things are very difficult to change. Castro's revolution had promised reforms in every facet of Cuban life, from the rights of women to racial equality, but when it came to gays, things got worse. Long viewed as anti-social, immoral counterrevolutionaries, they were the outcasts they had always been in Cuban society.

Through interviews with everyone from officials to gays themselves, this documentary describes the changes that are slowly but surely taking place in people's perceptions of gays as well as the growing acceptance of their way of life. International pressure has apparently had its effects on party policy towards homosexuals, and this is reflected in the new openness with which they lead their lives. The positive way in which the people on the street speak of their gay fellow-citizens also attests to that change at all levels of society.

Girón (The Bay of Pigs) Manuel Herrera / ICAIC, 1972, B&W, 120 min. *Music:* Sergio Vitier, Carlos Fernández Averhoff and ICAIC's Grupo de Experimentación Sonora.

Using interviews with soldiers who participated in the battles, newsreels and reconstructions, this documentary presents a vivid overview of the failed Bay of Pigs invasion staged by Cuban exiles in 1961. This testimonial stars the common people who took part in the action coming back to the scene of the battles; they tell their stories, which are then reproduced as they speak.

In a way, *Girón* proves just how important the cinema is as a tool to reach the masses. As one of the fighters relates the story of having to throw a hand grenade for the first time, he states that he considered pulling the pin with his teeth, "like they do in the movies." Fortunately he reconsidered, realizing that the move would have cost him his teeth and his jaws. In another instance, a woman relates her experiences hand-delivering a message from a unit to field headquarters. As she was walking by a beach, she heard some strange noises, and like a cinema heroine put the message in her mouth and tried to swallow it. She ended up chewing the unsavory, unyielding paper longer than expected.

Director Manuel Herrera Reyes was born in Santa Clara, Cuba, in 1942. He has done many short subject films and documentaries dealing with practical matters, such as *Cría porcina* (The Raising of Pigs, 1965) and *Papel, vidrio y metal* (Paper, Glass and Metal, 1966).

Giselle. Enrique Pineda Barnet / ICAIC, 1964, B&W, 88 min. *Music:* Adolphe Adam. *Cast:* Alicia Alonso and the Cuban National Ballet, Fernando Alonso, Azary Plisetsky, José Parés, Mirta Plá, Loipa Araujo, Vania Mischvek, Ana Marini, Josefina Méndez, Margarita de Sanz.

Choreographed and interpreted by Alicia Alonso, Cuba's prima ballerina, the film brings this outstanding performance to a general public that might not have had access to the ballet before. This film is part of the effort by the revolutionary government to bring the arts to the people.

Director Enrique Pineda Barnet was born in Havana in 1933, the cousin of famous novelist Miguel Barnet. Writer, journalist, radio personality and theater worker, he is one of the founders of the "Nuestro Tiempo" group, opposed to the Batista regime.

Golpes a mi puerta (Knocks at My Door) Alejandro Saderman, Carlos González / ICAIC, 1992, Color, 105 min. *Music:* Julio D'escriván. *Cast:* Elba Escobar, Juan Carlos Gené, Verónica Oddo, José Rodríguez, Frank Spano, Ana Castell, Eduardo Gil, Dimas González, Mirta Ibarra.

In this Cuban-Venezuelan-Argentine-British co-production, an anti-government radical is taken in by two tolerant and generous nuns, Ana and Úrsula, who shelter him from the police and from Church authorities. The town mayor, desiring to keep his relations with the local Church undiminished, refuses to search the nuns' home, and although he suspects they are hiding something, he accepts their explanation. The inevitable bad guy, a captain that believes neither in the mayor nor in the powers of the Church, forces his way into the home, finds the radical, and has him shot. Now everyone even remotely involved in the affair (the mayor, Ana the nun) is in deep trouble.

The main characters, both the altruist nuns and the sinister politicians, are presented as well-rounded, complex individuals who are constantly beset by trepidation about their actions. From the beginning scenes, where a Mass is held for a victim of the government, the savvy viewer will easily predict the upcoming turn of events. This latest victim of the local death squads happens to be a priest, a situation that makes the compromising mayor decide to leave the nuns alone. The mayor, played very well by Juan Carlos Gené, is an intricate and nuanced character that one expects to be a one-sided bad guy, but surprises in his apparent empathy with the victims of torture. He seems appalled, for example, when he learns that the local school has been turned into a torture chamber. He also looks the other way when the radical escapes. The nuns are also well-defined characters. The young Úrsula has feelings of repressed desire towards this young, handsome radical whom she observes as he sleeps and for whom she buys cigarettes; the older Ana brings her maternal instinct to bear, both in her protection of the rebel and in her supervision of the young and impressionable Úrsula. With the presence of a male in her home Ana herself remembers that she is a woman. At one point she openly regrets never having had "a man's love." This in a way begets the ambience of competition that develops between the two women. The movie was adapted from a two-act play by Juan Carlos Gené, who gives an outstanding performance as the mayor. The 1982 stage production of the play in Caracas also featured Verónica Oddo; she has successfully transferred her talents to film.

Guantanamera Tomás Gutiérrez Alea, Juan Carlos Tabío / ICAIC, 1995, Color, 102 min. *Music:* José Nieto. *Cast:* Mirta Ibarra, Jorge Perugorría, Carlos Cruz, Conchita Brando, Raúl Eguren, Pedro Fernández, Suset Pérez Malberti, Luis Alberto García.

This sexy road movie opens as a mid-level bureaucrat meets with his committee and acquaints them with his scheme to save the government important resources. He gets the chance to put his scheme to practice when his wife's aunt Yoyita, a popular singer living in Havana, drops dead as she is about to make love to her old flame Cándido. The problem is that Yoyita has died in Santiago, but she wished to be buried in Havana, hundreds of miles away. Her niece Georgina, using her best logic, proposes hiring a hearse and transporting the body to Havana, but her bureaucrat husband needs to put his theories into practice. Using a precise mathematical model, they will cross the island with the body, changing hearses at each province so the cost of fuel will be distributed evenly, and the costly trip of the empty hearse back to Santiago will be avoided.

In a parallel story, two lorry drivers set out from Santiago towards Havana following the same route. One of the drivers turns out to be Georgina's old student, who has harbored amorous feelings for her since his school days. The two caravans cross paths several times as they traverse the island, giving a clear account and strong criticism of the destitute state of the nation.

Habanera (Havana Woman) Pastor Vega / ICAIC, 1984, color, 101 min. *Music:* Carlos Fariñas. *Cast:* Daisy Granados, Ely Menz, Marcia Barreto, Adolfo Llauradó, Miguel Benavides, César Évora, Parmenia Silva, Linda Mirabal, Hilda Oates, Raúl Eguren, Elvira Cervera, Amarilis Pumeda, Zaida Castellanos, Shenda Román, Aarón, Herón and Hiran Vega.

A middle aged female psychiatrist, devoted wife and mother, seeks the help and advice of a friend when she learns that her husband is having an affair. What makes matters worse is that the affair is with one of her own patients, a beautiful young Brazilian student. A period of self-questioning ensues in which the psychiatrist unveils her idealistic past and compares it with her present. The portrayal of her tribulations gives the director a chance to explore contemporary Cuban society.

Hacerse el sueco

The world of a young psychiatrist (Daisy Granados) is shattered (along with her mirror) when she learns that her husband is having an affair with one of her patients in Pastor Vega's *Habanera*.

Director Pastor Vega Torres was born in Havana in 1940. He learned acting beginning in 1958 at Havana's Teatro Estudio, and he's performed in important films such as *La decision* (José Massip, 1962). Besides his work as an actor, he began to work as assistant director in ICAIC films beginning in 1960. He has headed ICAIC's International Relations Unit and has been in charge of the Havana Film Festival.

Habrá una vez (There'll Come a Time) Roberto H. Flores / Escuela Internacional de Cine y Televisión (EICTV) (Cuba), 1997, color, 10 min. *Cast:* Pablo Hare and Edgar Soberón Torchia.

A science fiction short, the story is set in a post-nuclear-holocaust world where the survivors have been reduced to hunting and gathering among the ruins. The individuals living in this hellish environment go by colorful names like Batuk and Atón. The human inquisitive spirit is not lost after the disaster, however, as a young hunter goes around exchanging food for books.

Hacerse el sueco (Make Believe You're Swedish) Daniel Díaz Torres / ICAIC–Arthaus–TVE, 2000, color, 105 min. *Music:* Edesio Alejandro and

Gerardo García. *Cast:* Peter Lohmeyer, Enrique Molina, Mijail Mulkay, Coralia Veloz and Ketty de la Iglesia.

In this Cuban-Spanish-German co-production, an enterprising burglar has a brilliant idea: he'll pull off a spectacular jewel heist in Cuba while posing as a Swedish literature professor. In a standard formula in Cuban films, love puts a wrench in the plans: the thief falls in love with the daughter of a retired cop and virtually becomes a part of her family. With Havana as a backdrop, the story then becomes a comedy of errors where the would-be jewel thief must play the innocent tourist-academic and is even forced to give a highly amusing, spontaneous lecture on Pippi Longstocking.

He finally pulls off the heist and high tails it to the airport with the loot, his sweetheart's dad hot on his heels. At that point he begins to have second thoughts as to what he should do: split with the booty, or give it up and return to the real treasure that awaits him in the form of a young Cuban beauty.

Hanoi, martes 13 (Hanoi, Tuesday the 13th) Santiago Álvarez / ICAIC, 1967, color, 38 min. *Music:* Leo Brouwer.

The background to this documentary is the poetry of Cuban national hero José Martí. The narrative begins on Tuesday the 13th, the day Hanoi began to be bombed by the U.S. Air Force early in the Vietnam conflict. It follows the daily lives of normal Hanoi residents as they try to cope with the unusual circumstances of bombs falling from above, destroying their city and disrupting their lives. The heroic music and the poetry leave the viewer with a feel for the gallant and laudable struggle of regular people trying to survive under very unusual circumstances.

Hasta cierto punto (Up to a Certain Point) Tomás Gutiérrez Alea / ICAIC, 1983, color, 80 min. *Music:* Leo Brouwer. *Cast:* Oscar Álvarez, Mirta Ibarra, Omar Valdés, Coralia Veloz, Rogelio Blain, Ana Viña, Claudio A. Tamayo, Luis Celerie, Lázaro Núñez and Elsa Medina.

Oscar is a scriptwriter working on a film about the persistence of machismo in Cuban society. He and Arthur, the director, choose the port of Havana to elaborate their story, feeling that among the brawny port workers the age-old macho culture will have its maximum exponents. Oscar is married to Marian, who supports her husband in every way and is quite attractive. While doing his research at the port, Oscar meets Lina, a checker at the port who is the single mother of a ten-year-old. This self-sufficient woman appeals to Oscar at a level in which his neo-bourgeois wife does not, and he is taken by her rustic charm. They begin a love affair, but it soon becomes apparent that Lina will not sit idly by while Oscar remains in his neat, stable relationship at home: it's either all or nothing. She is not the type that will become the kept woman waiting for her married lover to spare some time for her.

In spite of Oscar's problems, he still manages to film several interviews with dock workers who talk of their experiences with women. One says that although he agrees with the concept of women's liberation, he will never be comfortable with the idea of having a liberated woman as his wife. Another tells the story of a dockworker who kept his wife at home, afraid she would find a lover if she worked, but with the large amount of free time she had on her hands she started an affair that destroyed his marriage.

The film gives a pessimistic account of the effort by the government to change basic attitudes in the population. It seems to say that, in its battle against age-old mind-sets and entrenched values, the government is losing. This is brought home when we see that even the scriptwriter falls prey to the attitudes he was planning to combat in his documentary.

Hasta la victoria siempre (Onwards to Victory) Manuel Octavio Gómez / ICAIC, 1967, B&W, 19 min.

A melodramatic documentary shot right after the death of Che Guevara in Bolivia at the hands of the CIA and Bolivian Army Rangers. It portrays the general misery of the Latin American poor and the efforts of the guerrilla leader to better their lot.

Havana Sydney Pollack / Mirage–Universal, 1990, color, 145 min. *Writing credits:* from a story by Judith Rascoe. *Music:* Dave Grusin. *Cast:* Robert Redford, Lena Olin, Alan Arkin, Tomas Milian, Raúl Julia, Daniel Davis, Mark Rydell, Tony Plana, Betsy Brantley, Lise Cutter, Richard Farnsworth, Vasek Simek, Fred Asparagus, Richard Portnow, Dion Anderson, Carmine Caridi, James Medina, Victor Rivers, David Rodríguez, Alfredo Vorshim, Bernie Pollack, Daniel Vázquez, Miguel Ángel Suárez, Sharon Velez, Segundo Tarrau, Franklin Rodríguez, Mildred I. Ventura, Karen Russell, Owen Roizman, Raúl Rosado, Darlene Wynn, Alex Ganster, Carmen de Franco, Félix Germán, David Gibson, Enrique Chao Barros, Miguel Bucarelly, Anthony Bayarri, Giovanna Bonnelly, René Monclova, Bonita Marco, Salvadore Levy, Carlos Miranda, Adriano González, Pepito Guerra, Joe Lala, Tera Hendrickson and Hugh Kelly.

This is a U.S.–made movie with a Cuban theme. If the story seems awfully familiar, it is because *Havana* was conceived as a re-telling of *Casablanca*. In this film, Robert Redford plays Jack Weil, a professional gambler who wishes to cash in on the anarchic last hours of dictator Fulgencio Batista's regime. Once in Havana, he inevitably meets a beautiful woman who is an entrenched communist's wife. They fall in love, of course, a situation that makes Redford have to choose between his self-serving desires and the common good.

If one can look beyond the politicization of the story, one will be able to enjoy the evocative, late 1950s Havana atmosphere, complete with Meyer Lansky types, strippers, corrupt officials and dark, awe-inspiring women. One of its good points is the original score by jazz great Dave Grusin, nominated for the Academy Award as well as the Golden Globe.

Havana Widows Ray Enright / Warner Bros., 1933, B&W, 63 min. *Cast:* Joan Blondell, Glenda Farrell, Guy Kibbee, Lyle Talbot, Allen Jenkins, Frank McHugh, Ruth Donnelly, Hobart Cavanaugh, Ralph Ince, Maude Eburne, George Cooper, Charles Wilson and Garry Owen.

A very attractive Warner Bros. film, *Havana Widows* features Joan Blondell and Glenda Farrell as two devious beauties that make a living by extorting money from vulnerable elder gentlemen. And what better place to do it than in Havana, the sin capital of the Caribbean. What makes this a comedy is their target: a self-proclaimed, puffed-up defender of ethical principles who, as it turns out, is more inclined to drink and women than to saving souls. The snag, of course, is that somebody falls in love: the swindle is ruined when Blondell falls in love with the target's son Bob, played by Lyle Talbot. As we all expected, everybody lives happily ever after.

Hello Hemingway Fernando Pérez / ICAIC–Metro, 1990, color, 90 min. *Writing credits:* From a story by Maydo Royero. *Music:* Edesio Alejandro. *Cast:* Laura de la Uz, Raúl Paz, Herminia Sánchez, José Antonio Rodríguez, Micheline Calvert, María Isabel Díaz, Caridad Hernández, Enrique Molina and Marta del Río.

Director Fernando Pérez has conceived a charming story about Ernest Hemingway's teenaged next door neighbor (Laura de la Uz in a fine performance). Poverty-stricken, the girl finds escape from her surroundings by reading Hemingway's *The Old Man and the Sea* and dreaming of getting a scholarship to a school in the United States. But even her simple dreams prove to be too far-fetched and unreachable in the stagnant social environment of Batista's Cuba. The film won First Prize at the 1990 Havana Film Festival.

Historia de un ballet (The Story of a Ballet) José Massip / ICAIC, 1962, color, 30 min. *Music:* Original pieces by the Yoruba Ballet.

Much of the black Cuban population descends from the Yoruba tribe of the region around the Gulf of Guinea. In the spirit of recapturing the non–Spanish side of Cuban culture and bringing it to the fore, Afro-Cuban director José Massip filmed this documentary starring the dance company of the Cuban National Theater. They perform four pieces by choreographer Ramiro Guerra that are inspired by Yoruba customs, religion and culture in general. The music is heavy with drum beats and complicated African rhythms, the dancers are clothed in straw skirts and other items that remind us of deepest Africa, and the dance routines are compelling and dynamic.

Historia de una batalla (History of a Battle) Manuel Octavio Gómez / ICAIC, 1962, B&W, 39 min.

The main story in this documentary follows the massive mobilization of 100,000 young people who went into the interior and erased illiteracy in the country. This feat was accomplished in a year between 1961 and 1962. Cheerful youngsters, armed with pencils and notebooks, invade the countryside and leave a legacy of hope for the future among the people whose lives they touch.

Other aspects touched upon in this documentary are the hard work of common people building socialism, the battle against the Bay of Pigs invaders, and the historic confrontation with the U.S. at the Punta del Este Conference in Uruguay.

Historia de una descarga (Story of an Unloading) Melchor Casals / ICAIC, 1981, color, 24 min.

In January of 1981, a Soviet ship reaches the southern-coast port of Cienfuegos with 2,000 tons of paper pulp. The problem is that nobody knows where the pulp is destined. On top of that the port has no storage room available, and the longer the ship remains unloaded, the more money has to be paid out to the shipping concern. This documentary brings to light the continuing problems produced by the gigantic Cuban bureaucracy and the shortcomings of the central government's inexorable persistence on micromanagement.

Historias clandestinas en La Habana (Clandestine Stories in Havana) Diego Musiak / Adagio Films, 1998, color, 76 min. *Music:* Leonardo Lebas. *Cast:* Susú Pecoraro, Jorge Perugorría, Ulises Dumont, Luis Alberto García, Verónica Lynn, Humberto Páez, Jorge Martínez, Laura de la Uz.

A Cuban-Argentine co-production, this feature has an attractive

Argentine businesswoman, played with skill by Susú Pecoraro, visiting Cuba for the first time. She travels with some emotional baggage: back home in Buenos Aires she is divorcing her husband, a situation that partly explains her predisposition to become romantically involved with a Cuban taxi driver named Frank. In a sub-plot, a grieving garment business owner named Francisco, having lost his family, has traveled to Cuba, of all places, in order to commit suicide. In an unexpected twist, the taxi driver's mother recognizes Francisco as the passionate young lover who in her younger years got her pregnant and then abandoned the scene.

The filmmaker's exploration of relationships then touches upon homosexuality. As a gay couple argues over their coming out of the closet, the filmmaker showcases the problems inherent to a type of bond that is still ridiculed and maligned in Cuban society.

This is the line of the drama; it reveals a certain naïve simplicity punctuated by coincidence, a simplicity that in a way masks the complexity of the tensions implied. Certainly, the situations presented don't count as much as the intimations of personal feelings, moods and doubts that are the substance of the film.

Historias de la Revolución (Stories of the Revolution) Tomás Gutiérrez Alea / ICAIC, 1960, B&W, 81 min. *Music:* Carlos Fariñas (first episode), Harold Gramatges (second episode) and Leo Brouwer (third episode). *Cast:* First episode: Lilian Llerena, Reinaldo Miravalles and Eduardo Moure; second episode: Francisco Lago, Blas Mora, Enrique Fong, Encarnito Rojas, Tomás Rodríguez and Pascual Zamora; third episode: Calixto Marrero and Miriam Gómez.

In 1960 it was agreed that ICAIC should make its feature debut with a film that depicted key moments in the recently concluded revolutionary war. *Historias de la Revolución* gives us three key episodes in the story of that struggle: "El herido" (The Wounded Man), "Rebeldes" (Rebels) and "La batalla de Santa Clara" (The Battle of Santa Clara).

The first story deals with the assault on the Presidential Palace carried out by the radical group Directorio Revolucionario on 13 March 1957. Following the assault, a young rebel, shot in the leg, searches for a place to hide from the police. Upon seeing the wounded man, another character runs away, fearful of getting involved.

The second episode, "Rebeldes," is based on a story told to the director, Gutiérrez Alea, by Che Guevara. It takes place in the Sierra Maestra mountains in 1958. Rebels endure the bombardments from the Cuban Air Force and stick by their fallen comrades, giving the viewer a lesson in revolutionary solidarity.

The last episode, "La batalla de Santa Clara," is the most accomplished of the three. It was shot on location in Santa Clara with a montage that gives a clear idea of the progress of the battle. Scenes such as the capture of the military train, the battle between the infantry and the tank brigade, and the exploding Molotov cocktails amid the general chaos of armed action capture the intensity of battle. This episode has a conventional sentimental ending, as a woman rebel, while celebrating the victory and honoring a fallen comrade, discovers that the dead hero is her lover.

All things considered, the film, although set in a Cuban context, generalizes human conflict, as the ideological reasons why the killing is taking place takes a back seat to the price that individual human beings have to pay when violence is used to obtain change.

It is important to note that ICAIC and Gutiérrez Alea hired Otello Martelli to manage the cameras. Wanting their enterprise to be as un–American, as un–Hollywood as possible, the idea was to generate images in the Italian neo-realist style of the 1940s, something not unlike Rossellini's *Paisà* (a 1946 feature also shot by Martelli). The fact that *Historias de la Revolución* does not have a neo-realist feel to it may be due to the fact that Martelli was moving artistically closer to Hollywood in the '50s, both in his photographic style as well as in his lighting techniques. The abundant lack of experience at ICAIC's laboratory may well have contributed to the inadequately lit interiors that plague the film, particularly the first episode.

Holiday in Havana Jean Yarborough / Columbia, 1949, B&W, 73 min. *Writing credits:* from a story by Morton Grant. *Music:* Desi Arnaz, Ervin Drake, Doris Fisher, Albert Gamse, Fred Karger, Paul Mertz, Allan Roberts, Jimmy Shirl, René Touzet and Miguelito Valdés. *Cast:* Desi Arnaz, Elsa Lorraine Zepeda, Sig Arno, León Belasco, Argentina Brunetti, Cecilia Callejo, Ann Doran, Martín Galarraga, Nacho Galindo, Steven Geray, Fred Godoy, Mary Hatcher, Lillian Molieri and Tito Renaldo.

This movie is essentially a showcase for the talents of one Desi Arnaz. It is built on the weak storyline of a bandleader who splits up with his girl just before a big performance, giving him the freedom to paint the town red with happy-go-lucky pals. The film also stars Mary Hatcher and Ann Doran, but the real star here is Desi, who wrote the title song and also performs five other tunes.

Desiderio Alberto Arnaz y de Acha III, "King of the Rumba Beat," was born in Santiago de Cuba, Oriente Province, on 2 March 1917. His wealthy parents, Desiderio Jr. and Dolores de Acha, were well-known figures in Oriente, owning much land and involving themselves (especially the father) in politics. Desi's father was elected mayor of Santiago de Cuba in 1923, and senator to the National Congress in 1932. The 1933 riots that ousted dictator Gerardo Machado from power hurt the Arnaz family, which was fully identified with the people in power. Dolores and kids fled the family home only moments before an angry mob set fire to it; their property was confiscated and Desi's father was thrown in jail, where he spent six months.

Having lost everything, the Arnaz family fled to Miami as soon as the elder Arnaz was released from jail. In Miami they survived doing menial jobs and trying their hand at small businesses, such as importing bananas. One day Desi had a couple of dollars in his pocket and decided to enter a Miami pawnshop. Therein something caught his eye: a guitar, which he bought on the spot. This action would be the most momentous decision of his life. He fine-tuned his playing and got his father's friend to arrange for an audition with a rumba band called the "Siboney Septet," a house band at the Roney Plaza hotel. That's where he was spotted by Catalonian bandleader Xavier Cugat, who offered him a job provided he finished high school first. Six months later Desi had graduated and landed a job with Cugat at the very respectable rate of $25 a week.

After a year touring with Cugat, Desi decided to return to Miami, but he got Cugat to allow him the use of the "Xavier Cugat Orchestra" name for a $25 a week royalty payment. He thrived at the famous La Conga restaurant-nightclub, where his act was caught by Lorenz Hart (of Rodgers and Hart fame), who liked it so much that he returned to see Desi when he went to perform in New York. Taken by his talent, Hart became Desi's friend and began to teach him acting skills, finally casting him as "Manuelito" in the stage production of *Too Many Girls*. The play was a success and Desi and his conga line became the talk of the town.

RKO bought the film rights to *Too Many Girls* and cast Desi in the lead role, along with Richard Carlson, Ann Miller and Frances Langford. On the set his eye caught a nicely-built girl in tight slacks and a sweater. She would be playing the part of the ingénue and her name was Lucille Ball. Their relationship began almost immediately and they would marry on 30 November 1940.

After *Too Many Girls* Desi Arnaz starred in *Father Takes a Wife* (1941) with Adolph Menjou and Gloria Swanson. The plan was to have Desi sing the ballad "Perfidia" in the film to his own guitar accompaniment, but someone in the studio had the bright idea to have an Italian operatic singer dub his voice. The result was a ridiculous rendering of the song and the movie flopped.

His next film role was a dual one. He played a prince and a taxi driver in *Four Jacks and a Jill* (1942), and though the film did well at the box office, Desi once commented that he hoped nobody would remember it. This same year he starred in *The Navy Comes Through*, a story about a Merchant Marine vessel battling the Germans. With him starred George Murphy, Carl Esmond, Pat O'Brien, Jane Wyatt and Jackie Cooper.

Arnaz began touring this year (1942) for the Army and Navy Relief, raising money for the widows and orphans of American men killed in action. With him were figures such as Laurel and Hardy, Bob Hope, Groucho Marx, Charles Boyer, Eleanor Powell and Joan Blondell.

In 1943 Desi starred in MGM's *Bataan*, a job for which he was recognized with the Photoplay Award. After *Bataan* he enlisted in the Army Air Force, where he would spend much time doing latrine duty and other menial tasks as punishment for fighting with fellow soldiers. As a "Hollywood type," he was treated quite roughly by the other soldiers, but the hot-blooded Cuban would always fight back and, as a result, get into trouble.

While he was away in the Air Force, Lucy, pursuing a successful career back in Hollywood, filed for divorce (Sept. 1944). It seems that she had learned that Desi had had numerous affairs with many of the women who had worked with him. Desi obtained a temporary leave of absence and went to see Lucy, convincing her to withdraw the divorce papers. He was discharged from the military on 16 November 1945.

Back in Hollywood, without new prospects, Desi bought out his MGM contract and formed a band. He toured widely, ending at Ciro's of Hollywood; it was here that Howard Welsh, producer for Universal Studios, offered Desi the lead role in the musical *Cuban Pete*, co-starring Don Porter, Beverly Simmons and Joan Fulton. The film brought his band national recognition and he went on tour, ending at New York's famed Copacabana. His hits included "Babalú" and "Cuban Pete." It was during this period that Desi filmed *Holiday in Havana*. On 24 December 1949 Lucy and Desi appeared together on the "Ed Wynn Show."

By 1950 CBS was talking to Lucy about moving her hit radio show *My Favorite Husband* to the television screen. She convinced the producers to cast Desi as her husband, and the series *I Love Lucy* was born. Desi's idea to have the episodes captured on film rather than done live is the reason we can watch reruns today of programs that, in 1950, were not saved for posterity. For years, the show was number one in the nation.

In 1956 MGM released *Forever Darling*, starring both Lucy and Desi, with James Mason and Louis Calhern. By this time the Arnaz business interests had become an empire, and Desi insisted on running it himself. The pressure was overwhelming, and he began drinking heavily and spending weekends away from home. But business was booming, and Desi was able to buy RKO Studios and turn it into Desilu.

By 1959 the pressure overwhelmed Desi and he wanted out. Perhaps to get his mind off the work, he drank more than ever and had several affairs. In November of 1959 he asked Lucy for a divorce, blaming the constant rush and excessive work for the couple's woes. With "Lucy Meets the Mustache Man" the series *I Love Lucy* came to an end on 1 April 1960. Divorce was finalized on 4 May 1960. Desi later married Edie Hirsch and retired from television.

He made occasional appearances on talk shows like "The Sam Yorty Show" and the *Nosotros Awards Show*. With Sam Yorty he looked very ill, and after a commercial break it was announced that Desi would not return because he was not feeling well. He also appeared, with better results, on *The Dean Martin Show, The Tonight Show* and *The Danny Thomas Show*. In March of 1982 the U.S. Hispanic community made him guest of honor at a carnival, televised on the show *Siempre en domingo*. There, he performed a song with his children, Desi Jr. and Lucie.

Ill, he accepted what he probably knew would be his final performance, a part on the film *The Escape Artist* (1982), a Frances Ford Coppola production starring Raúl Julia, Joan Hackett and Jackie Coogan. In 1983 his wife Edie died of cancer, and so did he on December 2, 1986.

Un hombre de éxito (A Successful Man) Humberto Solás / ICAIC, 1986, color, 116 min. *Music:* Luigi Nono. *Cast:* César Évora, Raquel Revuelta, Daisy Granados, Rubens de Falco and Jorge Trinchot.

Humberto Solás envisions his movies as ample portrayals of slices of Cuban life during particular eras. This film is no different, as he attempts to capture a quarter century period beginning in the 1930s and ending with the Revolution. This is done through the story of two brothers, Javier and Darío, their days in school, their dreams for the future. The paths these two brothers take couldn't be more different. While politics and its world enchant Javier, Darío is progressively drawn to the world of radical revolutionary action. Javier learns to play the game of bourgeois politics and, putting aside all his scruples, ascends the ladder of political and economic success. He seduces the women that will help him climb, marries a newspaper magnate's daughter, and plots and schemes his way to the top of Cuban society. Darío, on the other hand, increases his radical activity of spreading leaflets and placing bombs, and he pays with his life.

So which of the two brothers is the successful man? In this rudimentary Cain and Abel saga it is easy to surmise that the word "successful" has to be taken with a grain of salt. Darío is the one who has led a life of principle and sacrifice, giving his life for a cause. Javier has an existence empty of principles, devoid of ethics or positive feelings. It is Darío who has "succeeded" in making his life mean something, to himself and to others.

Although the plot turns out to be trite and clichéd, the director has managed to capture the ambiance of 1940s Cuban society, with the opulence of the ruling classes and the defiance of the insurgent working classes.

El hombre de Maisinicú (The Man From Maisinicú) Manuel Pérez / ICAIC, 1973, B&W, 124 min. *Music:* Leo Brouwer, Silvio Rodríguez and the Grupo de Experimentación Sonora del ICAIC. *Cast:* Sergio Corrieri, Reinaldo Miravalles, Adolfo Llauradó, Raúl Pomares, Alberto Graverán, Rigoberto Águila, José Hermida, Enrique Molina, Mario Balmaseda, Raúl Eguren, Enrique Domínguez, Alfredo Perojo and Rogelio Blain.

The story is told as a flashback, starting with the hero's death. Alberto Delgado was a farm administrator who infiltrated the anti–Communist rebels fighting the Castro government early in 1964 in the Escambray mountains, his intention being to destroy them. Or was he really a counterrevolutionary fighting against the changes being instituted on the island? The story follows the 14 months prior to his death, slowly untangling his mysterious relationship with the anti–Castro rebels, but shedding little light on his true stance. The rebels are destroyed before they establish contact with United States operatives, and in the end we don't know if Delgado has been killed by Castro's forces or by the rebels themselves.

Director Manuel Pérez Paredes was born in Havana in 1939. He directs one of the three main subdivisions of the ICAIC.

Hombres de Mal Tiempo (The Men of Mal Tiempo) Alejandro Saderman / ICAIC, 1968, B&W, 32 min. *Music:* Carlos Fariñas. *Cast:* Miguel Benavides, René de la Cruz, Pedro Rentería, José A. Rodríguez, Omar Valdés and the old veterans of Cuba's war of independence.

Veterans of the famous battle of Mal Tiempo, between the Cuban rebel army and the Spanish colonial army, tell the story of the legendary engagement. These fellows are all over 90 years old, and they include a 108 year old ex-slave and a Galician who also participated. They reconstruct the battle for the crew, taking the cameramen through the fields and giving the details of how the battle developed and their particular role in it. Perhaps the best feature of this film is the intervention of these elder heroes, whose faces show the pride they feel at being a part of history.

Jíbaro (Wild Dog) Daniel Díaz Torres / ICAIC, 1985, color, 95 min. *Music:* Leo Brouwer. *Cast:* Salvador Wood, René de la Cruz, Adolfo Llauradó, Flora Lauten, Ana Viña, Enrique Almirante, Alejandro Lugo, Miguel Gutiérrez, Javier González, Gilberto Reyes, Orlando Casin, Raúl Pomares, Nancy González, Alberto Molina and Humberto García Espinosa.

In the beginning years of the Castro regime, in the early 1960s, a famous wild dog hunter named Felo starts having problems with all the changes being introduced by the Agrarian Reform and, generally, with revolutionary ideology. He has a misunderstanding with an old friend because of a woman. Before things get out of hand, he is able to put his personal issues on the back burner and use his dog-hunting skills to hunt down the malevolent counterrevolutionary farmers who are fighting the government in the Escambray Mountains.

El joven rebelde (The Young Rebel) Julio García Espinosa / ICAIC, 1962, B&W, 83 min. *Music:* Leo Brouwer. *Cast:* Blas Mora, Wember Bros, Carlos Sessano, José Yedra, Leonel Alleguez, Luis Oropesa, Inocencio Téllez, Rolando Menéndez, Reinaldo Miravalles, Amanda López and Ángel Espasande.

The film follows an original script by Cesare Zavattini, and tells the story of Pedro, a 17 year old rustic who leaves hearth and home to join the revolutionaries in their fight against the Batista government. Before setting off, he decides to steal a gun belonging to his friend's uncle, but he is unsuccessful. On the road, he is given a ride by a "guajiro" who intuits that the boy is attempting to join the rebels. At a village, they are stopped by soldiers looking for people who might be bringing supplies covertly to the rebels. The savvy peasant covers for Pedro, and the youngster sets off on his own again.

Stopping at a bar, Pedro steals a gun from a soldier, who notices the theft and gives chase after the boy. Cornered, Pedro shoots and wounds the soldier, and as the camera focuses in on his face, we see a mixture of self-satisfaction and apprehension.

A girl, who turns out to be a boy, brings him into the rebel camp where his gun is taken from him. To the young man's surprise, the apparent commander of this rebel unit is a black man named Artemisa. Pedro is quickly learning many lessons. First of all, things are not what he expected them to be, as the girl-boy shows him. Second, a black can assume a position of power and decision. Third, in the coming society the concept of property will be greatly transformed, as his gun — he is told — does not belong to him but to the Revolution.

Soon the stubbornness that conveyed Pedro to the mountains begins to produce negative results: in order to avoid the "humiliation" of attending a rebel school for peasants, he claims to be able to read already; eventually he fails to read an inscription on a bomb after a bombing raid.

Pedro is then sent on an expedition to a salt manufacturing plant near the sea, but on the way there he stops at a village and becomes acquainted with a young woman who is washing clothes at a pond. In a scene awash in sensual symbolism, the girl asks Pedro to bring her back a seashell from the shore, creating a deep sense of erotic anticipation in Pedro. Pedro (apparently he is one of the select handful of Cubans who've never seen the sea) fills his sack with the stolen salt and walks over to the sea to retrieve a seashell. Astonished by the vastness of the ocean, Pedro hangs around in a daze and, as the audience was anticipating, is seen and shot at by guards. All ends well, though, as he is able to run off into the underbrush and join his comrades.

On his way back he finds that the seashell girl's village has been bombed, and there is a general exodus taking place. He extracts the shell from his sack to hand it to the girl; it is now more a promise of victory than a symbol of passion. Back in camp, Pedro continues his education in revolutionary ethics as he is admonished for uttering racist insults and censured for picking fights when things don't go his way.

The film ends when, in the midst of battle, Artemisa is killed and Pedro takes over the machine gun he was manning. The audience now recalls Artemisa's last words to Pedro: "*This* is where you earn your gun."

Kid Chocolate Gerardo Chijona / ICAIC, 1987, B&W, 20 min.

This documentary follows the life of Kid Chocolate, the most famous boxer in Cuban history. Speaking in a sure, melancholic voice, "Kid" tells us that "to remember is to live again," and this is exactly what he does on camera, just before his 80th birthday. We follow his rise to fame in the U.S. boxing circuit, his championships, and we get a glimpse at his philosophy of life, his opinions about sports, women, fame and friendship.

Kleines Tropicana-Tropicanita (Little Tropicana) Daniel Díaz Torres / ICAIC–BMG International, 1998, color, 112 min. *Cast:* Carlos Cruz, Vladimir Cruz, Peter Lohmeyer, Corina Mestre, Enrique Molina, Jorge Molina and Thais Valdés.

A Cuban cop named Lorenzo has a strange job: he is a specialist in grave robberies. So when Hermann, a Cuban of German descent, is found dead and dressed like a bird in a grave that is considered holy by the locals, he is sent to investigate. He reports back to his boss, major Anancio, who seems thoroughly bored by the whole thing. The excessive number of characters makes the movie hard to enjoy passively, as one is constantly trying to remember characters and events.

Lorenzo investigates Hermann's landlady Dora, who is also an elevator operator, Águila and Silvia, cultural affairs workers, and Chrissy, a British "internationalist lover" who has interpreted her socialist internationalist mission as granting sexual favors to as many Third World types as she can. The long list of suspects is topped off by Xiomara (Hermann's mother), a dwarf, Nazis, neo–Nazis, Santería priests, a false Guatemalan who is a rapist, and a drag queen.

From the myriad of characters and the chaotic situation, one can surmise that *Tropicanita* is a microcosm of the greater chaos that is Cuba (remember that Díaz Torres also directed *Alicia en el pueblo de las maravillas*). The action proceeds from Lorenzo's report to his boss, whose imminent slumber is an unintended parallel to the public's mood after viewing this film.

Lágrimas negras (Black Tears) Sonia Hermann Dolz / Endirectocom, 1997, color, 75 min.

A warm and intimate documentary where legends of Cuban music narrate their experiences and give a history of the island's many contributions to the rhythms of Latin America. We follow these masters as they rehearse, go on tour, and talk about their experiences.

Spanish filmmaker Sonia Hermann Dolz had already explored the soul of Latin music in her 1993 film *Romance de Valentia*. In *Lágrimas negras* she creates a biography of sorts: the interviews with the musicians of the "Vieja trova santiaguera" (ages 62–84), as she follows them around Cuba and on tour in Europe, give us an intimate view of these five musicians, their hopes and dreams, their families, their women and their love of Fidel. But it is the music that gives this documentary its special charm.

"It is La Vieja Trova Santiaguera's love of son (Cuban pop music)—and their enthusiasm in playing and singing it—that Dolz uses to link the dozens of bits and pieces of 'Black Tears' into such a delightful, swinging film" (Philip Elwood, *San Francisco Examiner*, 30 April 1998).

Latino Bar Paul Leduc / ICAIC–Universidad de los Andes–Ópalo Films, 1991, color, 84 min. *Music:* Joan Albert Amargos, Gerardo Batiz, Benny Moré, J. Antonio Méndez, Tabu Ley Rocherau and Consejo Valiente. *Cast:* Juana Bacallao, Cecilia Bellorín, Milagros Carías, Antonieta Colón, Pedro Durán, Dimas González, Ernesto Gómez Cruz, John Johny, Jesús Liendo, Raúl Medina, José Elías Moreno, Marcos Moreno, Dolores Pedro, Nirma Prieto, Lisette Solorzano, Roberto Sosa, Janet Thode and Dianina Vargas.

I'm not sure of what Paul Leduc is trying to do in this Cuban-Spanish-Venezuelan co-production. There is absolutely no dialogue in the film, although the rich ambient background music sets the tone for the "action." The characters are the inhabitants of a derelict bar and brothel in Venezuela, and their aphasic nature responds, I can only guess, to their lack of voice in the capitalistic society in which they exist. There is a sort of love story in which a woman working the bar falls for an ex-con. The viewer sees the plight of these people, which presumably needs no explanation, and draws his own conclusions. This type of extravagance needs more insight and resources to pull off successfully.

LBJ Santiago Álvarez / ICAIC, 1968, B&W and color, 18 min.

This documentary takes a satiric look at U.S. society and political culture, whose true character is shown through the assassinations of Martin Luther King and John and Robert Kennedy.

Lejanía (Parting of the Ways) Jesús Díaz / ICAIC, 1985, color, 100 min.
Cast: Verónica Lynn, Jorge Trinchet, Isabel Santos and Beatriz Valdés.

Susana left Cuba ten years ago, abandoning her son Reinaldo. She now returns trying to recover her relationship with her son and erase the chasm that has opened up between them. The two have very different ideas

Jorge Trinchet and Isabel Santos in a scene from *Lejanía* (Parting of the Ways), directed by Jesús Díaz. A Cinema Guild Release.

as to what the outcome of their encounter should be. For him, it is imperative to recover the image he had of her as a loving, dedicated mother. For her, the most important thing is to take her son back to the U.S. to try to recover the lost years. They both eventually come to realize that it is too late: Reinaldo cannot bring back the young woman who nurtured him, Susana cannot bring back a son that now has a family of his own. In the end, both mother and child come to understand that time can't flow backwards, that some things are lost that can never be recaptured, that they must go their separate ways.

This could have been a film of epic proportions, given its subject. Cuba went through a civil war that split families and sent one million Cubans into exile. The weak acting and the shallow and artificial way in which this agonizing subject has been handled has prevented ICAIC and Señor Díaz from telling a remarkable story.

Leo Brouwer José Padrón / ICAIC–Sociedad General de Autores y Editores Españoles, 2000, color, 57 min.

Winner of the prestigious *El Mégano* Award for the year 2000, this documentary follows the life and career of Cuban musician extraordinaire Leo Brouwer. A very well-documented piece, it follows a career spanning 22 years, his main concerts, practice sessions, guitar classes and music festivals. This is a filmed dramatization of events in the musician's life that is expertly mixed with footage of Brouwer's many musical deeds. In this "dramatization" the actor is Brouwer himself, and he is interviewed, for example, in his car as he talks with some omnipresent interlocutor. In another scene he visits his friend, guitarist-composer Jesús Ortega, and the two reminisce and look at photographs. In yet another, his grand uncle speaks with him about his childhood, and later on a pajama-clad Brouwer leads us through his disordered library in search of an old document and again reminisces about the old times.

This accomplished, remarkable documentary began to take shape in the mind of José Padrón in 1996, when he began to put together all the materials that would coalesce, four years later, into the product we see today.

Leyenda (Legend) Rogelio París / ICAIC, 1981, color, 96 min. *Cast:* Ramoncito Veloz, Mario Balmaseda, Nelson Villagra, Raúl Pomares, Germán Pinelli, Aramis Delgado, Susana Pérez, Samuel Claxton, Manuel Porto, Ángel Espasande, René de la Cruz, Luis Alberto García, Rogelio Blaín, Omar Valdés and Ángel Toraño.

A Cuban counterrevolutionary working for the CIA is found dead in a yacht in the high seas. The story then becomes a reconstruction of the dead man's life, from his youth to the time he became an anti–Castro CIA operative. It gives viewers a close-up view of what makes a subversive tick, what motives generate his deeds.

Una leyenda americana (An American Legend) Mario Rivas / ICAIC, 1984, color, 9 min. 44 sec. *Animation:* Adalberto Hernández. *Music:* Daniel Longres.

In the beginning, in the time when only beautiful birds populated the earth, an ugly bird appeared. All the other birds knew not what to do with this unattractive individual, but at last they took pity on him and helped him transform into a magnificent bird. Thus endowed, the formerly ugly bird now began to act as a superior being. As if beauty were enough, it shunned learning and wisdom and began to create bad feelings among his peers, and between them and some strange ringed tigers that float around, stiff and open-mouthed, in the eccentric cosmos of Cuban animation.

Lista de espera (Waiting List) Juan Carlos Tabío / ICAIC-DMVB France–Canal Plus France–Producciones Amaranta Mexico–Road Movies Filmproduktion Germany–Tabasco Films–Tornasol Films de España–Vía Digital, 2000, Color, 106 min. *Writing credits:* Arturo Arango, based on his story. *Music:* José María Vitier. *Cast:* Vladimir Cruz, Thaimí Alvaiño, Jorge Perugorría, Saturnino García, Alina Rodríguez, Antonio Valero and Noel Valero.

A Cuban-Spanish-French-Mexican co-production, the film is set at a bus stop in the middle of nowhere in present day Cuba. On one side we can see a beautiful beach on the Caribbean where the tourists go to sun themselves, while at the other we spy the extreme poverty of a rural community. Every once in a while a bus comes by, the only means of transportation out of the impoverished town. But the buses are usually full, or can take one or two extra passengers, a situation that causes friction among the numerous would-be travelers waiting at the stop. People hoping to get to Havana or Santiago keep accumulating there, and the town's own bus, an ancient vehicle imported from the "Soviet bloc," is missing a part that is no longer available.

The situation sums up the predicament that the regular Joe-on-the-street faces daily in Cuba. Transportation is a basic necessity, be it to get to a job, to go back home to the family, or whatever the need, a necessity that is not met under current conditions on the island. As if underlining the basic human indignity of circumstances not supposed to be prevalent in a revolutionary society, a character yells at the beginning of the film:

"What is this, a capitalist or a socialist country?" The rest of the movie can be thought of as a quest for an answer to that question, an answer that proves extremely elusive.

At another point, an exasperated character exclaims: "I wonder if our destiny will be the same as that of characters in a movie I saw once, where the people could not exit a room although the doors were open." The reference is to Luis Buñuel's *El ángel exterminador* (The Exterminating Angel, 1962), where a group of bourgeois ladies and gentlemen is trapped by their own anguish, just as this group of workers and peasants is captive, metaphorically as well as physically, in a rural Cuban bus stop. Few situations can be more metaphorically significant, in present day Cuba, than a group of people from all walks of life unable to travel, unable to move, languishing in the inert morass of what should have been a platform from which to board a vehicle that would take them to their destination. The bus stop is for Tabío a social laboratory in which to take the pulse and temperature of his countrymen.

When a bus finally arrives (full), people will board according to how strong and athletic they are, a Darwinian situation given a Marxist twist: each will board, they exclaim, "according to his possibilities."

Lucía Humberto Solás / ICAIC, 1969, B&W, 160 min., 16 mm. *Writing credits:* Julio García Espinosa, Nelson Rodríguez, Humberto Solás. *Music:* Leo Brouwer. *Cast: Lucía* 1895: Raquel Revuelta, Eduardo Moure, Idalia Anreus and Silvia Planas; *Lucía* 1933: Eslinda Núñez, Ramón Brito, Flora Lauten and Rogelio Blain; *Lucía* 1960 s: Adela Legrá, Adolfo Llauradó, Teté Vergara, Aramis Delgado and Flavio Calderín.

Lucía is Cuba's first film spectacular, compared at times with *Gone With the Wind*. This is an epic, three-part feature film that dramatizes three separate periods in the struggle for national liberation, placing special emphasis on the role played by women in that struggle. The first part is set in 1895, with Lucía (played brilliantly by Raquel Revuelta) implicated in a tale of love and betrayal in the chaos of Cuba's war of national independence from Spain. This first Lucía is rapidly approaching that age in which the Cuban woman loses all hope of marriage. With most eligible bachelors off fighting the war for independence, Lucía falls for a married Spaniard just arrived from Spain. To encourage her feelings for him, the Spaniard assures her that he is politically neutral in the conflict between Cuba and Spain. He then proposes they flee together to her family's coffee plantation, thus sparing Lucía the humiliation of living openly with a married man. Because her brother is hidden in the plantation with his band of rebels, she feigns not to know where the plantation is located. Finally

Raquel Revuelta as the first of three Lucía characters in Humberto Solás' 1969 film *Lucía*. She walks the streets hiding a dagger with which she will soon kill the Spaniard who betrayed her love and is responsible for her brother's death.

relenting, she leads the Spaniard to the plantation, but they are followed by Spanish forces that destroy the rebel band and kill her brother. In a fit of madness, she stabs her Spanish lover to death in a public square. Issues of repressed sexuality and the exploitation of women are finely addressed in this part of the film. The epic battle scenes, with the Cuban soldiers riding naked against the Spaniards in their fancy uniforms, underscores the theme of a people fighting for freedom against the disciplined, well-paid minions of a colonial power.

The second part is set in 1933, with Lucía (played here by Eslinda Núñez) falling in love with a young man who is active in the clandestine struggle to overthrow the dictator Gerardo Machado. Leaving the safety (and boredom) of her middle-class environment, she begins to take an active part in the struggle, taking a menial job in a tobacco factory in order to support herself and her lover. Machado falls from power, but things don't change much, so her lover rebels against the new government and is killed for his trouble. In the end, we are left to ponder whether Lucía goes back home or continues to work against the status quo.

In this second part the violation of middle class sexual values is not

Lucía (Raquel Revuelta) falls in love with Spaniard Rafael (Eduardo Moure), a married man who makes her his mistress and eventually betrays her love and causes her brother's death. (ICAIC)

an issue, and even the machismo that is evident in part one is played down, as the male lover is as innocent and inexperienced in sexual matters as Lucía. As a woman, this Lucía has evolved from the almost childlike individual of part one to a more rounded, active and self-reliant person.

The third section, weakest of all three due to the blatant intrusion of official ideology, has Lucía (Adela Legrá) being taught to read and write during the literacy campaign waged by the revolution in the 1960s. Despite being married, she goes forth to learn of her newly acquired rights within the new socialist society. The social strains caused by the changing roles of men and women are embodied in Lucía's marital problems. Her husband, jealous of the young man who teaches Lucía, becomes violent and even beats her. He also feels that her desire to work reflects badly on his capacity to provide for her. He eventually begins to drink and continues to deteriorate as a human being. Eventually, he begins to realize that his wife's new independence and freedom bring him freedom as well. As we leave them still bickering at the end of the film, we understand that Solás is calling for a new mind-set, especially among men, in order to make the new society a viable one. The filmmaker is saying that socialist culture cannot be created while old value systems still prevail. This last Lucía, then, is immersed in a struggle to overcome her husband's *machismo*, a product of social values to be overcome by the socialist culture. Her husband, in his way, represents an added barrier to be conquered by women after the triumph of the Revolution.

Solás' achievement has been to capture the "feel" of each historical epoch through the peculiar visual style he assigns to each part of the film. In all three parts, the themes of love and war reach epic proportions. As we have seen, Solás brings to the fore the social and cultural attitudes that have traditionally given women second-class status. The film gives reason to expect a brighter future for Cuban women: each section gives an increasing role to the heroine in the events that shape the nation, such that the Lucía of the 1960s is more empowered than her homonym of 1895. Solás explains his film in this way: "*Lucía* is not a film about women but about society. In that society I selected the most vulnerable character, the one that is most obviously affected at any given moment by contradictions and changes" (Marta Alvear, "Interview with Humberto Solás," *Jump Cut*, no. 19).

He goes on to say, "I began to prepare *Lucía* right after the premiere of *Manuela*. This group of stories is not what appeared originally in the first project. Only the first remains. The second and third (those concerning the Republic and the Revolution) were not accepted. Truthfully, it was a very different film from the present one. And I'm really happy that the project as a whole was not approved. Neither of the rejected stories has ceased to interest me: a satire on the Republic seen through the eyes of a couple trying to find a place to make love one day in Santiago de Cuba, and a dramatic story on the difficulties of a pair of lovers (him married, her single) who work in the same firm. But with the passage of time, I feel that the stories that have been substituted for these give the film a much richer and more harmonious structure" (Teresa Fernández Coca, "Interview with Humberto Solás," *Granma*, 23 October 1968).

One of the film's more complex features is the musical score created by maestro Leo Brouwer. The challenge was to capture the atmosphere of each different time period, and for this Brouwer followed the evolution of musical tastes in Cuba from 1895 to the 1960s. In the first part of the film, for example, he develops the score based on a Schumann theme; in the second the flute renders a Chopin prelude, while the third part is permeated by the sounds of the guitar and the popular Cuban ballad "Guantanamera." A roving minstrel (Pablo Milanés) also sings a ballad that provides commentary on the events portrayed.

The film has many techniques one would associate with the documentary. One such procedure is the interview carried out in the manner of a television report, with the interviewee on camera and the person asking the questions off-screen. A group of patriots discusses the events, introducing themselves to the camera one by one. A rebel walks up to people in the streets, asking them to give their opinions about the independence movement, acting as an interviewer of sorts. There are also interviews of soldiers and of the governor of the island, among others. There is even a documentary series on the machete itself, its ancestry and applications, making of this utensil a type of historical character in its own right.

Lucía can be thought of as an example of what in Latin America is called *cine rescate* (a film that attempts to rescue historical events from the quandary where they've been placed by bourgeois culture). It is also *cine encuesta* (a form of cinema that attempts an in-depth inquiry into a historical subject).

Lucía won several prizes and brought Solás international recognition, yet the Cuban government's "parametrización" (the discredit and persecution of homosexuals and other "anti-socials") during the early '70s, robbed him of that recognition in his own country for some time.

Maluala Sergio Giral / ICAIC, 1979, color, 95 min. *Music:* Sergio Vitier. *Cast:* Samuel Claxton, Miguel Navarro, Roberto Blanco, Miguel Gutiérrez, Raúl Pomares, Adolfo Llauradó, Nicolás Reynoso, Hilda Oates, Jorge Ryan, Julio Hernández, Elio Mesa, Jorge Losada, Mercedes Planas, Grupo Folklóroco "Combate" and the Cuban National Ballet.

During colonial times, runaway slaves called "cimarrones" set up communities in the most remote parts of the island. These communities, called "palenques," at times became well populated and strong, as was the case with the one called Maluala in the eastern mountain region. Reluctant to send his forces into the easily defended, forested mountains, the Spanish governor tries a policy of "divide and conquer" in order to subdue the runaways. He offers a favorable pact to one leader of a "palenque," Coba, and convinces him to oppose Gallo, the king of Maluala. In the end, Coba's men are decimated and Gallo succeeds in defeating the Spanish forces in an ambush. Myths of African origins mingle with history in the epic story of Maluala.

Director Sergio Giral Rivas was born in Havana in 1937. He studied the arts and lived for many years in the United States.

The Mambo Kings Arnold Glimcher / Alco Films–Arnon Milchan–Le Studio Canal Plus–Regency Enterprises–Warner Bros., 1992, color, 100 min. *Writing credits:* Oscar Hijuelos, from his novel *The Mambo Kings Play Songs of Love*. *Cast:* Armand Assante, Antonio Banderas, Cathy Moriarty, Maruschka Detmers, Desi Arnaz, Jr., Celia Cruz, Roscoe Lee Browne, Vondie Curtis-Hall, Talisa Soto, Joe Petruzzi, Theodora Castellanos, Lázaro

Pérez, Miller P., Julie Pinson, Dawn McKinster, James Medina, Valerie McIntosh, Jessica Neal Ortiz, Jocelyn O'Brien, Salvador Miranda, René Monteagudo, Adrián Martínez, Ron Thompson, William Thomas, J.T. Taylor, Yul Vázquez, Martin Charles Warner, Tito Puente, Cynthia Santos, Marcos Quintanilla, Susie Stillwell, Suzanne Smith, Maiquel Suárez, Debra Scott, Natalie Zimmerman, Scott Cohen, Helena Carroll, Pablo Calogero, Joe Conzo, Jonathan Delarco, Jessica Z. Diamond, Karen Assante, José Alberto, June Brown, Stephanie Blake, Anita Banderas, Doug Barron, Diane Manzo, Billy Hopkins, John Herrera, Mario Grillo, Pete MacNamara, Ryan Howell, Ralph Irizarry, Thomas F. Duffy, José Duvall, Ahn Duong, Frank Grillo, Cordelia González, Colleen Fitzpatrick and Carlos Gómez.

Arnold Glimcher, a New York art dealer who had never directed a film, directed this romatic U.S.–French co-production about two Cuban brothers who leave their home country in the 1950s, coming to the USA with the hope of becoming famous musicians. Their trip is not entirely voluntary: they have been forced to leave the island, the profitable nightclub circuit in Havana and even a well-loved sweetheart after rubbing some mobsters the wrong way. In New York, their dreams are put on hold as they are forced to work as meat packers while trying to put a band together. Eventually the brothers organize their band and begin to have success in the New York music scene, each one falling in love with very different women. But their personalities seem to upset those around them, and ultimately they are kicked out of the New York nightclub circuit, ending up playing bar mitzvahs just to survive. When Desi Arnaz (played by Desi's son) discovers them, their future seems brighter than ever. Nostalgia for their homeland doesn't abate, and when one of them dies abruptly at the end, the other is left alone to pursue "the dream" on his own.

The story doesn't seem to hang together well; it comes apart from the heavy burden of the contrived plot lines and lumbering performances by Assante and Banderas. The "feel" of the 1950s is nicely captured, though, and cameos by Celia Cruz and Tito Puente add much needed credibility to the production. The music is most enjoyable.

El maná (Manna) Jesús de Armas / ICAIC, 1960, color, 3 min. 40 sec. *Animation:* Hernán Henríquez.

In 1959 and in anticipation of the U.S. embargo, an organ was set up by the revolutionary government to buy products that might be impossible to obtain in the future. This organization was called the Bank of Foreign Commerce, and some of its hastily imported products from the U.S. were a Mitchell camera, a special effects optical camera, an animation table and sundry laboratory equipment. This equipment allowed ICAIC to set up an animation department whose crew included Jesús de Armas, Hernán Henríquez, Eduardo Muñoz and Australian-Cuban Harry Reede. This department quickly produced two four-minute cartoons, *El maná* and *La prensa seria*.

El maná is a cartoon in line with the efforts of the new government to instill good work habits in the rural population. It tells the simple story of a peasant who sits to wait for his needs to be met while others work. In the end, others reap the product of their toil while the peasant in question ends up empty-handed. (In other words, don't expect the state to do everything for you.)

Las manos (The Hands) Juan Padrón / ICAIC, 1976, color, 5 min. 7 sec. *Animation:* Leonardo Piñero and Erasmo Juliachs. *Music:* Lucas de la Guardia.

This is a short animation without dialogue that shows a number of ways in which a worker can injure his hands. Different industrial equipment pieces are shown along with the dangers of their improper or incautious use.

Manuela Humberto Solás / ICAIC, 1966, B&W, 41 min. *Music:* Tony Taño. *Cast:* Adela Legrá, Adolfo Llauradó, Olga González, Luis Alberto García, Ruddy Mora, Flavio Calderín and Juana Albuquerque.

Manuela's farm has been burned to the ground by the evil forces of the wicked capitalist regime. She decides that she can no longer stand idly by in this battle of good versus evil, so she goes to the mountains to join Castro's guerrilla fighters, who, for her, have become the representatives of all that is good. Once there, she becomes the friend of "la gallega" and meets "el mexicano," with whom she falls in love. After a firefight with government soldiers, enraged villagers want to lynch a government informer, but the virtuous guerrilla fighters prevent it. Manuela doesn't understand and would have preferred to see the informer lynched. The guerrillas then undertake an attack on an important military convoy, where Manuela is mortally wounded. El mexicano vows revenge, but Manuela herself reminds him that, as a guerrilla, he must let virtue govern his actions. The time she has spent as a guerrilla fighter has made her a better person.

This is a visually stunning and accomplished film, in spite of the immoderate ideological content.

Maracas y bongó (Maracas and Conga Drums) Max Tosquella / Producciones Mussie del Barrio, 1932, B&W, 15 min. *Music:* Neno Grenet,

Trío Matamoros, Armando Valdés, F. Collazo. *Cast:* Yolanda González, Fernando Collazo, José Manuel Valdés, Elpidio Valdés, Jacinta Oliva and Septeto Cuba.

The first with a soundtrack produced in Cuba, this film presents the kaleidoscopic world of the "solar," the shared patio of a Cuban communal house. A number of love relationships serve as the backdrop and the excuse to break out into song and dance routines. The film gives an interesting glimpse into the musical scene of early 1930s Cuba.

María Antonia Sergio Giral / ICAIC, 1991, color, 111 min. *Cast:* Alina Rodríguez and Alexis Valdés.

Set in 1950s Cuba, this is the story of a prostitute who falls for a boxer and becomes devoted to him, caring for him and nurturing him in the good times and in the bad. As the boxer becomes ever more successful, he begins to chase other women and neglects the one who loves him passionately. She does everything in her power to steer him back to her, but to no avail. She then becomes despondent and deteriorates spiritually. It becomes apparent that the world she lives in admits no positive feelings, that there is no room for such things as love in this underworld jungle of the urban lower classes.

María la O Adolfo Fernández Bustamante / Amador Films, 1948, B&W, 80 min. *Music:* Ernesto Lecuona and Antonio Díaz Conde. *Cast:* Emilio Tuero, Issa Morante, Oscar López, Rita Montaner, Linda Gorraez, Armando Borroto, Ernesto Vilches, Fanny Schiller, Manuel Noriega, Oscar Pulido, Elvia Pedroza, Leopoldo Francés and Mary Cristy.

This Cuban-Mexican co-production is set in Havana in the 1840s. It is a feature film that tells the story of the love affair between María la O, a beautiful mulatto woman, with Fernando, the young, white heir to a fortune. Although Fernando has a fiancée from his own race and social class, the *mulata* comes between them and seduces the young man, who ends up proposing to her. Upon learning of his son's infatuation, the Marqués del Palmar reprimands him and makes him repudiate María la O. She, with the help of black associates, plans to take her terrible revenge, but decides against it when she finds out that she is pregnant by Fernando. Shunned by other blacks for carrying the baby of a white man, María la O now does not belong to either white or black society: she is the ultimate outcast. Fernando learns of María la O's predicament and rejoins her, but passions are still running hot and he is mortally wounded, dying in her arms. María la O vows to commit suicide.

Adolfo Fernández Bustamante has made a memorable film out of the tragic and beautiful fundamentals of human behavior. With the fervor of a poet and the skill of a magnificent cameraman, he examines a theme that lies close to the Cuban heart, the grim and ceaseless struggles of a society trying to come to terms with its multi-racial makeup. Fernández expels everything that is artistically alien to the camera, employing only one ally, and that is the remarkable music of Ernesto Lecuona and Antonio Conde Díaz.

Mariposas en el andamio (Butterflies on a Scaffold) Luis Felipe Bernaza and Margaret Gilpin / Kangaroo Productions, 1996, color, 75 min.

The butterflies in the title refer to the members of the Havana gay community which, after decades of persecution, are beginning to "come out." This documentary takes us to the "La Güinera" neighborhood where women in positions of power have encouraged gays to express themselves in their own creative ways. They fashion dresses out of sacks, manage to make false eyelashes from carbon paper and go on stage. Interviews with local politicians, community leaders and the homosexuals themselves bring out a backdrop of lingering insecurity and fear of free expression in a society which, until recently, labeled gays as anti-social deviants.

El Mégano Julio García Espinosa and Tomás Gutiérrez Alea / Moisés Ades, 1955, B&W, 20 min. *Music:* Juan Blanco. *Cast:* The inhabitants of the village of El Mégano, in the Zapata swamp, Pastor Álvarez, Cheo Lazo, Arencibia San Judas, Sibila Lazo, María Leila Lazo, Berto and Nelson Álvarez, Sixto Cruz, Eusebio Lazo and Menia Martínez as the tourist.

This is a documentary that uses neorealist reconstruction to condemn the inhuman conditions endured by a sector of the Cuban labor class. In the midst of the Ciénaga de Zapata marshes, on the southern coast of what was then Las Villas province, charcoal burners work under arduous conditions. We see their moments of leisure also, kids playing and dancing while tourists idle. A revolt breaks out when the laborers are to be paid but are instead robbed of their earnings.

The invitations to the film's premiere, at the Enrique José Varona amphitheater in the University of Havana, had it as the first attempt at neorealism in Cuban cinema. The movie became a *cause célèbre* when the authorities seized it after only one screening. García Espinosa was taken to police headquarters in Havana and was released when he agreed to bring the film back to the police. He scrambled to make a copy before having to comply with the order, but the police were in no mood for waiting. The head of the secret police interviewed the director: "Did you make this film?" the agent asked. "Do you know this film is a piece of shit?" "Do *you* know," replied an irritated García Espinosa, "that this film is an example of neorealism?" and he proceeded to give a detailed explanation to the policeman, who patiently listened to everything. "Not only is the film a piece of shit," replied the cop, "but you also talk a lot of shit. Stop eating shit and go make films about Batista!" García Espinosa recalls that exchange as "my first intervention as a theorist" (Michael Chanan, "Interview With Julio García Espinosa," in *The Cuban Image*, p. 82).

Mella Enrique Pineda Barnet / ICAIC, 1975, color, 110 min. *Music:* Carlos Fariña. *Cast:* Sergio Corrieri, Norma Martínez, Armando Soler, Juan Carlos Romero, Genaro Goss, Mario Martínez Casado, Ángel Espasando, René de la Cruz, Carlos Pérez Peña, Enrique Santiesteban, Mariano Castro, Ramón Brito, Justo Vega, Alejandro Lugo, Omar Valdés and Raúl Eguren.

Julio Antonio Mella (1903–1929) was a student communist leader responsible for many innovative ideas. He is largely responsible for founding the Workers' University and the Cuban Communist Party. Long before Castro and his people, Mella introduced Cubans to the practice of dehumanizing anyone who might not think like you or have your values. He would publicly call his opponents lackeys, traitors to the homeland, insects, pirates, troglodytes and other miscellaneous designations. General Machado attempted to get Mella on his side, but the young man was too principled to join the man who would later become a despised dictator. His opposition to Machado got him expelled from the University of Havana and thrown in jail for terrorist activities. He went on a hunger strike, and after a couple of weeks in which he did not eat a thing, Machado ordered him to be freed. Hoping to avoid further run-ins with the law, Mella fled to Mexico, where he fell madly in love with Tina Modoti, a comrade from the Party. After a severe fallout with the Communist Party, Mella began a media campaign against Machado from Mexico; Machado's people, in turn, began a campaign to ruin his reputation. In one instance, it was widely publicized that Mella ripped down a Cuban flag and wiped his feet on it during Mexico City's "Cuban Night" festivities. A distressed Mella ran to the offices of Western Union and cabled Sergio Carbó, editor of the weekly *La Semana*, asking him to clarify the situation, because he would never dishonor the national symbols. That same evening, as Mella was exiting a nightclub in the company of Tina Modoti, he was shot several times. It was said that the killer had been José Magriñat, a known hit man for the Machado government. Mella himself, as he lay dying, exclaimed, "Machado has killed me. I die for the revolution." The mysterious death of Tina Modoti a short while later gave rise to the theory that the Soviets had a hand in the disappearance of the two lovers.

This film is a scrupulous recreation of the main events in Mella's life, and although the screenwriter has romanticized much of it, it is an informative document for those interested in this intriguing period in Cuban history.

Melodrama Rolando Díaz / ICAIC, 1995, color, 55 min. *Cast:* Verónica López, Héctor Eduardo Suárez, Javier Ávila, Carlos Cruz, María Isabel Díaz, Humberto Páez and Carmen Daysi Rodríguez.

Esperanza is a pretty successful television weather forecaster who dreams of having a child. An unfortunate accident forces her to make a choice that will change her life forever.

Memorias del subdesarrollo (Memories of Underdevelopment) Tomás Gutiérrez Alea / ICAIC, 1968, B&W, 97 min. *Writing credits:* Edmundo Desnoes, based on his novel *Memorias del subdesarrollo*. *Music:* Leo Brouwer. *Cast:* Sergio Corrieri, Eslinda Núñez, Daisy Granados and Omar Valdés.

Sergio (Sergio Corrieri) seduces the young woman (Eslinda Núñez) for which he'll be accused of rape, in Tomás Gutiérrez Alea's ***Memorias del subdesarrollo***.

Bourgeois intellectual Sergio (Sergio Corrieri) walks around Havana contemplating the new society brought forth by the Revolution. He has a lot of free time on his hands, as he is living off the rental of his apartment and most of his family has fled to Miami. Sergio is also a non-committed intellectual, a passive spectator who tries to understand the new intellectual activity taking place in Havana. Attending a writers' conference at the Hemingway Museum where a roundtable of Marxists (Desnoes included) throw concepts around without reaching any clear objective, Sergio comments, "Words devour words and leave you in the clouds."

The ever-idling Sergio seduces frivolous young Elena (for which he's accused of rape and eventually acquitted), contemplates his past, reviews his erotic daydreams about his cleaning lady, considers the difficulties with his alienated wife, and thinks of his future and his career. The Bay of Pigs invasion and the ensuing Missile Crisis serve to reveal a disquieting fact to Sergio: he no longer belongs to the old society that has perished, but he doesn't have the will or the inclination to work towards the construction of the new one. "Sergio is benumbed by the Revolution. Perhaps this is ultimately Alea's message — that [in the new Cuba] there is little room, if any, for individuals, for disaffected intellectuals" (Ronald Schwartz, *Latin American Films, 1932-1994*, p. 160).

Although the protagonist is anything but likeable, he does leave a strong impression. Perhaps this is due to the fact that he represents so many others trying to cope with new, alien circumstances, members of a newly marginalized class that must relegate its values to the dustbin of the past.

Memorias salvadas del olvido (Memories Saved from the Past) Marcos Castillo / EITV, 1999, color, 12 min.

This documentary takes the feature *Memorias del subdesarrollo* and its protagonist Sergio as a background to give a skeptical and frustrated perspective on the capitalist furor that has gripped the island during the last decade.

La mesera del café del puerto (The Waitress from the Docks Café) Juan Orol / España Sono Films de Cuba–Juan Orol (Mexico), 1955, B&W, 94 min. *Music:* Rosendo Ramírez. *Cast:* Martha Rams, Julio Capote, Bertha Montesinos, Juan José Martínez Casado, Elisa Araujo, Augusto Martín, Chino Wong, Julio Martínez, Armando Bringuier and Alicia Rico.

In this Cuban-Mexican melodrama, Adelita, a lame waitress at the café on the Havana docks, becomes the protector of young Ricardo, a destitute composer who desperately needs Adelita's financial help. With the help of a Chinese businessman (Chino Wong) he gets a job playing the piano and singing. A considerable talent, he quickly becomes well esteemed by the music hall dancers. Gloria comes on the scene and wants to drive him away from Adelita, believing that his relationship with the limping waitress will only hold the young man back and keep him from achieving his objectives. Ricardo moves to New York and becomes a success, while the distraught Adelita remains in Havana and decides to undergo a risky operation to correct her gait. An incomplete phone call leads Ricardo to believe that Adelita has died, but upon returning to Cuba he finds her well, beautiful and no longer lame. Gloria, of course, is now sorry for the role she played in separating Ricardo and Adelita and agrees to be a witness to their wedding.

Director Juan Orol García was born in El Ferrol, Galicia, Spain, in 1897. Director, producer, actor, and distributor of his own films, he worked mostly in Mexico, where he died in 1988.

Mi pañoleta (My Shawl) Juan Padrón and Erasmo Juliachs / ICAIC, 1974, color, 6 min. *Animation:* José Reyes, Erasmo Juliachs and Gabriel Ramos. *Music:* Lucas de la Guardia.

This cartoon has a pioneer (young student) on his way to school along with a dog and a cat. The animals help the youngster keep his triangular shawl clean in spite of all the obstacles they find along the way. The shawl is a distinctive feature of young Cuban scholars, who wear it over their shirt collars.

Miel para Oshún (Honey for Oshún) Humberto Solás / ICAIC–El Paso Producciones (Spain), 2001, color, 90 min. *Cast:* Isabel Santos, Jorge Perugorría, Mario Limonta and Saturnino García.

Roberto (Jorge Perugorría) is a Cuban-American man who has lived in the United States since he was seven years old. He had always believed that his mother had abandoned him. When his father dies, he learns that this was not true, so he decides to return to the island from which he was taken—it turns out—illegally by his father. In the search for his mother (and, by extension, for his roots) he is helped by a taxi driver (Mario Limonta) and a cousin (Isabel Santos). He travels the length of the island, getting acquainted with its people and culture.

With this film Humberto Solás introduced the Cuban film industry to the digital camera. As per Sergio Benvenuto Solás (*Cine cubano*, 151, p. 34), the text for *Miel para Oshún* was written by his mother, Elia Solás, sister of Humberto Solás, in 1993. But the project met a great number of obstacles, and year after year the text was changed and reworked. In the first months of 1999 Humberto Solás traveled to Mexico to explore the possibilities of filming his next work with a digital camera. He had previously gone to Madrid to meet with Tote Trenas, a man who was able to operate the camera by hand, without the need for a steady cam. Solás went back to Cuba in the middle of the year 2000 convinced that his next film would be done with a digital camera.

Production began immediately after his return, beginning in Havana and then travelling east to Varadero, Sancti Spíritus, Camagüey, Holguín, Gibara, Guantánamo, La Farola and Baracoa. During the six weeks of filming the crew moved more than one thousand kilometers in the middle of the Cuban summer. At the end of the second week Trenas had to abandon the project and was replaced by Porfirio Enríquez on the digital "betacam." He proved an asset to the production.

In the end, *Miel para Oshún* gives a charming account of a young man looking for his origins while flanked by a couple of very aesthetically appealing characters.

Miradas (Glances) Enrique Álvarez / ICAIC, 2001, color, 100 min. *Cast:* Jaqueline Arenal, Alfredo Alonso, Raquel Casado, Mihail Mulkay, Miguel Navarro, Alina Rodríguez, Samuel Claxton, Manuel Porto and Paula Alí.

A frustrated photographer has a fit and decides to destroy all his work. Just as he finishes obliterating his photos he puts a gun to his head, shuts his eyes, and ... the telephone rings. It is his girlfriend, who informs him that a New York art gallery wants to exhibit his work, a chance of a lifetime. He now has 24 hours to replace the photographs, so he goes out with his camera and starts to shoot away. The film then becomes the story of the city and its faces, as the photographer attempts to capture their essence.

Morro Castle, Havana Harbor Edison Manufacturing Company, 1898, B&W, 15.24 meters long.

"A most excellent picture of the grim old fortress which stands at the entrance to Havana Harbor. The high ramparts and lofty battlements look very formidable. Parts of the stronghold date back to the seventeenth century. While the yacht from which the picture is taken sails around the promontory, an excellent view is afforded of the entire fortress. Waves are seen dashing up against the rocks at the foot of abutments. The lighthouse and sentry-box are so near that the guard is plainly seen pacing up and down. The photograph is excellent; and in view of a probable bombardment, when the old-fashioned masonry will melt away like butter under the fire of 13-inch guns, the view is of historic value" (*Edison Catalog,* 1898).

Apparently the reviewer felt he was witnessing the last vistas of the Spanish fortress before the U.S. Navy blasted it into oblivion. The film was released on 20 May 1898.

Muerte al invasor (Death to the Invader) Santiago Álvarez and Tomás Gutiérrez Alea / ICAIC, 1961, B&W, 15 min. 30 sec.

This documentary uses actual footage from the failed Bay of Pigs invasion of March 1961. It gives an interesting account of the three days of battle, but a heavy dose of partisan ideology wrests some credibility and seriousness from the presentation; in its extreme subjectivity, it portrays the invaders as evil criminals intent on the destruction of a peace-loving, just society. One is reminded here of the more strident U.S. World War II documentaries.

La muerte de Joe J. Jones (The Death of Joe J. Jones) Sergio Giral / ICAIC, 1966, B&W, 12 min.

This is a short three-part documentary that follows the life of a typical American, whom they call Joe J. Jones. Joe indulges in the "American way of life," which includes fascist ideology, fast and irresponsible sex, and a general disregard for others. Joe, as one might expect, dies young and violently. The image of a smiling Joe dressed in fatigues and carrying two large machine guns is the most memorable image Cuban viewers will perceive from this "typical" American.

La muerte de un burócrata (Death of a Bureaucrat) Tomás Gutiérrez Alea / ICAIC, 1966, B&W, 85 min. *Music:* Leo Brouwer. *Cast:* Salvador Wood, Manuel Estanillo, Silvia Planas, Gaspar de Santelices, Pedro Pablo Astorga, Carlos Gargallo, Fausto Rodríguez, Laura Zarrabeitia, Tania Alvarado, Roberto Gacio and Rafael Sosa.

A comedy where an exemplary worker, a rebel fighter against the Machado dictatorship and inventor of a machine to mass produce busts (of José Martí, of course) dies and is duly buried with all corresponding tributes and praise. The problem is that his union comrades decided to bury this exceptional laborer with his union card in his pocket; without it, his widow cannot collect any pension money. When all attempts at exhumation are interrupted by red tape, she and her nephew decide to rob the grave. The enterprising nephew enlists the after-hours aid of cemetery workers eager to earn an extra peso, and they proceed to disinter the body. But, alas, the night watchman discovers them with the casket already up on a dolly. As his cemetery confederates flee, the nephew watches incredulously as the unsecured dolly begins rolling down the hill with the newly commuting coffin on it. The watchman, standing near the gate, sees the strange vehicle speeding towards him and gets out of the way as the coffin shoots down the hill and out of the gate. As the watchman returns with the police, the apprehensive nephew, locked outside the cemetery, has to return home pushing the unusual cart, which he has covered in branches to hide its contents. The aunt has mixed emotions about her nephew's achievement: delighted to have the union card in her possession, she's not thrilled by her husband's unanticipated return home.

The young man now faces an even greater bureaucratic nightmare: how is he going to re-bury his uncle? Unsympathetic cemetery workers will not bury a body that, according to the records, was already put in the ground. Desperate, they get a funeral director to show up with the coffin at the cemetery, but he is stopped at the entrance by a group of bureaucrats. The ensuing discussion causes a backup of bereaved families in funeral processions trying to enter the cemetery. The whole thing degenerates into a brawl between these families and the uncompromising bureaucrats at the gate. Finally, nephew and aunt are forced to return home with the coffin.

In spite of the old woman's constant efforts at maintaining a suitable supply of ice inside the casket, the number of vultures that circle the house and alight on the roof is noticeably increasing. Circumstances forcing him to persevere, the nephew now finally obtains the exhumation order that had been denied before, and he telephones his aunt telling her to bring the body. Once at the cemetery, the director insists on exhuming a body, since the order is for exhumation and not interment. In spite of the nephew's protests, he proceeds and finds an empty tomb, accusing the nephew of fraud. At this point the young man becomes a raging lunatic and attacks everyone he can get his hands on.

The final scene has a funeral procession (in all likelihood the nephew is being buried) attended by well-dressed bureaucrats (probably the same people who caused his demise); after them follows a decaying old hearse (hopefully bearing the uncle's remains) with a lonely figure trailing it: the aunt. The audience expects this to be the end of the ordeal ... but is it really?

The film is an eminent portrayal of the rigid and at times absurd character of the socialist bureaucratic system in the first years of the Revolution. The protagonist nephew is a hero of sorts, determinedly striving to adhere to the system's requirements but constantly disappointed by its shortcomings. Meaningful is the fact that he is forced to break the law in order to act logically. In all, this is a very entertaining film.

Mujer ante el espejo (Woman Before a Mirror) Marisol Trujillo / ICAIC, 1983, color, 17 min.

This documentary deals with the difficult role of the typical woman in the new society brought forth by the Revolution. When Rosario Suárez, a successful dancer with the Cuban National Ballet, has a child, her life becomes complicated as she strives to cope with her job, her obligations to society, and her responsibility towards this new being that is absolutely dependent on her. It is an inside look at the intimate world of the Cuban professional woman: she dances, she works, she breast-feeds.

Mujer transparente (Transparent Woman) Héctor Veitia, Maya Segura, Mayra Vilasís, Mario Crespo and Ana Rodríguez / ICAIC, 1989, color, 78 min. *Cast:* Isabel Moreno, Verónica Lynn, Mirta Ibarra and Leonor Arocha.

The directors, all documentary filmmakers, shot this work of fiction that has a real-life documentary feel to it. It consists of five stories of women coping with modern (late 1980s) society. Issues include the struggle for self-esteem, relationships with men, hopes for the future, nonconformity and relationships with friends.

Una mujer, un hombre, una ciudad (A Woman, a Man, a City) Manuel Octavio Gómez / ICAIC, 1978, color, 99 min. *Cast:* Idalia Andreus, Mario Balmaseda, Raúl Pomares, Omar Valdés, Alden Knight and Ramoncito Veloz.

Nuevitas, in northern Camagüey province is, along with Havana and Matanzas, one of the major ports on the northern coast of Cuba, an energetic and lively city with a population of urbane, forward-looking individuals. It is the story of two of these individuals that the film gives us, intertwined with the story of the city itself. This is an interesting look at the life of a medium-sized Cuban city, with its problems and its unique appeal.

Mulata Gilberto Martínez Solares / Mier y Brook, 1954, B&W, 80 min. *Writing credits:* Roberto Oliveira Márquez, based on his novel *Mulatilla*. *Music:* Manuel Esperón. *Cast:* Ninón Sevilla, Pedro Armendáriz, René Cardona, Fanny Schiller, Ricardo Román, Jorge Mondragón, Lolita Santa Cruz, José Muñoz and Digna Sevilla.

A beautiful half-breed named Caridad sets men on fire (not literally) and incites the profound jealousy of other women, who dream of looking like her and possessing her charms. Caridad falls in love with a Mexican sailor (this *is* a Mexican co-production) who brings her to Veracruz to work in a cabaret. He then leaves her. She eventually joins him again; she is head over heels in love with him. Caridad falls ill and the sailor is forced to leave her in Havana, but the infatuated girl feels she's been abandoned again. He returns to pick her up, but too late: the tragic beauty ends up dying on his boat. Ninón Sevilla in blackface reminds us of the limits put on black Cubans in every facet of social life.

Nada (Nothing) Juan Carlos Cremata / ICAIC, 2001, color, 90 min. *Cast:* Thais Valdés, Nacho Lugo, Daysi Granados, Paula Alí, Verónica López, Luis Manuel Iglesias and Raúl Pomares.

Carla works at the post office, where she dedicates her time to helping others in a number of ways. Her family has signed up for the visa lottery, a system set up by the U.S. government whereby U.S. visas are granted to Cubans through a lottery. Carla must decide whether to leave Cuba and the people she selflessly helps, or stay in Cuba and be separated (forever?) from her dear family. This topic was played out a decade ago, and this film is uninspired and humdrum.

Nadie escuchaba (Nobody Listened) Néstor Almendros and Jorge Ulla / Cuban Human Rights Project, 1984, color, 90 min.

A U.S.–made, fiercely anti–Castro documentary that seeks out and takes testimony from many people that have been victimized by the errors and excesses of the revolutionary government.

Among those interviewed are Pedro Luis Boitel's mother, talking about the horrible and constant torture of her son in Castro's prisons and his eventual death. Members of the old Cuban Communist Party are also interviewed in Miami, where they fled Castro's "pseudo communism." The film's title, *Nobody Listened*, refers to the civilized world's refusal to listen to the cries of all those being victimized by Castro's authorities.

"Parts of *Nobody Listened* are visual firsts. Never before, for instance, have outsiders seen plantados prisoners crunched in their small cells, wearing only their underwear. It's the ideal eye-opener for all the naives who still believe that Castro is a victim of a vicious campaign by Right Wing 'Imperialists'" (Carlos Verdecia, *The Miami Herald*, 18 Feb. 1988, p. 19A).

A Night in Havana: Dizzy Gillespie in Cuba John Holland / Chisma Productions–Cubana Bop Partners, 1988, color, 84 min. *Cast:* Dizzy Gillespie and Allen Honigberg (interviewer).

This is not just a documentary about Dizzy's trip to the Fifth International Jazz Festival in Havana. Forty years after he first brought Cuban rhythms to jazz, and 30 years after his first visit to the island, this jazz great returns to the well, as it were, holding a private interview with Castro and reconnecting with the people. Ordinary Cubans recognize him and seem eager to talk with him. Dizzy becomes a professor of sorts, explaining to admiring Cubans how it was on their island that the African connection was kept alive, for the drum holds the key to African culture, and unlike the situation in Cuba, in North America the drum was banned. One of the most sought-after explanations is the reason why Dizzy's cheeks blow up when he plays the trumpet. His explanation combines a little fact with much comedy. He meets Cuban trumpeter Arturo Sandoval (who later defected to the U.S.), of whom he has spoken very highly on several occasions.

No hay sábado sin sol (There's No Saturday Without Sun) Manuel Herrera / ICAIC, 1992, color, 92 min. *Cast:* Eslinda Núñez, Mario Balmaseda, Alejandro Lugo, Salvador Wood, René de la Cruz and Humberto García Espinosa.

The Revolution put a number of social-construction policies in place. In many cases, the application of those policies was hindered by people who were entrenched in their ways and resisted change. This film tells the story of María, a young worker stationed in the village of "El Mamey," who must battle folks with deep-rooted, outdated ideas and get them to move to a newly built village. Her patience, tenacity and revolutionary zeal finally pay off.

Las noches de Constantinopla (Constantinople Nights) Orlando Rojas / ICAIC–El Paso Producciones (Spain), 2001, color, 109 min. *Music:* Pavel Urkiza. *Cast:* Rosita Fornés, Raquel Revuelta, Liberto Rabal, Paco Rabal, Verónica Lynn, María Isabel Díaz, Verónica López, Natacha Díaz, Zulema Hernández, Vladimir Villar and Jorge Alí.

The late Spanish actor Paco Rabal stars next to his grandson Liberto in this comedy about Hernán (Liberto Rabal), a writer of erotica who is keeping his creative activities a secret from his conservative family, especially from his aunt. Hernán wins the Boccaccio Prize for erotic literature and his aunt, after learning of her nephew's peculiar skill, goes into a coma, but not before punishing Hernán by making him responsible for the family mansion, "Villa Florida." The less-than-ethical family members descend on the mansion, and the inevitable voluptress, by the name of Manón, seduces the naive writer. In order to pay for his new expenses, Hernán sells off his aunt's important art collection. Unexpectedly, the aunt begins to recover from her coma, and Hernán and company have to figure out a way to replace the looted masterpieces. The idea is to set up an underground cabaret, where the clients can enjoy themselves thoroughly to the beat of Cuban music. The whole thing turns out to be a great success, and the money is used to make copies of the looted art. When the aunt returns, she is so impressed by her family's good management of the mansion that she decides to sell her "masterpieces" in order to repay them for their loyalty. This new state of affairs presents novel challenges for the writer, who now has to go back to the drawing table.

A nice feature of this film is the acting of Rosita Fornés, a grand lady of Cuban film. Fornés has been entertaining Cuban audiences for almost six decades, having begun her career in 1938 at the *La Comedia* theater with the musical comedy *El asombro de Damasco* (Damascus Astonishment). Her silver screen career began in 1939 with *Una aventura peligrosa* (A Dangerous Adventure), directed by Ramón Peón, followed in 1941 by *Romance musical* (Musical Romance), directed by Ernesto Caparrós. From 1945 to 1959 she starred in a number of Mexican films, returning to the Cuban screen in 1983 with *Se permuta* (For Trade), directed by Juan Carlos Tabío. She is also considered one of the founders of Cuban television, being involved in diverse programs (comedies, dramas, musicals) since 1952.

Nosotros la música (We the Music) Rogelio París / ICAIC, 1964, B&W, 66 min. *Cast:* Elena Burke, Celeste Mendoza, Bola de Nieve, Ana Gloria, Charanga Francesa, Septeto de Ignacio Piñeiro, Silvio y Ada, Quinteto Instrumental de Música Moderna, Orquesta Chapotín, Comparsas del Cocuyé y el Orilé.

A must-see for lovers of Cuban music, this documentary gives a short but very informative history of its forms and styles. With the first-hand accounts of musicians like Bola de Nieve and Elena Burke, with dance numbers and songs performed by top artists, this film steps beyond the boundaries of a simple documentary and comes alive with sound and movement. Here is a good example of the revolutionary government's drive, through ICAIC, to bring Cuban popular culture to the masses and counteract many decades of foreign cultural interference.

In *Nosotros la música* you will not find the great story of a national culture, but you will discover a simple story that has been splendidly told. The cast members, permitted to talk, shrug, breathe and cough as human beings instead of actors, bring a freshness and gaiety of spirit that is generally hard to find in documentaries of this or any other sort. The skill of the director, Rogelio París, and the excellent camera work only serve to enhance the quality of the performers.

Una novia para David (A Girlfriend for David) Orlando Rojas / ICAIC, 1985, color, 103 min. *Writing credits:* Senel Paz and Orlando Rojas. *Music:* Pablo Milanés. *Cast:* Jorge Luis Álvarez, María Isabel Díaz, Francisco Gattorno, Thais Valdés, Linda Mirabal and César Évora.

A young man named David arrives in Havana to begin his high school studies. He becomes fast friends with Miguel, who gets him a date with a girl. Ofelia, an unappealing girl in David's class, falls for the young man, but David is persuaded by his classmates to pursue Olga. Olga is a beauty whose pride is resented by the other students. The idea is to have David seduce Olga and dump her, or to have Olga reject David. Either situation would create much entertainment and mirth. As we all suspected, David eventually becomes attracted to homely Ofelia as he begins to recognize her inner beauty and her honesty.

Director Guillermo Orlando Rojas Feliz was born in Santa Clara, Cuba, in 1950. He studied physics and French literature at the University of Havana, and he was very active in the student "cineclubs" there. Rojas worked on the sets of Humberto Solás' *Cantata de Chile* (1975) and Tomás Gutiérrez Alea's *Los sobrevivientes* (1978).

Now! Santiago Álvarez / ICAIC, 1965, B&W, 6 min.

A documentary that uses file footage, both moving pictures and stills, to trace the long struggle of African Americans in the United States to gain equal rights. Major incidents in this struggle are shown, as well as President Johnson's meeting with prominent black leaders, including Martin Luther King. Lena Horne sings the movie's title song "Now!"

La nueva escuela (The New School) Jorge Fraga / ICAIC, 1973, Color, 89 min.

This documentary tells the story of a challenging government project to build hundreds of new secondary education schools throughout the island in the early '70s. It begins with the departure, in the 1960s, of wide-eyed secondary school students to teach literacy and the revolution's ideals to peasants in the countryside. Castro himself is shown explaining to worried parents that the task their children are performing is essential in the construction of the new society.

There follows a portrayal of the inequalities of education prior to the Revolution, and an explanation of how education in a revolutionary society serves to advance the interests of the community, not of individuals. The film argues for the creation in these schools of the new socialist man, one who has internalized the ideals of the Revolution and will dedicate himself unselfishly in the pursuit of its goals.

A long segment follows in which the location of the schools is given, the techniques for building them, the record time in which they were completed, and so on. These new schools are located in rural areas but comfortably close to urban centers, and they house 250 boys and 250 girls in separate quarters. On weekends the kids return home to their families.

As largely "voluntary brigades" of construction workers built the schools, some scenes show these workers gaily celebrating the completion of one such educational institution with the students. It seems nothing is left out, as we are bombarded with details as to curriculum, student activities, organization, collective agricultural tasks, dorms, mess halls, and the strict military discipline they observe. In short, we are made witnesses to socialist theory being put into pedagogical practice. "The film gives the impression that all Cuban junior high school students attend the new school, thrive on military discipline and regimentation, master a rigorous academic curriculum, and learn to like daily agricultural labor. This is clearly not the case.... The film is after all a propaganda film intended to portray, convince and motivate others to emulate the Cuban example" (R. Paulston, "The New School," in *A Guide to Cuban Cinema*, ed. Alan Adelman).

Nunca llegará el final (It Will Never End) Marcelino Pérez / EICTV, 1994, color, 25 min. *Cast:* (All being interviewed) José Borrás, Elio Mesa, Fernando Pérez, Julia Yip and Nelson Rodríguez.

A poignant documentary where Cuban filmmakers and technicians talk about the old days and their lives in the world of film. Not all is nostalgia, however, as they look forward to the future. Thus the film's title, *It Will Never End*.

Ociel del Toa (Life on the River Toa) Nicolás Guillén Landrián / ICAIC, 1965, B&W, 17 min. *Music:* Roberto Valera.

Ociel del Toa is a documentary with a cogent poetical quality to it. It portrays the life of peasants in the Toa River Valley, in the eastern province of Oriente, and the changes brought to it by the Revolution (this is the substantial element in the film). Inclusion rather than exclusion and prohibition is the norm: being Communist doesn't prevent the person from going to Mass. Rural scenes are skillfully presented, and they include a funerary procession on canoe down the river and the inevitable music and dance.

Director Nicolás Guillén Landrián was born in 1938 and is the nephew of famous poet Nicolás Guillén.

La odisea del general José (General José's Odyssey) Jorge Fraga / ICAIC, 1969, B&W, 64 min. *Writing credits:* Antonio Maceo, based on one of his letters. *Music:* Armando Guerra. *Cast:* Miguel Benavides, Carlos Pérez Peña, Idalia Anreus, José Antonio Rodríguez, René de la Cruz, René Arisa, Silvano Rey, Alfredo Ávila and Georgina Almanza.

After the beginning of the last war of independence, in 1895, General José Maceo, brother to the national hero Antonio Maceo, begins an insurgency movement in Oriente province with a small army of rebel fighters. To join the larger liberation army, he and his men must traverse regions full of Spanish soldiers and other dangers. With ingeniousness and knowledge of the country, Maceo's army undertakes the perilous journey.

La ola (The Wave) Enrique Álvarez / ICAIC, 1995, color, 70 min. *Cast:* Xenia Cruz and Igor Urquiza.

Two youngsters walk aimlessly through Havana trying to construct a story for themselves. Outlandish yarn indeed.

Omara Fernando Pérez / ICAIC, 1983, color, 26 min.

United States music enthusiasts might remember Omara Portuondo as one of the artists spotlighted in the recent and very popular film *Buena Vista Social Club*. Like the other singers and musicians portrayed therein, she has been around for many decades now and has become one of the legendary names in the history of twentieth century Cuban music. Nube Negra, a subsidiary of Intuition Records, recently released *Palabras,* a compact disc with many of her well-known interpretations.

This documentary is a personal and intimate look at Omara the person, from her infancy in a loving home to her happy years singing with Elena Burke and Moraima Secada. Through her relations with other artists and family members, Omara begins to develop her artistic sensibilities. Today she is one of the respected elders of the Cuban musical tradition.

Director Fernando Pérez Valdés was born in Havana in 1944. He studied the liberal arts in the Soviet Union, and he is a well-known film critic on the island.

Operación Fangio (Operation Fangio) Alberto Lecchi / ICAIC–El Paso Producciones (Spain)–El Puente Producciones (Argentina)–Hasta la Victoria S.A. (Argentina)–Tesela P.C. (Spain)–INCAA (Argentina) and TVE (Spain), 1999, color, 105 min. *Music:* Iván Wyszogrod. *Cast:* Darío Grandinetti, Laura Ramos, Héctor Alterio, Ernesto Tapia, Fernando Guillén, Arturo Maly, Gustavo Salmerón, Óscar Bringas, Susana Pérez, Néstor Jiménez, Glenmys Rodríguez, Luis Enrique Quiñónez, Diego Álvarez, Hirán Vega, Osvaldo Doimeadiós, Adrián Pellegrini, Serafín García Aguilar, Hilario Peña, Jorge Martínez, Luis Sartor, Nieves Santana, Julio

Prieto Rodríguez, Elvira Cervera, Victoria Yins, Carmen Adela Martínez, Samuel Claxton, Aduvice Fuentes, José Worel and Carlos Acosta.

Based on a true event, *Operación Fangio* tells the story of a group of young Cuban revolutionaries who kidnap Argentine racing great Juan Manuel Fangio before a Formula 1 race in Havana. They hope to bring world attention to their cause by keeping one of the world's all-time greatest racers from competing. Batista, Cuban strongman at the time, sends his men out on a brutal search for Fangio, but the revolutionaries, through sheer luck, manage to avoid them.

Make no mistake: the kidnappers are the good guys. They actually help their victim by keeping him from harm at the hands of Batista's henchmen, a group of tough hombres who would like nothing better than to kill the racer and blame it on the revolutionaries.

Otra mujer (Another Woman) Daniel Díaz Torres / ICAIC, 1987, color, 98 min. *Music:* Daniel Longres. *Cast:* Mirta Ibarra, Jorge Villazón, Susana Pérez, Raúl Pomares, Alejandro Lugo, Dagoberto Lainza and Carlos Paulín.

During the early years of the revolution, Juan returns to his village after having fought in the ranks of the revolutionary army. Still residing in the village are his wife Eugenia and his mistress Dulcina. But the life to which he returns is very different from the one he left behind when he went off to fight in the war. His work as a truck driver is no longer available to him, so he is given the opportunity to take a job managing a store that has been seized by the new government. But Juan does not take well to the new state of affairs, and the strain begins to interfere with his personal and social interactions, especially hurting his relationship with his wife Eugenia. Eugenia will progressively turn into … another woman.

El otro Cristóbal (The Other Christopher) Armand Gatti / ICAIC, 1963, B&W, 115 min. *Music:* Gilberto Valdés. *Cast:* Jean Bouise, Alden Knight, Bertina Acevedo, Pierre Chaussat, Marc Dudicourt, Carlos Ruiz de la Tejera, José Antonio Rodríguez, Eduardo Manet, Agustín Campos and Eslinda Núñez.

The film is an allegory of dictatorship in Latin America and the revolutionary struggles to free its people from oppression. It appeals to the folklore and archetypes of the region in order to put context into what is otherwise an unremarkable film.

El otro Francisco (The Other Francisco) Sergio Giral / ICAIC, 1974, B&W, 103 min. *Writing credits:* Anselmo Suárez y Romero, from his novel *Francisco*. *Music:* Leo Brouwer. *Cast:* Miguel Benavides, Alina Sánchez,

Ramoncito Veloz, Margarita Balboa, Adolfo Llauradó, Alden Knight, Samuel Claxton, Omar Valdés, Gerardo Riverón, Armando Bianchi, Ángel Toraño and Patricio Manns.

Adapted from the first anti-slavery novel written in Cuba, it follows the drama of a slave couple denied the most basic of human comforts while foregoing the romatic, sentimental elements contained in the novel. The film opens at a literary salon presided over by Domingo del Monte, who has invited English intellectual Richard Madden to read Suárez y Romero's new novel *Francisco*. Madden is in Cuba investigating alleged violations of a treaty between Spain and Britain regarding the suppression of the slave trade. Events in the novel are portrayed in the film, and they are portrayed again a second time as a sort of philosophical counterweight to the original novel. This second presentation of events purports to show the events without the romantic-sentimental element and more in tune with the reality of slave life in Cuba. This explains the title of the film, *The Other Francisco*. As the Englishman travels around the island, he begins to meet the characters in the novel.

The basic story has Ricardo fall in love with his slave Dorotea, but she rejects his advances. In order to get Dorotea to submit he decides to torture her black lover, Francisco. Dorotea is eventually sent to Havana while Francisco commits suicide in utter desperation. The absolute disregard for the blacks' humanity and the subsequent squalor in which slaves are kept are the most striking elements in this beautifully photographed historical film. The negative has to be the glaring overacting by just about every actor involved.

Pablo Víctor Casaus / ICAIC, 1978, color, 105 min. *Writing credits:* Pablo de la Torriente Brau, from his letters. *Cast:* Lorenzo Hernández, Giraldo Cárdenas, Emilio Porto and Eduardo Rodríguez.

Pablo de la Torriente Brau was born in San Juan, Puerto Rico, on 12 December 1901. One of the most outstanding Cuban journalists of his time, he was able to capture the mood and atmosphere of a whole epoch of Cuban life in his articles and stories. Considered one of the founders of the testimonial genre in the novel, he was one of the paramount chroniclers of the first third of the twentieth century. A fighter against the Machado regime and the first Batista government, the last part of his life was spent in Spain, where he worked as a journalist covering the Spanish Civil War for several Latin American publications. He died on the Majadahonda front on 18 December 1936 aiding in the defense of Madrid against the onslaught of Nationalist troops.

Among his works are the short story collection *Batey*, the chronicles

La isla de los 500 asesinatos, Presidio modelo, and *Peleando con los milicianos,* the novel *Las aventuras del soldado desconocido cubano* and a collection of letters published in a volume with the title *Cartas cruzadas.* The film is based on the biographical data taken from his work.

Los pájaros tirándole a la escopeta (The Tables Have Turned) Rolando Díaz / ICAIC, 1984, color, 90 min. *Music:* Juan Formell. *Cast:* Reinaldo Miravalles, Consuelo Vidal, Alberto Pujol, Beatriz Valdés, Silvia Planas, Néstor Jiménez, Filiberto Romero, Carlos Gómez, José Blanco, Ana Domínguez, Pedro Fernández, Roberto Viña and Lucía Myrna Bernal.

Emilio and Magdalena are two young workers at the Construction Ministry who begin to like each other and eventually fall in love. As their relationship develops, they decide to meet each other's families. At the meeting one thing is clearly established: the young people think very differently from their elders. While the young are open and more liberated in their beliefs, the old folks are entrenched in their old mores and are more traditional. But when Emilio's mother and Magdalena's father begin their own love affair, Emilio and Magdalena categorically reject it, showing that the kids, given the right situation, can be just as conservative and close-minded as their parents.

Director Rolando Díaz is the brother of better-known filmmaker Jesús Díaz. Rolando was born in Havana in 1947 and was a radio and telegraph operator during his time in the military. He began to work at the ICAIC in 1969 in the sound department; he is also a well-regarded film critic.

Papeles secundarios (Supporting Roles) Orlando Rojas / ICAIC–Televisión Española, 1989, color, 117 min. *Writing credits:* based on the play *Requiem por Yarini* by Carlos Felipe. *Music:* Mario Daly. *Cast:* Rosa Fornés, Juan Luis Galiardo, Luisa Pérez Nieto, Ernesto Tapia, Leonor Arocha, Carlos Cruz, Cristóbal González, Miriam Socarrás, Micheline Calvert, María Isabel Díaz, Elio Mesa, Francisco Gattorno, Paula Alí, Leonor Borrero, Susana Marrero, Dolores Pedro, Fernando Bermúdez, Pedro Hernández, Hilda Rabilero, Antonio Puelma and the voice of Mario Balmaseda.

Rosa Soto is the director of one of the best theater companies in Havana. Alejandro, after spending years in a miserable cabaret out in the provinces, comes to direct the classic play *Réquiem por Yarini,* the story of one of Cuba's most infamous pimps. The set is full of intrigue as a high-ranking inspector comes to pay a visit. Mirta, a longtime supporting actress, gets a chance to read for a leading role, a job contested by a promising young actress. Amorous schemes intertwine with professional jealousies as the troupe moves forward with its project.

Papeles son papeles (Paper Is Only Paper) Fausto Canel / ICAIC, 1966, B&W, 90 min. *Music:* Leo Brouwer. *Cast:* Reinaldo Miravalles, Sergio Corrieri, Lilian Llerena, Manuel Pereiro, René de la Cruz, Elio Martín, Carlos Ruiz de la Tejera, Olga Navarro, Salvador Wood and Ugo Ulive.

This comedy takes place in the cabarets, luxury hotels and other places for the "beautiful people" in Havana during the first years of the Revolution that brought Castro to power. A group disguised as militiamen go on a swindling rampage, as people are mostly concerned with two things: money and a way to get out of the country. But the first concern for safeguarding money might prove futile: the Revolutionary authorities' forthcoming currency change could make their money simple, worthless pieces of paper. (In 1961 the government changed currency in order to devalue clandestine bank notes that were freely circulating in the country.) The narrative suffers from absolute lack of coherence; this is a severely unaccomplished production of what was a very promising concept.

Director Fausto Canel was born in Havana in 1939. He was a film critic before and after the triumph of the revolution. He went into exile after the making of *Papeles son papeles*.

Paraíso bajo las estrellas (Paradise Under the Stars) Gerardo Chijona / ICAIC–Ibsermedia–Wanda Films (Spain), 1999, color, 90 min. *Music:* Carlos Faruolo, José María Vitier and Carlos Fernández. *Cast:* Thais Valdés, Vladimir Cruz, Amparo Muñoz, Enrique Molina, Daisy Granados, Santiago Alfonso, Jacqueline Arenal, Litico Rodríguez and Alicia Bustamante.

Those curious as to the workings of world-famous Havana nightclub Tropicana must not miss this one. The title *Paradise Under the Stars* refers to the open-air nightclub; the music is fantastic, the colors exhilarating and the women divine. Romance and race make up the weak storyline, which is overwhelmed by the music and the colorful spectacle of the Tropicana show.

El parque de Palatino (Palatino Park) Enrique Díaz Quesada / Empresa del parque de diversiones "Palatino Park," 1906, B&W, 1 min.

This one-minute fragment of a promotional short is the only extant work of film pioneer Enrique Roque Manuel Silverio Díaz Quesada, the "father of the Cuban cinema." Its images show us the popular Palatino Amusement Park, open to the public in Havana on 8 March 1906. Filmed on 25 March 1906, the film shows several spectators that watch those who are experiencing the thrills of the Ferris wheel as two others, hat in hand, enjoy themselves next to the miniature-train tracks. The camera pans from right to left, beginning at a coffee stand where a crowd gathers, attracted by the large sign that announces "CAFÉ"; the carousel tent is surrounded by a fence and another sign tells us "CABAÑAS, CIGARROS SIEMPRE BUENOS"; another crowd gathers in front of a stand announcing "MANTECADO CON BARQUILLO," a favorite treat for Cubans of the period. Now mounted on top of one of the stores, the camera pans toward the right, showing the Tívoli theater and the imposing structure of the roller coaster. In with the crowd now, the camera travels along with two men and a little girl and arrives at a slide where kids and adults, dressed in their Sunday best, glide happily down to the waiting arms of an attendant. Not far, men slide down a cable.

That day, March 25, 1906, Díaz Quesada was a 23-year-old who was exploring the possibilities of that new artifact, keen to recreate the excitement that he himself was experiencing when he visited the newly opened theaters in Havana that showed moving pictures, venues like the Irijoa Theater or the Florodora. Díaz Quesada showed artistic talents from a very early stage in his life. As a kid he used to hang about in a shop owned by José García González, maker of illuminated signs since the late nineteenth century. It was here that Díaz Quesada made his first acquaintance with the film world, as García González bought a "Chronophotograph" machine from Georges Demeny, to which the enterprising Cuban fitted clockwork in order to experiment with animated promotional matter. He also bought a "Cinematograph Lumière," the one bearing number 247.

Díaz Quesada also worked with Cuban film pioneer José E. Casasús in his production of *Un brujo desapareciendo* (A Disappearing Warlock) in 1898. The young Díaz later founded (1905) the *Moving Pictures Company* with businessman Francisco Rodríguez. His company would produce the series *Cuba al día*, a program specializing in local news items and forerunner of the Cuban newsreel; the Martí and Albisu theaters were the principal locations for viewing his work. His productions also include *Salida de las tropas para Santiago de Cuba durante la Guerra racista* (Troops Leave for Santiago de Cuba During the Racist War). This film — according to many who were able to see it before it was lost — captured dramatic footage of the Cuban Army's operations in Oriente Province. From 1906 to 1909 Díaz Quesada produced a number of films with his brother Juan, and in 1910 he released his *Criminal por obcecación*, a huge success that played to packed houses and opened on 26 March at the Montecarlo Theater. He also filmed *Juan José*, a movie that featured a story by Juan Dicenta and starred Gerardo Artecona and María Luisa Villegas.

Díaz Quesada would then fix up the attic of a house at 356 Calzada de Jesús del Monte, making it the first film studio on the island. The house's first floor became the laboratory where the film was processed. By 1912 the U.S. had decided to recover the remains of the battleship *Maine*, which had sunk in Havana Bay in 1898. American cameramen came with the U.S. expedition, and José G. González got the contract from the Cubans to film the event. As recounted by Pepito González, Jose's son, his father would get seasick easily, leaving Enrique Díaz Quesada behind the camera to capture the details of the operation. The result was the film *Epílogo del Maine* (Epilogue for the *Maine*), whose debut at the Payret Theater only a couple of days after the end of the salvage operation was a great success.

His growing fame got him the contract to film the first feature film in Cuban history, *Manuel García, rey de los campos de Cuba* (Manuel García, King of the Cuban Countryside), underwritten by entrepreneurs Santos and Artigas with Gerardo Artecona in the lead role. The production took six months and at its debut, on Wednesday, 6 August 1913, it was perceived as a remarkable accomplishment. In 1914 Santos and Artigas spent $4,000 on another film directed by Díaz Quesada, *El capitán mambí o libertadores y guerrilleros* (The Mambí Captain or Liberators and Guerrillas); it was first shown on 26 January 1914 at the Polyteama Theater. All this time Díaz Quesada kept filming documentaries, like the ones from the *Riquezas de Cuba* (Cuban Natural Resources) series, the most important of which was *La industria del azúcar de caña* (The Sugar Cane Industry).

Santos and Artigas keep funding Díaz Quesada's efforts, and in 1916–17 they traveled to Camagüey, in midwestern Cuba, to film *El rescate del brigadier Sanguily* (The Rescue of Brigadier-General Sanguily). The text was written by Eduardo Varela Zequeira, and to make the work more realistic, they got Colonel Julio Sanguily, the hero's son, to lend the orthopedic equipment his father used. The film's debut was at the Payret Theater on 9 January 1917, and the Havana Town Hall awarded a gold medal to the producers, Santos and Artigas, for having fashioned a film worthy of the history of the nation. Some of its scenes featured very violent gunfights, and although the blasts couldn't be heard in this silent epic, it was reported that the impression given by some of the soldiers, who appeared to be firing directly at the moviegoers, made many people anxious.

Díaz Quesada went on to film *La hija del policía, o en poder de los ñáñigos* (The Policeman's Daughter, or In the Power of the Ñáñigos) in 1917, the first film that dealt with an Afro-Cuban theme. This same year he also directed *El tabaquero de Cuba o El capital y el trabajo* (The Cuban Tobacco Worker or Capital and Labor), a film which demonstrates Díaz Quesada's social-nationalistic preoccupations, a film in which he also worked the camera. The Afro-Cuban topic introduced three years earlier was such a hit that the same subject was used in a subsequent endeavor, *La brujería en acción* (Witchcraft in Action) in 1920, again produced by Santos and Artigas. This was the last film in which Díaz Quesada cooperated with producers Santos and Artigas. The two entrepreneurs decided to focus their efforts on their highly successful circus, which they had founded in 1916, and on improving the revenues they received from the string of movie theaters that they owned throughout the island. This rupture did not stop Díaz Quesada, who moved on with the series *Los genios del mal* (Evil Minds) produced from 1919 to 1920.

In 1922 he directed and produced *Arroyito*, based on the life of the mythical outlaw of the same name. Full of action and "spectacular adventures," the film again featured Díaz Quesada's brother Juan behind the camera, and it opened to a packed house on 24 April 1922 at the Capitolio Theater.

Díaz Quesada was now ready to achieve his most enduring and timeless production, the epic *El Titán de Bronce* (The Bronze Titan), based on the life of Cuban national hero Antonio Maceo. With a text written by Varela Zequeira, he had again obtained the support of Santos and Artigas for the project, and everything was set to go. But Díaz Quesada died. He had been filming outdoors when it began to pour. The young director refused to stop the shoot, and as a result caught a bad cold that developed into double pneumonia. The "Father of the Cuban Cinema" died on 13 May 1923; he was 40 years old. His disappearance was a blow to the fledgling Cuban film industry, for the young man had had a hand in 17 of the 40 titles in fiction produced on the island up to that point. The baton would be picked up by Ramón Peón, who at that point was already responsible for five films. Santos and Artigas abandoned the film industry altogether, and some time later a fire destroyed the warehouse where all of Díaz Quesada's original negatives were stored. Miraculously, as if to remind the world of Díaz Quesada's genius, the one-minute promotional film *El parque de Palatino* survived the voracious flames.

El paso del Yabebirí (The Yabebirí Pass) Tulio Raggi / ICAIC, 1987, color, 8 min. *Writing credits:* Horacio Quiroga, based on his tale. *Animation:* Noel Lima. *Music:* Juan Márquez.

Based on an Horacio Quiroga tale, this short cartoon tells the story of a man who becomes friendly with the fish; they've saved him when he was being attacked in the Yabebirí River by some ferocious tigers. The theme is solidarity with those in danger of being devoured by powerful and violent neighbors.

Pata negra (Black Leg) Luis Oliveros / ICAIC–El Paso Producciones (Spain), 1999, color, 100 min. *Cast:* Enrique Almirante, Yamilé Blanco, Irela Bravo, Gabino Diego, Baudilio Espinosa, Fernando Echevarría, Javier Gurruchaga, Néstor Jiménez, Hilario Peña, Santiago Ramos, Ulises Toirac and Carlos Treto.

Filmed in Havana and scenic Valle Viñales in Pinar del Río Province, this is the story of a company representative who is sent to a country in Latin America to find new business opportunities for his bosses. His company happens to sell the famed "Pata negra" hams. He has trepidations, for he's not well acquainted with the region, he's heard horror stories as to what goes on in that part of the world and, as we are all about to laugh at his naïveté, all his feared plights come true. Once at his destination, everybody seems to be trying to kill him, from the government to the guerrillas to the drug lords. Even his romantic liaison will become a danger to him. The film has some funny moments.

Patakin Manuel Octavio Gómez / ICAIC, 1985, color, 108 min. *Music:* Rembert Egucs. *Cast:* Enrique Arredondo, Miguel Benavides, Jorge Losada, Carlos Montezuma, Hilda Oates, Assenah Rodríguez, Litico Rodríguez, Alina Sánchez and the Danza Nacional de Cuba.

A Cuban musical not unlike those '60s beach party movies produced in the United States. Music and voluptuous bikini-clad women abound in a story where a certain Shangó Valdés, a womanizing macho man, lives off his wife and has as much fun as he can. At a party in an agricultural enterprise, Shangó attempts to seduce Caridad, wife of Ogún Fernández, but when she refuses his advances he sabotages the affair. We follow Shangó and his friend Elegguá in a series of misadventures, until the climax, a boxing match between Shangó and Oggún and the appearance of Señor Death. The music is outstanding and there are some very funny moments.

Director Manuel Octavio Gómez Martínez de Lahidalga was born in Havana in 1934, and he died there in 1988. He studied Advertising, Journalism, Sociology and Theater, and he was with the ICAIC since its foundation. He was also a film critic, publishing in *La Tarde* and *Diario Libre*.

Patty Candela Rogelio París / ICAIC, 1976, color, 91 min. *Cast:* Raúl Pomares, Salvador Wood, Rogelio Blain, Noel García, Marcos Miranda, Carlos Gili and Luis A. Ramírez.

Operation Patty Candela was a CIA-sponsored plan to kill Raúl Castro on 26 July 1961 as he gave a speech at Maceo Stadium in Santiago de Cuba. Cuban CIA operatives named Izaguirre, Pujals and Baudin, inside the island, would organize anti–Castro resistance while another counterrevolutionary, Aurelio Oslé, would fire mortar shells into the U.S. naval base at Caimanera (Guantánamo), giving the U.S. an excuse to intervene. Another mortar would fire on Cuban positions close to the U.S. base, hoping that the Cubans would fire on the Americans in self-defense. Later that same day, other operatives would kill Fidel himself and some of his closest assistants, paving the way for a generalized insurrection against the revolutionary government. The Cuban Secret Service (G-2) was able to dismantle the plan and 159 anti–Communists were captured and neutralized. This film gives the Cuban government's version of the historical plan to topple the Castro brothers from power.

Pedro, cero por ciento (Pedro, Zero Percent) Luis Felipe Bernaza / ICAIC, 1980, color, 20 min.

Pedro Acosta manages a dairy farm named "Ñame Uno" near Fomento, in the province of Sancti Spíritus. He is important to the Revolution because under his care, for over seven years, his farm has not lost even one calf or cow (zero percent loss). This documentary shows the daily toil of this dedicated man and the difficulties he endeavors every day to overcome.

Una pelea cubana contra los demonios (A Cuban Fight Against Demons) Tomás Gutiérrez Alea / ICAIC, 1972, B&W, 130 min. *Writing credits:* Fernando Ortiz, based on his folk story collection. *Music:* Leo Brouwer. *Cast:* José Antonio Rodríguez, Raúl Pomares, Silvano Rey, Mares González, Olivia Belizaire, Reinaldo Miravalles, Verónica Lynn, Armando Bianchi, Ada Nocetti, Elio Mesa, Luis Alberto García, Donato Figueral and Vicente Revuelta.

The region of Remedios, in the province of Las Villas, is the place where the demons are let loose in the seventeenth century. An enterprising priest siezes the occasion to try to get rid of the residents and do some land speculation. Only a smuggler sees through the scheme and actively opposes the land grabbing scheme, but to no avail, as the backwardness and blind faith of the villagers leads them to destruction.

Tomás Gutiérrez Alea was born in Havana in 1928. One of the founders of ICAIC, he began turning out experimental short subject films when he was only 20 years old. After studying law, he went to Rome's Centro Sperimentale di Cinematografia in 1951. Afterwards he began making documentaries for an association called "Nuestro Tiempo," a group of intellectuals opposed to the Batista regime. He, along with Julio García Espinosa, was instrumental in setting up the army's film department, precursor of the ICAIC. He then turned out the first documentary and first feature film of the revolution and went on to have an exceptional career as a director. With his death in 2000, Cuba lost its most accomplished filmmaker.

Plácido Sergio Giral / ICAIC, 1986, color, 96 min. *Writing credits:* Gerardo Fulleda León, from his play *Plácido*. *Music:* Sergio Vitier. *Cast:* Jorge Villazón, Mirta Ibarra, Rosita Fornés, Miguel Benavides, Ramón Veloz Jr., Miguel Gutiérrez and Orlando Casín.

In 1841 and 1842, black slaves staged bloody insurrections, rebelling on a coffee farm named "Perseverancia" and in the sugar mills "Alcancía," "Luisa," "Trinidad," Las Nieves" and "La Aurora." They came together and presented a unified battle front as they advanced towards the more populated regions of the island. At the battle of "Bemba Road" in the province of Matanzas they were confronted by a company of Spanish army lancers and soundly defeated. The survivors were given chase by the soldiers and shown no mercy, being cut down wherever they were found. Many of them committed suicide. In November of 1842 another generalized slave revolt saw the sugar mills of "Triunvirato," "Acana," "La Concepción," "San Miguel," "San Lorenzo" and "San Rafael" burn while its slaves united and went on a bloody rampage. Again they were routed in a pitched battle with the disciplined Spanish battalions, after which the survivors, exhausted and defeated, took to the wooded hills where they were hunted down and exterminated like animals.

In December of 1843 a female slave who was her owner's lover told him of a plot by the slaves to rebel during the Christmas festivities, only a few days away. The alarmed slave owner, a man named Santa Cruz de Oviedo, contacted the authorities; these unleashed a terrible investigative campaign that employed all types of intimidation and cruelty to get to the truth. Thousands of trials took the judicial system to the brink of collapse, and hundreds of slaves (and some free men), many of them presumably innocent, went to their deaths.

Among the accused was one Gabriel de la Concepción Valdés (Plácido). Plácido was a mulatto who looked almost white. He was the bastard son of a light-skinned mulatto named Diego Ferrer Matoso, a hairdresser, and a Spanish ballerina named Concepción Vázquez. He was born in Havana on 18 March 1809, and he may have been abandoned by his white mother, because it was his father and his paternal family that brought him up. As a young man Plácido wrote a sonnet against slavery that became very popular. After some time his poems were all the rage among the most liberal intellectuals on the island as well as among the most humble classes. His anti-slavery, anti–Spain stance as well as other supposed subversive activities served as the pretext to accuse him of treason, of participating in the conspiracy later named "La Escalera." The District Attorney, Pedro Salazar, brought certain accusations that had Plácido serving as viceroy in a new Black Republic of Cuba. The poet apparently named names in a desperate attempt to save his life. The trial lasted over six months, after which he was sentenced to death. While awaiting his turn to face the firing squad, Plácido wrote some of the most lyric and moving poems in the history of Cuban literature. On the 28th of June 1844 he died with dignity reciting a poem, in spite of the fact that 20,000 curious thrill seekers came to see the poet and ten others die. Slave owners were advised to bring their slaves to witness the price to be paid for challenging the authority of Spain.

This film follows the life of this gentle, talented patriot with affection and admiration. Jorge Villazón in the lead role borders on brilliance.

¡Plaff!, o demasiado miedo a la vida (Plaff!, or Too Afraid of Life) Juan Carlos Tabío / ICAIC, 1989, color, 110 min. *Music:* Nicolás Reynoso. *Cast:* Daisy Granados, Thais Valdés, Raúl Pomares, Jorge Cao, Alicia Bustamante, Ana Vivian Mora, Rolando Núñez, Natasha Díaz, Blanquita Contreras, Miriam Socarrás, Gastón Palmer, Néstor Jiménez, Sonia Elena Prado, Amarilis Pumeda, Rosa María Alonso, Gerber Couso, Annia Ibáñez, Johan Gómez, Héctor Rodríguez, Elvira Valdés, Cristobalina Arrieta, Daniel Chavarria, Juan Carlos Hernández, Ricardo Ávila, Susana Ríos, Icay Romay, Jaqueline Arenal, Idalmis del Risco, José L. Rodríguez, Luis Lima Barreto, and María Elena Barreto.

In this strange comedy, Concha, a superstitious woman who lives under the same roof with her son and his wife, is having a hard time accepting her new daughter-in-law. In fact, Concha has always been afraid of change, and this fear has been the fundamental component of her life. The problem is that someone is throwing eggs at Concha, and it is not clear who it is or what the purpose might be. Is it her scientist daughter-in-law? Is it the taxi driver with whom Concha has fallen in love? *Plaff!*, which refers to the sound of splattering eggs, is a clumsy, poorly made comedy that plays on the fact that its low budget has not allowed for a better quality production. The actors execute their parts normally even when the camera crew is seen in the mirror or when encountering a crew member on screen or requesting a prop from someone off-camera. The implicit censure of Castro's bureaucracy and the portrayal of the inferior living conditions suffered by Cubans are of interest.

Polvo rojo (Red Dust) Jesús Díaz / ICAIC, 1982, color, 112 min. *Music:* José María Vitier. *Cast:* Adolfo Llauradó, René de la Cruz, José Antonio

Rodríguez, Cristina Obin, Tito Junco, Luis Alberto Ramírez, Enrique Molina, Salvador Wood, Nelson Villagra, Carlos Montezuma, Miguel Gutiérrez, Rogelio Blain, Reinaldo Miravalles, Paloma Abraham, Aarón Vega and Alberto Molina.

During the first years of the revolution, the rebel authorities nationalize a large nickel producing concern owned by Americans. As most of the workers resolve to leave for the U.S., one engineer, a mulatto from the lower classes, decides to stay and help the new authorities maintain and improve the enterprise with his expertise.

Por primera vez (For the First Time) Octavio Cortázar / ICAIC, 1967, B&W, 10 min. *Music:* Raúl Gómez.

The revolutionary government set up "Cinemóvil" units that brought film to the most remote places in the country. This documentary follows one of these units as it works in Los Mulos, in the remote Baracoa area of Oriente Province, a place where many people had never seen a movie. Their impressions, opinions and facial expressions give a compelling account of a community coming into the twentieth century.

People in the village are interviewed — kids in the schoolroom, older women in the street — and their reactions to the film-viewing experience portray a refreshing naïveté, as a woman states: "Film is ... well, lots of things happen in the cinema. You see snakes and you see beautiful girls and you see weddings, horses, war and all that." "And then we see them watching a film — Chaplin's *Modern Times*. The sequence with the automatic lunch machine has them in tears of laughter. We see faces gazing in wide-eyed amazement and delight.... Old men and women look as if they cannot believe the cinema has really come to them, and a little girl bites her finger in excitement" (Michael Chanan, *The Cuban Image*, pages 11–12).

Director Octavio Cortázar was born in Havana in 1935. He worked in advertising and on television (CMBF Channel 7). He was also director of the popular series *The Popular Encyclopedia*, and subsequently studied film in Prague's FAMU.

La prensa seria (The Serious Press) Jesús de Armas / ICAIC, 1960, B&W, 3 min. 20 sec. *Animation:* Hernán Henríquez. *Music:* José Iglesias.

Castro and his revolution have come under fire from liberal-capitalist circles for controlling the press. In this cartoon, Cuban adults and children alike see how the so-called "free-press" or "serious press" can take an event and turn it on its head. Isn't it better — the viewer begins to ask — if the state corrects the misrepresentations and distortions that the uncontrolled press is bound to fabricate?

El primer paso de papá (Dad's First Step) Tulio Raggi / ICAIC, 1977, color, 5 min. 9 sec. *Animation:* Erasmo Juliachs. *Music:* Juan Blanco.

As is bound to happen in every home, one day the wife has to be absent (she went shopping). The father is left on his own and has to do the housework, something with which he is obviously not conversant. After many failed attempts at accomplishing the tasks at hand, the husband finally gets the job done. He also shows his young son that a real man can do housework. A didactic cartoon for young and old alike.

La primera carga al machete (The First Machete Charge) Manuel Octavio Gómez / ICAIC, 1969, B&W, 80 min. *Music:* Leo Brouwer and Pablo Milanés. *Cast:* José Antonio Rodríguez, Adolfo Llauradó, Idalia Anreus, Carlos Bermúdez, Julián Martínez, Omar Valdés, Eduardo Moure, Raúl Pomares, Ana Viñas, Felipe Santos, Alfredo Perojo, Eslinda Núñez, Eugenio Hernández, Miguel Benavides, Pablo Milanés, Rigoberto Águila and Aramis Delgado.

Set during Cuba's first War of Independence, begun in 1868, this is the story of the insurgents' legendary taking of the town of Bayamo, in Oriente province. To counteract them, the colonial governor sends two columns of Spanish troops to put an end to their adventure. The first column is forced to retreat through clever strategy, while the second is defeated when the Cuban forces charge with machetes in their hands.

The story then follows the epic story of the machete as it becomes the Cubans' main weapon against the Spanish army, beginning with that first fateful charge in Bayamo led by General Máximo Gómez. The film is done using documentary techniques, with interviews of both Spanish and Cuban "participants," hand-held cameras taking in the action and direct sound. At the end of the film, balladeer Pablo Milanés comments, in song, on the action.

"*La primera carga al machete* is Cuban experimental cinema at its best. The film not only recaptures the past, but brings its anti-war and proud nationalistic message home to the present. It is a worthy cinematic experience" (Ronald Schwartz, *Latin American Films, 1932–1994*, p. 205).

Las profecías de Amanda (Amanda's Prophecies) Pastor Vega / ICAIC, 1999, color, 102 min. *Cast:* Daisy Granados, Laura Ramos and Consuelo Vidal.

This is an interesting look at "santería," that very Cuban, syncretic interpretation of the spiritual realm. This feature tells the story of Amanda, a middle-aged practitioner of santería whose prophecies are presented in a series of vignettes. The story of her life, from her early years to maturity in the present, is also told in a realistic, down to earth style.

Los que se quedaron (Those Who Stayed Behind) Benito Zambrano / EICTV, 1995, color, 15 min.

Benito Zambrano is a Spaniard who studied and graduated from Cuba's International School of Film and Television (EICTV). This documentary is his thesis project, and it tells the dramatic story of a mother who disowns her son after his escape from the island during the 1980 Peruvian embassy incident.

Quiéreme y verás (Love Me, and You'll See) Daniel Díaz Torres / ICAIC, 1995, color, 100 min. *Cast:* Reinaldo Miravalles, Rosita Fornés, Raúl Pomares and Litico Rodríguez.

At the end of the year 1958, a group of thieves plans a daring heist in one of Havana's most important banks. But the inevitable voluptress gets in the way and the plans have to be put off. As January 1, 1959, rolls around, everything changes: the revolutionaries enter Havana and the heist can never be pulled off. Thirty-five years later, three of the would-be bank robbers get together to remember their plans, tactics and strategy, and the events of that fateful January 1959 that would change the island's history forever.

Quinoscopio I Juan Padrón / ICAIC, 1985, color, 6 min. 40 sec. *Animation:* Mario García-Montes. *Music:* Daniel Longres.

This cartoon short is based on seven jokes by the famed Argentine comedian Joaquín Lavado, also known as "Quino." One has to do with a traffic cop, another has a military band with a very special singer, a third deals with a lion hunter, and yet another with a modern dentist, an explorer in the Andes, and a little old lady with good lungs. The type of jokes and the nature of the cartoon characters (bare-chested women with voluminous breasts, for example) make evident that this animation is for a more mature audience.

Raíces de mi corazón (The Roots of My Heart) Gloria Rolando / Imágenes del Caribe, 2001, color, 50 min. *Music:* Jorge Maletá, "Vocal Baobab" group and Junius Williams. *Cast:* Monse Duane, Sonia Boggiano, Zoraima Segón, Renny Arozarena, Luz María Collazo, Jorge Prieto, Aimeé Despaigne, Manuel Oña, Nora Rodríguez, Francisca Loredo, Ileana Chávez, Simone Balmaseda, Luz Marina Delis, Aloima Rodríguez, Darwin L. Duane and Elvira Cervera (cameo appearance).

In the early days of the Republic, a hard-line group of Afro-Cubans, many of its members veterans of the independence wars, begin advocating violence in order to see its demands met. Among its leaders are two veterans, Pedro Ivonet and Evaristo Estenoz. This group sees race as the main vehicle for achieving their goals, not the class struggle or the struggle for true democracy. Their fight, it was made clear, was against the white race. Their philosophy was formed by centuries of dealings with the white population of the island; any attempt at unity with the whites, it was argued, would only benefit the whites, possessors of the wealth and education. These groups kept their organizations closed to whites, advocated blacks-only beaches and parks, industries, businesses and schools. Sports organizations were set up only for blacks only, and consumer cooperatives were being planned for an exclusively black membership.

This group took the name "Asociación Independiente de Color" (Independent Association of Color), and quickly developed into a political party. But the black majority would not back their project, and in the 1908 elections the party, expecting widespread support from the Afro-Cuban majority, suffered a resounding defeat. Helping in their defeat was the hostility shown them by prominent black Cubans like Senator Martín Morúa Delgado and statesman Juan Gualberto Gómez.

On top of this, the Cuban Senate then passed a law prohibiting parties and organizations that based their membership on race. By 1912, frustrated by its poor showing in the polls and the new prohibition, the party took to arms and thousands of blacks went to the mountains of Oriente Province, where many white farm families were slaughtered. The United States became alarmed at the situation and landed troops against President José Miguel Gómez' wishes. The Cuban president, wanting to avoid another full intervention by the U.S., unleashed the full force of the newly formed Cuban National Army against the black insurgents, who proved no match for the professional soldiers. In a few weeks the rebellion was smashed, 6,000 blacks were dead and their leaders were being dissected by army doctors looking for physiological clues to their behavior.

This is all told in this film through the story of Mercedes, an Afro-Cuban woman who seeks her roots by looking through old photographs, newspaper clippings and her mother's stories. She finds that her forebears took part in the rebellion, a movement that was branded as racist until the revolution's revisionist historians restored the incident, showing that blacks had abundant justification to rebel.

Rancheador (Runaway Slave Hunter) Sergio Giral / ICAIC, 1977, color, 95 min. *Writing credits:* Cirilo Villaverde, from his novel *Diario de un rancheador*. *Music:* Leo Brouwer. *Cast:* Reinaldo Miravalles, Adolfo Llauradó, Samuel Claxton, Omar Valdés, Salvador Wood, Carlos Bermúdez, Luis

Rielo, Heriberto Velázquez, Eduardo Macías, Argelio Sosa, Daniel Jordán, Elio Mesa, Armando Borroto, Alejandro Díaz, Ana Viña and Adela Legrá.

A ranceador is a man charged with finding and returning runaway slaves to their owners. Francisco Estévez is a bold and fearless man who not only terrifies the slaves, but becomes a tool of the powerful against the farmers and villagers. His obsession is Melchora, the elusive leader of the runaways. His excesses in the end cause his downfall.

The film captures the spirit of the Cuban salon very nicely. This was the place where, in the early 1800s, the Cuban upper classes went to learn about the latest fashions, literary styles and philosophies coming from Europe; there they also showed off the dresses and jewelry brought back from shopping sprees in the old continent. The contrast between the life of the salon and that of the slave quarters is made quite evident in this film. It also captures the mind-set of the ruling classes on the island: while in South America the bourgeois had largely joined in the fight against the Spanish colonial authorities, in Cuba those same authorities were seen as a safeguard against a black, Haiti-like rebellion that would result in the massacre of anyone with white skin.

Realengo 18 Oscar Torres, Eduardo Manet / ICAIC, 1961, B&W, 60 min. *Writing credits:* from a story by Pablo de la Torriente Brau. *Music:* Enrique Ubieta. *Cast:* Teté Vergara, René de la Cruz, Pablo Ruiz Castellanos, José A. Rodríguez, Ester Guerra, Rita Limonta, Giraldo González, Nicomedes Milanés, Roberto Sánchez and José Limeres.

A "realengo" is an ownerless tract of land that is settled by dispossessed peasants. The film deals with historical events during a peasant revolt in Oriente province during the 1930s. After the death of his father, a young man decides to join the local guard against his mother's wishes. When an American sugar company wants to claim the land and the peasants resist, the young man has to point the gun at his own neighbors which are led by his defiant mother. This 60-minute film looks quite crude, but the use of non-professional actors, some of whom actually experienced the events depicted, is a refreshing novelty.

Puerto Rican director Oscar Torres had done a documentary for ICAIC before tackling *Realengo 18*. Like Gutiérrez Alea and García Espinosa, Torres had studied at the Centro Sperimentale in Rome, and he came to Cuba sporting aesthetic and social ideas comparable to his two Cuban counterparts. The documentary in question is called *Tierra olvidada* (Forgotten Land) and, like its famous precursor *El Mégano*, it deals with life in the Zapata swamps of the southern coast. But things are not the same as before: the new government is clearing the land, dredging the swamp, caring for the charcoal workers, and generally improving the lives of the rural population there.

A short time after completing *Realengo 18*, Torres returned to Puerto Rico, where he died a very young man.

El recurso del método (Long Live the President!) Miguel Littín / ICAIC–K.G. Productions (France)–FR3–Conacine (Mexico), 1979, color, 164 min. *Writing credits:* Alejo Carpentier, from his novel of the same name. *Music:* Leo Brouwer. *Cast:* Nelson Villagra, Katy Jurado, Alain Cuny, María Adelina Vera, Salvador Sánchez, Ernesto Gómez Cruz, Reinaldo Miravalles, Raúl Pomares, Idelfonso Tamayo, Gabriel Retes and Ignacio Retes.

The president of the Republic wants to be an enlightened despot, able to deal with the many pressures from the Americans while paying lip service to the many aspirations of his people. Looking to France as the cradle of democratic liberties, he travels to Paris and lives in a luxurious apartment close to the Arc de Triomphe, but while there he sleeps in a hammock like most of his countrymen. This unsavory character puts down a rebellion and even orders a massacre in order to remain in power, while the breakout of the First World War makes the world ignore him and his country's economic boom. He ends up in exile in Paris, where his daughter has transformed his apartment. He dies and is buried in Montparnasse.

This film is one of ICAIC's first co-productions with Latin American companies and directors like Miguel Littín, a Chilean.

Redonda y viene en caja cuadrada (It's Round and It Comes in a Square Box) Rolando Díaz / ICAIC, 1979, color, 10 min.

This short documentary attempts to capture the emotion and the passions that a typical baseball game in any town in Cuba is bound to generate. The unparalleled ardor and enthusiasm of the crowd might amaze those not conversant with Cuban mores.

Reina y Rey (Queen and King) Julio García Espinosa / ICAIC, 1994, color, 92 min. *Music:* Pablo Milanés. *Cast:* Rogelio Blain, Coralia Veloz and Consuelo Vidal.

Reina is old and lonely. Her only companion is her dog Rey. The problem is that Rey disappears into thin air, and the old lady, now lonelier than ever, despairs. Unexpectedly, her old employers, who had left Cuba for Miami 20 years ago, turn up at her door wanting to spend some time with her and reminisce. They also try to convince her to go back to the U.S. with them, but the woman, faced with the prospect of spending what's left of her life in an alien environment with people who've become strangers, decides to stay in Cuba, loneliness and all.

Retrato de Teresa (Portrait of Teresa) Pastor Vega / ICAIC, 1979, color, 103 min. *Music:* Carlos Fariñas. *Cast:* Daisy Granados, Adolfo Llauradó, Alina Sánchez, Raúl Pomares, Eloísa Álvarez Guedes, Alejandro Lugo, Idalia Anreus, Miguel Benavides, Mario Limonta, Samuel Claxton and Elsa Gay.

Teresa is the group leader of a particularly efficient production unit in a textile mill. She is also the union representative and leader of the factory's dance troupe, an accomplished group that is involved in national competitions. By all accounts she is the liberated, "new" woman ushered in by the Revolution, but is she really? When she gets home at night she finds Ramón, her husband, who has not shed the old bourgeois social values and is having problems with Teresa's freedom. His biggest problem is with the dance troupe, and he tells his wife that she is shirking her sacred responsibilities to her children and her husband.

Teresa goes to her mother for advice, but she is still entrenched in the old ways and offers no practical help. Eventually, the exasperated Ramón leaves the home and begins an affair with another woman. Although he will attempt reconciliation with his wife, she confronts him with the knowledge of his affair, and asks him what he would feel if she herself had an affair. Ramón cannot answer. In the end, Teresa decides to spend the rest of her life without Ramón: her freedom and her responsibilities as a full-fledged member of society take precedence over her love for Ramón.

This is a film in which the characters fasten themselves to one's mind, not as actors, but as real persons with real problems. Performances are deserving of praise, especially that of Daisy Granados as Teresa, Adolfo Llauradó as Ramón, Alina Sánchez as Ramón's lover and Raúl Pomares as Teresa's factory supervisor.

El ring (The Ring) Oscar L. Valdés / ICAIC, 1966, B&W, 20 min.

A short documentary that gives a very general view on the sweaty and painful world of boxing and of the men who have made a career out of that popular sport. Two fighters spotlighted are the famous Kid Chocolate and Fermín Espinosa.

Río Negro (Black River) Manuel Pérez / ICAIC, 1977, color, 140 min. *Music:* Juan Márquez. *Cast:* Sergio Corrieri, Nelson Villagra, Alejandro Lugo, Mario Balmaseda, Raúl Eguren, Sergio González, René de la Cruz, Elio Martín, Raúl Pomares, Luis Rielo and Rogelio Blain.

"*Río Negro*, Manuel Pérez' second feature, is a Cuban western set on a ranch in the Escambray at the time of the Bay of Pigs, in which Tirso, a revolutionary militiaman, son of a peasant whose land was siezed in the bad years before the Revolution, slugs it out with Chano, a counterrevolutionary who had been involved in the land seizure. The greatest delights in this last film are the superb performances of Sergio Corrieri as the self-searching Tirso, and the Chilean actor Nelson Villagra as the thwarted Chano, but the genre format — and especially the spectacular shoot-out with which the film ends— overwhelms the attempt that had been made to mould the character of Tirso differently from the conventional genre hero, above all by introducing contradictions in his personality and a level of political discourse which Hollywood would never permit. Sergio Corrieri, like Nelson Villagra an actor of exceptional qualities, internationally renowned for the lead in *Memorias del subdesarrollo*, also played the Man from Maisinicú. After these films he withdrew from screen acting, to avoid getting typecast as Cuba's principal male lead" (Michael Chanan, *The Cuban Image*, p. 277).

El romance del palmar (Romance Under the Palms) Ramón Peón / PECUSA (Películas Cubanas, S.A.)–Antonio Perdices, 1938, B&W, 92 min. *Music:* Gonzalo Roig, Ernesto Lecuona, Gilberto Valdés, Félix B. Caignet, Moisés Simons, Bola de Nieve, Antonio Fernández and Alberto Villalón. *Cast:* Rita Montaner, Alicia Rico, Carlos Badías, José M. Linares Rivas, Alberto Garrido, Federico Piñero, Julio Gallo, Nena Núñez, María de los Ángeles Santana, Julito Díaz, Lolita Berrio, Marta Elba Fombellida, G. Delfino, Orquesta Habana Casino, Orquesta Películas Cubanas, Trío Pinareño and Hermanas Álvarez.

A pretty young woman named Fe (Faith) dwells in an idyllic setting in the Cuban countryside, insouciant and free. She lets herself be seduced and she and her seducer wind up in Havana, where Fe lands a job as a cabaret singer. She ends up quarreling with her seducer and commencing a sentimental relationship with another man, while back at the ranch, her father does his best to get her to return home. Rita Montaner and the superb music provide the most pleasing moments in this melodrama, one of the most popular ever produced on the island.

Director Ramón Peón García was born in Havana in 1897. He worked in the sugar industry as a young man, and afterwards became a dancer. His film career is divided between Cuba and Mexico; in this second nation he was production assistant to Antonio Moreno in the films *Santa* (1931) and *Águilas frente al sol* (1932). He moved to Puerto Rico in his mature years, where he died.

La rosa blanca (The White Rose) Emilio Fernández / Comisión del Centenario de José Martí–Películas Antillas S.A., 1954, B&W, 121 min. *Music:* Antonio Díaz Conde. *Cast:* Roberto Cañedo, Gina Cabrera, Julio Capote, Raquel Revuelta, Dalia Íñiguez, Julio Villarreal, Alicia Caro, Juan José Martínez Casado, Rodolfo Landa, Rebeca Iturbide, Andrés Soler, Jorge Casanova, Gaspar Pombo, Celestino San Gil, Rafael Alcaide, Miguel Inclán, Arturo Soto Rangel, Palma de Ribera, Agustín Campos, Santiago Ríos, Raúl Díaz, Pedro Martín Plana, Manolo Riera, Enrique Medina, Jorge Max and Manuel Noriega.

This feature film deals with the thorny issue of the life of José Martí, Cuba's revered national hero. Set in the 1870s, we see a young Martí condemned to forced labor for opposing the Spanish domination of Cuba. After being freed and on his way to exile in Spain, he falls in love with a Cuban girl in Mexico. Later on, in Guatemala, he accepts the adoration of a young Guatemalan girl, but remains faithful to the Cuban, whom he has married. Deported a second time, Martí goes to New York, where he works diligently to further the cause of Cuban independence, giving speeches and raising funds. Far from his wife and son, Martí decides to go to Cuba and join in the fighting, thus evading the criticism that he is not the most courageous of rebels, safe in New York while others were giving their lives for Cuba's independence. In the end he dies in battle and the Spaniards, his enemies, give him a hero's funeral.

This film was a co-production with Mexico. One would expect better quality, the film having been directed by one of that country's leading directors, "El Indio" Fernández, and having obtained government patronage. Planned as an official tribute to Cuba's national hero, it starred a Mexican actor (Roberto Cañedo) who bore no resemblance whatsoever to Martí, and offered a maudlin storyline that only succeeded in irritating many perceptive Cuban viewers.

La salación (Bad Luck) Manuel Octavio Gómez / ICAIC, 1965, B&W, 77 min. *Music:* Roberto Valera. *Cast:* Blanca Contreras, Josefina Henríquez, Lorenzo López, Idalia Anreus, Dinorah Anreus, Pedro Pablo Astorga, Marta Farre, Rigoberto Aguila, Antonia Peña, Miguel Borrego.

Manuel Octavio Gómez's feature debut is vaguely reminiscent of English New Wave films, with a slow narrative style and B&W photography that reminds one of films like *Loneliness of the Long Distance Runner*. It is the story of a young couple in the first years of the Revolution that is trying to cope with a number of problems, not the least of which is the fact that each partner comes from a different social class. The girl's family, middle class before the Revolution, disapproves of her relationship with a working-class boy. The boy's family, full of working-class pride, would rather he not get involved with a representative of the old order. His father dead, the young man is reluctant to get married because he must support his mother and two younger brothers on a mechanic's salary. In the most evocative scene of the film, the two young lovers enter a large house in order to make love while the thunder and rain outside keep the streets empty. The house, reminiscent of a time gone by, of class power and privilege, prevents them from consummating their love. The large house, in a way, is the physical presence of the social relations of the past, of the bourgeois morality that frowned upon furtive love. Back in the small family apartment, the couple struggles to find a bit of privacy, retreating to the balcony while in the background one hears the rest of the family arguing over the noise each person is making. Gómez is a keen observer of the new social space brought in by the Revolution and the strain it puts on relationships, of the fact that the implementation of social reforms can create other, new problems (overcrowding, lack of privacy) with which to contend. *La salación* is the new revolutionary society as seen through the eyes of two young lovers, two largely innocent individuals whose apolitical perspectives give us an honest view of the reality of the new Cuba.

Santera Solveig Hoogesteijn / ICAIC–Alter Films–CNAC–Gona TV–Macu Films–RCTV, 1997, Color, 97 min. *Music:* Víctor Cuica. *Cast:* Laura del Sol, Hirma Salcedo, Víctor Cuica, Gladys Ibarra.

Shot in conjunction with Spain and Venezuela, this feature tells the story of Paula, a social worker from Spain played by Laura del Sol, who travels to Venezuela in order to work in a women's prison there. Slowly becoming acquainted with the individual personalities that populate the prison, Paula notices that one woman is very different from the others. This woman is always alone, shunned by the others, mysterious and alluring. Her name is Santera Soledad (played by Hirma Salcedo), and as her name aptly announces, she is a santera (practices Santería) and is usually alone (Soledad).

After Santera is tortured by prison guards, Paula feels pity and approaches her. She learns that the inmate's Santería witchcraft has deep cultural roots and that she has a learned spiritual guide named Eulogio and a family back in her jungle village.

The film contains much of the Santería rituals, dances and practices and strives for authenticity, but at times it has the feel of a tourist promotional short, an informative piece for Europeans and for the uninitiated.

Se permuta

Se permuta (For Trade) Juan Carlos Tabío / ICAIC, 1983, color, 103 min. *Music:* Juan Márquez. *Cast:* Rosita Fornés, Isabel Santos, Mario Balmaseda, Ramoncito Veloz Jr., Silvia Planas, Manuel Porto, Maritza Rodríguez, Litico Rodríguez, Rini Cruz, Mirta Ibarra, Luis García, María Elena Mariño, Miriam Lezcano, Paco Espinosa, Elsa Medina, Raúl García and Sergio San Pedro.

This is a comedy where Gloria, a single mother living in a run-down neighborhood of Havana, is worried about her teenage daughter Yolanda's love affair with a mechanic, whom she perceives as not worthy to marry her girl. She then puts a plan into effect that will separate her from the mechanic: she swaps her apartment for a better one in the finer neighborhood of "El Vedado." There, Yolanda meets Guillermito, an opportunistic bureaucrat who gets her to agree to marry him, although she is not very enthusiastic. Seeing how his future mother-in-law was successful in swapping her apartment for a better one in a fine neighborhood, Guillermito persuades her to initiate an elaborate house-swapping network where he and Yolanda will end up with a big, comfortable house. This complicated network rests on a little old lady who lives alone in a large house and dreams of moving to Matanzas to be close to her son.

Things get complicated when Pepe, an older black man, shows up at Gloria and Yolanda's apartment to knock down a wall. Young Yolanda instantly falls in love with him, and he is taken with the girl as well. In the following days she seeks him out at home and at work. A further complication is that Pepe is fiancé to María Cristina, Gloria's good friend.

As Gloria continues to engage people in her house-swapping scheme, the viewer feels that it will all be for naught, as her daughter becomes increasingly involved with Pepe. In the end, it all falls apart when the little old lady shows up in a taxi and informs the house-swappers that she is no longer interested in moving to Matanzas, as her son is coming to Havana to live with her.

The film is marked by the intrusion of an unidentified character whom I take to be the producer, who explains that the house-swapping story has gone on too long, and that now the film will "cut to the chase," as it were. The end of the story is now at hand, with Yolanda in bed with Pepe, Guillermito in bed with María Cristina (not only houses are swapped), and Gloria happy knowing that her little girl is with the man she really loves. At times some of the characters recognize the presence of the camera, as when Pepe flags down a complete stranger who promptly offers to drive him anywhere for free. Pepe looks at the camera in disbelief. The main storyline, that of the teenaged white girl having a love affair with an elder black man, says a lot about the elimination of racial and age prejudices in the new Cuban society; the house-swapping plot teaches the non–Cuban viewer how people change residence in an economy where private rent has been outlawed.

La segunda hora de Esteban Zayas (Esteban Zayas' Second Chance) Manuel Pérez / ICAIC, 1984, color, 105 min. *Cast:* Mario Balmaseda, Diana R. Suárez, Salvador Wood, Susana Pérez, Enrique Molina and Nelson Villagra.

Esteban Zayas runs a mill in a remote area of the northern coast of Oriente province, the easternmost part of the island. He's lived alone most of his life, missing out on the great events that have shaped Cuban history. With the advent of new times, he will now get a second chance to participate in the life of his nation.

Un señor muy viejo con unas alas enormes (A Very Old Man with Enormous Wings) Fernando Birri / ICAIC–Laboratorio de Poéticas Cinematográficas de Fernando Birri–Televisión Española, 1988, color, 90 min. *Writing credits:* from a story by Gabriel García Márquez. *Music:* Pablo Milanés, Gianni Nocenzi and José María Vitier. *Cast:* Daisy Granados, Asdrúbal Meléndez, Fernando Birri, Luis Alberto Ramírez, Adolfo Llaurradó, Marcia Barreto, Silvia Planas, María Luisa Mayor, Marabú, René Martínez and Rodrigo Utría.

As the result of a tropical storm, an old man with enormous wings is blown onto an island where he lands close to a family's home. The family, not knowing what to make of such a portent, shelters him in a chicken coop. A priest that comes to take a look promptly announces the creature is an evil thing, but the poor family, seeing the curiosity the strange creature excites, begins charging admission. The old man is exploited this way for six years, after which he fixes his wings and flies away.

El señor presidente (Mr. President) Manuel Octavio Gómez / ICAIC–SFP–TF1–French Ministry of Culture, 1984, color, 100 min. *Writing credits:* adapted from Miguel Ángel Asturias' novel *El señor presidente*. *Music:* Rembert Egües. *Cast:* Michel Auclair, Reinaldo Miravalles, Bruno Garcín, Florence Jaugey, Idalia Anreus, René de la Cruz, Alejandro Lugo, Dora Doll, Erdwin Fernández, Tania Pérez James, Francisca Miranda, Omar Valdés and Raúl Eguren.

A madman kills a colonel, friend and comrade of a Latin American dictator, a situation that gives the strongman an excuse to accuse the opposition and strike at his political enemies. The immoral activities of all those that surround the "president" are brought to the fore. A very predictable flick.

La serpiente roja (The Red Serpent) Ernesto Caparrós / Royal News (Félix O'Shea), 1937, B&W, 80 min. *Writing credits:* Félix B. Caignet. *Cast:* Aníbal de Mar, Pituka de Foronda, Carlos Badías, Roberto Insúa, Aurelio Cavia, Antonio Trigo, Pedro Segarra, Félix O'Shea, Ramón Valenzuela, Juan de Aragón, J. Ayala and Paco Alfonso.

In this first feature talkie in Cuban film history, famed detective Chan-Li-Po (Aníbal de Mar) investigates mysterious murders in a London mansion. The killer leaves behind the enigmatic graffiti "Red Serpent," and the number one suspect is the butler. Behind a secret door, a hideous man is discovered whose anomalous psychological disposition makes him do the butler's bidding. Thus, following his time-tested theory "Tenga paciencia, muuuucha paciencia," Chan-Li-Po gets to the root of the problem.

79 primaveras (79 Springs) Santiago Álvarez / ICAIC, 1969, B&W, 25 min.

Through the life and experiences of Ho Chi Minh, the viewer is treated to a short history of Vietnam's age-old struggle to be free. The Vietnamese leader is revealed in his different facets as a poet, soldier and politician. He is also shown as a sort of respected grandfather with a group of children, with whom he mingles freely. The title refers to his age.

Director Santiago Álvarez Román was born in Havana in 1919. A jack of all trades, he studied Medicine, Philosophy and Liberal Arts in the University of Havana, and later on studied Psychology at Columbia University in New York. He lived for many years in the U.S., and in 1942 he became a member of the Socialist Party. He worked at CMQ Radio in Havana and later went on to direct the ICAIC's Latin American news desk. From 1961 to 1967 he was ICAIC's director of short subject films. He is exclusively a documentary filmmaker.

Si me comprendieras (If You Could Only Understand Me) Rolando Díaz / Luna Llena, 1998, color, 87 min. *Music:* Marcos Castilla

Produced by a company from the Canary Islands, *Si me comprendieras* tells the story of a Cuban film director who is searching for the perfect leading lady for his new musical comedy. The requirements are that the woman be black or mulatto and a good singer and dancer.

For the sake of spontaneity, he prefers a fresh young face without much acting experience, so he searches through files in the Film Institute looking through its lists of extras. Out in the streets of Havana, he and his friends interview a number of prospects and get more than they bargained for: an honest, sincere look at the reality of contemporary Cuba as seen through the eyes of poor, black Havana women.

The result, then, is the story of the director and his film crew (who always remain behind the camera) interviewing people in the streets of Havana. This procedure helps them "create" the cast of the film as they go along, with all the real social problems and issues this "cast" brings with it. Never forgetting the fictional aim of the director, that is, to find a suitable protagonist for his film, very attractive music and dance numbers are included that in no way detract from the poignant portrayal of Cuban social problems in the late nineties, issues such as racism and emigration.

Si me comprendieras reminds one of the powerful social documentaries made in Cuba in the sixties; devoid of much of the stridency of some of them, it has that feel of artistic maturity that comes with forty years of experience in the genre.

Siboney Juan Orol / Aspa Films (Juan Orol y Asociados), 1939, B&W, 112 min. *Music:* Ernesto Lecuona, Rodrigo Prats, Sánchez de Fuentes, Rafael Barros and Rodríguez Silva. *Cast:* María Antonieta Pons, Juan Orol, María Luisa Morales, Jean Angelo, Jorgelina Junco, Consuelo Sainz de la Peña, Aurora Lincheta, Chela Castro, Diosdado del Pozo, Carlos Alpuente, Lolita Feliú, Ramón Pérez Díaz, Eustaquio Toledano, Amador Domínguez, Oscar Lombardo and Enrique del Río.

In the 1850s young Spaniard Gastón Montero, seeing the ill treatment suffered by slaves in Cuba, rebels against authority, setting off a quarrel with his father. Leaving home, he becomes business manager for Ligia, an opera singer. Gastón has to return home when his father dies and he frees the beautiful slave Siboney, who is eventually taught to sing by Ligia. Inevitably, love relationships become complicated when Ligia is spurned by Gastón, who has fallen in love with Siboney; Siboney, in turn, is seduced by the tenor Ricardo. Distraught, Gastón leaves for the countryside to join Carlos Manuel de Céspedes and his force fighting for independence from Spain. Mortally wounded, Gastón asks Ricardo to marry Siboney and make her happy.

Siempre la esperanza (There's Always Hope) Belkis Vega / ICAIC, 1991, color, 15 min.

This documentary follows the experiences of one Rodolfo Estévez, a truck driver who was sent as part of the Cuban army that fought the war in Angola. Estévez was made prisoner and spent many months in hell, much of the time in solitary confinement. After a time, he loses his will to live, yet hope springs eternal.

Siete muertes a plazo fijo (Seven Deaths on the Installment Plan) Manolo Alonso / Manolo Alonso S.A. (Ernesto Regueral), 1950, B&W, 90 min. *Music:* Osvaldo Farrés. *Cast:* Raquel Revuelta, Alejandro Lugo, Eduardo Casado, Ernesto de Gali, Hugo Montes, Rosendo Rosell, Julito Díaz, Juan José Martínez Casado, Maritza Rosales, Pedro Segarra, Manolo Fernández, Carmen Ignarra, Elizabeth del Río, Pepe Palomera, Enrique Alzugaray, Américo Castellanos, Humberto Suárez, Martica Díaz, Rolando Barral and the Orquesta Cosmopolita.

In this Cuban thriller, a mysterious character predicts the deaths of seven revelers. As the first one of them dies, the other six take the prediction very seriously and begin to panic. In the end, they all find out that the mysterious character was only an escaped lunatic.

El siglo de las luces (The Age of Enlightenment) Humberto Solás / ICAIC, 1981, color, 120 min. *Cast:* Jaqueline Arenal, François Dunoyer, Rustan Urazaeu and Frederic Pierrot.

In eighteenth century colonial Havana, three youngsters named Sofía, Carlos and Esteban come to age amidst the gracious decorum of a society influenced by French refinement and elegance.

Simparelé Humberto Solás / ICAIC, 1974, color, 30 min.

Haiti is the Western Hemisphere's poorest country. How could this situation prevail, in a country that was one of the first to shed colonial rule and to have a successful slave revolt? Marta Jean Claude, a top performer of Haitian folklore, attempts to answer that particular question in this documentary. Music, dance, theater and poetry unite to tell the story of this fascinating nation that shares so much with Cuba.

El sinsonte (The Mockingbird) Tulio Raggi / ICAIC, 1969, color, 8 min. 16 sec. *Animation:* Leonardo Piñero. *Music:* Lucas de la Guardia.

"To your own self be true," seems to be saying this little cartoon story, which has a mockingbird and a parakeet vie for control of a house. The mockingbird, the older resident, feels displaced by the arrival of the dynamic parakeet. To recover his former status, he begins to imitate the parakeet, but only succeeds in making a fool of himself.

Los sobrevivientes (The Survivors) Tomás Gutiérrez Alea / ICAIC, 1978, color, 130 min. *Music:* Leo Brouwer. *Cast:* Enrique Santiesteban, Reinaldo Miravalles, Germán Pinelli, Ana Viña, Vicente Revuelta, Carlos Ruiz de la Tejera, Leonor Borrero, Juanita Caldevilla, Carlos Montezuma, Armando Soler and Patricio Wood.

An aristocratic family decides to stay in Cuba after the 1959 revolution, remaining in their mansion until (they hope) the revolution fizzles out. They refuse to be contaminated by the ideas and way of life that are taking root outside their door, their property a small bourgeois enclave in a sea of socialism. But it will not be easy: their stored food is running out, so is their money, and the servants just don't behave like they used to. Day by day the family becomes more impoverished, but they hang on to their bourgeois values and way of life as if losing them meant losing their identity.

Son ... o no son (To Be or Not) Julio García Espinosa / ICAIC, 1980, color, 84 min. *Cast:* Enrique Arredondo, Leonor Borrero, Centurión, Alejandro Díaz, Daisy Granados, Carlos Montezuma, Eslinda Núñez and Carlos Ruiz de la Tejera.

A troupe is trying to put together a musical comedy. For obvious economic reasons, this Hollywood-style comedy is almost impossible to bring to the stage in a Third World country, so after a number of stumbling blocks and setbacks throw them off course, the production is all but stopped. The story then focuses on the troupe's reflections on the topic and the best ways to successfully bring the musical comedy to the stage.

Soy Cuba (I Am Cuba) Mikhail Kalatozov / ICAIC–Mosfilm, 1964, B&W, 141 min. *Music:* Carlos Fariñas. *Cast:* Luz María Collazo, Jean Bouise, Sergio Corrieri, José Gallardo, Raúl García, Salvador Wood, Alberto Morgan, Fausto Mirabal, Roberto García York, María M. Díez, Silia Rodríguez, Bárbara Domínguez, Iris del Monte, Rosendo Lamadriz, Mario González Broche and the voice of Raquel Revuelta.

The film is composed of four episodes set in pre-revolutionary Cuba. The first shows us Havana, with all its extravagant night life, its tourists, its sounds and its energy; a capital city with a rotten core under its seemingly happy environment, seething with corruption, violence and the debasement and objectification of women. Then, in the countryside, the "guajiro" or poor farmer must try to survive in an environment where those on top have everything and those who work don't know where their next meal will come from, a place where the United Fruit Company is the law. Back in Havana for the next episode, a group of students plots to kill a lieutenant of the dictator Batista. Fearing that their actions will endanger a group of nearby children, they nobly back off and don't go through with their plan.

The last episode shows the guerrilla fighters in the mountains of eastern Cuba, the famed Sierra Maestra, where they gallantly protect the poor peasants against the barbarous actions of the government forces.

The film is well made. It begins with a helicopter shot over the Cuban coast, capturing images of poverty before settling on a hotel rooftop, where a beauty contest is in progress. Afro-Cuban music fills the air as people dance. An American businessman (played by French actor Jean Bouise) spends the night with a beautiful prostitute only to awaken in the midst of a large makeshift village sunk in extreme poverty.

We are then acquainted with a grungy peasant (José Gallardo) who, as he looks out into a rainstorm, recalls how he lost everything. It turns out he was hoodwinked into leasing his sugar cane land only to have it sold out from under his nose to the powerful United Fruit Company.

The story then focuses on a young man (Raúl García) who, together with a group of students, is throwing Molotov cocktails at a drive-in screen showing a newsreel that celebrates U.S.–Cuba relations. The film ends in the beautiful and rugged Sierra Maestra Mountains: a peasant joins Castro's guerrillas after the government commits atrocities against his family.

There is a certain hallucinating poetry to the film that goes a long way to capture the viewer's imagination. Once you get past the first half-hour, which looks like Fellini on a bad day, you'll be treated to some of the most striking images shot in Cuba.

For this, the director takes a radical approach. An example of it is the first, apparently unbroken take that begins on the rooftop of the above-mentioned hotel, slips past the beauties participating in the pageant, goes over the edge of the deck and descends about four floors to another deck with a swimming pool. The camera comes to a bar, follows a waitress to a tourist table, and follows one of the tourists as she stands up and goes to the pool, where the shot ends, under water.

The socialist didactic bent is evident everywhere in the film, as Cuba is shown tortured under the yoke of Yankee imperialism. But workers, peasants and students rebel, and in the end there appears a great hero, a bearded man (guess who) who fights for justice and equality in the forested hills and is sheltered and supported by the peasants.

Melodrama is not lacking, as in the scene where the reluctant prostitute is offended by her Yankee john when he offers to buy her a crucifix, or worse yet, when they are found in bed by the prostitute's humble peasant fruit-vendor fiancé, who thought she was ... a virgin. Also, make sure to get out of the way of the American sailors (they're all drunk) who are chasing the women down the streets and causing general havoc.

The film is a product of its times. It portrays the age-old struggle of good against evil, with the absolute good represented by the anti-government elements, while absolute evil is clearly the government, its defenders, and the socio-economic system that gives it life. That year, 1964, is one of struggle and uncertainty. His ties with the United States severed, Castro has turned to the Soviet Union for support. Cubans are leaving their country in droves. The line has been drawn, seems to say the filmmaker; the old evil is gone and a new day dawns with the representatives of the absolute good (the ethical students, the exploited "guajiro," the altruist guerrilla fighters) now in power.

Spanish Volunteers in Havana American Mutoscope Company, 1898, B&W, 94.49 meters long.

This early silent was released in March of 1898. Filmed entirely in Havana, it shows a battalion of volunteers that the Spanish colonial authorities raised in the city to fight the rebels in the interior of the island during Cuba's second War for Independence.

Spirits of Havana Luis O. García and Bay Weinman / National Film Board of Canada, 2000, color, 92 min.

Riding the wave of interest and curiosity that things Cuban have generated in the 1990s, this Canadian documentary follows Canadian jazz musicians Jane Bunnet and Larry Cramer in their tuneful pilgrimage to the musical mecca of the Western Hemisphere, the prolific, fertile and immensely creative island of Cuba. Once there, they mix with the natives; early footage alternates with the Canadians' adventures, showing classic rhumba sessions and beautiful little villages full of turn-of-the-century folks. Cloud 9 breaks when a tearful Jane Bunnet believes her precious instruments have been swiped from her hotel room. All told, this is a naïve albeit entertaining look at Cuba by individuals who are completely alien to its culture and traditions.

Or, as Liz Braun sees it, "Jazz giants Jane Bunnett and Larry Cramer –it's a marital and musical partnership–are frequent travellers to Cuba. In *Spirits of Havana* they travel to the country, followed by the camera as they look up old friends and make new ones in the world of music. Bunnett hauls her instruments around to play music with the locals everywhere from town squares and someone's kitchen to the recording studio.... Along the way, Bunnett and Cramer capture the esence of complex Cuban music, which is a mixture of various elements. Tata Guines, a well-known conga maestro in his country, talks about playing music from age six onward. 'The teachers were the street corners, where everything passes by. Because then, what black person went to school?'" ("Music Is the Way of Life in Havana," *Toronto Sun*, 11 May 2001.)

The documentary also explains the conditions under which Cuban children must learn their music. In one school, for example, 14 students share a single flute.

Sueño tropical (Tropical Dream) Miguel Torres / ICAIC, 1993, color, 75 min. *Cast:* Alberto Pujols, Daisy Granados and Orlando Casín.

A Cuban man has a horrible nightmare. He is one who boasts about how much money he brings home, brags about how many women he has bedded, orders his wife about the house in front of his friends and, all things considered, is the essence of the Cuban no-nonsense macho. One day he has a terrible experience: he wakes up to a world in which a complete role-reversal has taken place. Women go about boasting of their sexual conquests, smoking, playing cards with friends and ordering their husbands around. When at last the macho wakes to find it has only been a dream, he is relieved and grateful to be a man.

Director Miguel Torres Espinosa was born in Havana in 1941.

El Super (The Building Superintendent) León Ichaso and Orlando Jiménez Leal / Arce–Ichaso–Max Mambrú Films Ltd., 1979, color, 90 min. *Writing credits:* from a play by Iván Acosta. *Cast:* Raymundo Hidalgo-Gato, Zully Montero, Raynaldo Medina, Juan Granda, Elizabeth Peña, Hilda Lee and Orlando Jiménez Leal.

A film produced by Cubans in the United States, it tells the story of an exile in New York who cannot get accustomed to his new country. He's got a job as a building superintendent in New York, a city he finds is too cold and too dirty. He lives in a tiny basement apartment in the building with his wife and daughter. Try as he might, he cannot understand the American way of life. His wife puts up stoically with the vicissitudes of their new life, but it is his daughter Aurelita who seems to be adjusting best. When confronted with the possibility of moving to Miami, Aurelita flatly refuses to leave, saying she has a life and friends in New York. To her father, Miami is the closest thing to old Cuba left in the world, and he longs to recapture his sense of belonging by moving there as soon as he can afford it. As family members die in Cuba and they cannot go to the funerals, their isolation becomes more acute and tangible. Their dreams of return collapse as they find out that Aurelita is pregnant. In a fit of anachronic outrage, he demands to know the name of the boy who got his daughter pregnant so he can repair his honor, but he soon realizes the futility of it. We leave him returning to his duties: picking up garbage and clearing the snow. A very poignant, human story.

Techo de vidrio (Glass Roof) Sergio Giral / ICAIC, 1988, color, 91 min. *Music:* José María Vitier. *Cast:* Susana Pérez, Miguel Gutiérrez, Samuel Claxton, Eduardo Macías, Jorge Villazón, Ana Viña, Salvador Wood, Roberto Perdomo, Miriam Socarrás, Mercedes Planas, Andrés Hernández, Idelfonso Tamayo, Jorge Losada, Ana Lillian Rentería and Jesús Terry.

A young lawyer is sent to investigate certain charges of embezzlement at a construction firm. The two people charged are good workers and good revolutionaries, although one of them is an engineer who is accustomed to the good things and certain privileges not available to everyone. The movie turns out to be an investigation into the workings of the human mind and how an individual who gets more than his neighbors might feel entitled to more and more advantages, disregarding the moral consequences and the legality of his pursuit of them.

Tercer mundo, tercera guerra mundial (Third World, Third World War) Julio García Espinosa and Miguel Torres / ICAIC, 1970, B&W, 90 min.

This is a documentary that explains the destruction being brought on the Democratic Republic of Vietnam by the imperialist forces of the United States. As we are taken to sites of bombings and other depredations, the narrator lets us know that the Vietnamese people's struggle is the most brilliant example of selfless sacrifice and resistance ever recorded in the annals of modern history.

Tesoro (Treasure) Diego de la Texera / ICAIC–Cinematográfica de Sotavento–Producciones C.A. de Venezuela–Taleski Studios (Puerto Rico), 1987, color, 106 min. *Music:* Eddie Palmieri and Jean-Claude Marta. *Cast:* Mayra Oloe, Javier Serbiá, Frank Aguilar, Ignacio Valdés, Julio Hernández de Armas, Yolanda Ruiz and Óscar Álvarez.

Three youngsters whose imaginations have run amok are hanging around an island searching for pirate treasure. Reality hits them in the face when some Haitians, trying to escape the terrible social and economic conditions in their country, land on the island. Unforthcoming at first, the youngsters and the refugees hit it off very nicely, beginning a relationship that blossoms into friendship. Yes, as you suspected, they found a treasure which is not gold and precious stones, but the trust and friendship they now share with the runaways.

The best part of this Cuban, Puerto Rican, Venezuelan, Panamanian co-production is the soundtrack.

El tiburón y las sardinas (The Shark and the Sardines) Jesús de

Armas / ICAIC, 1961, color, 16 min. 31 sec. *Animation:* Hernán Henríquez and José Reyes. *Music:* Jesús Ortega and Carlos Puebla.

An allegory of the United States in its relations with smaller countries, this cartoon tells the story of an unlikely shark (round with a huge mouth and rectangular, spaced teeth) and its subservient sardines, whom the shark exploits. One day a courageous sardine (guess what country it represents) escapes from the shark's kingdom, craving freedom and independence. The shark pursues the sardine everywhere, but the little fish manages to evade every trap the larger fish sets for him. Being unable to bring back and punish the escapee, the shark now fears for his privilege and power.

Tiempo de morir (Time to Die) Jorge Alí Triana / ICAIC–FOCINE (Colombia), 1985, color, 98 min. *Writing credits:* from a story by Gabriel García Márquez, dialogue by Carlos Fuentes. *Music:* Leo Brouwer and Nafer Durán. *Cast:* Gustavo Angarita, Patricia Bonilla, Sebastián Ospina, Jorge Emilio Salazar, María Eugenia Dávila, Lina Botero, Enrique Almirante, Carlos Barbosa, Mónica Silva, Héctor Rivas, Luis Chiape, Rodolfo Miravalles, Lucy Martínez, Edgardo Román, and Nelly Moreno.

Based on a García Márquez story, this Cuban-Colombian co-production tells the story of a man who committed a crime and spent 18 years behind bars paying for it. Released and believing he's paid his dues to society, he decides to go back to his village, the place where he did the deed. But the villagers have not forgotten, and now they *really* want to make him pay.

La tierra y el cielo (Heaven and Earth) Manuel Octavio Gómez / ICAIC, 1979, color, 87 min. *Writing credits:* Antonio Benítez Rojo, from his novel. *Music:* Sergio Vitier. *Cast:* Samuel Claxton, Tito Junco, José Díaz Diosnier, Idelfonso Tamayo, Daniel Josué Bernard, Martha Jean-Claude, Luis Alberto Ramírez, Trinidad Rolando and Alicia Mondevil.

Two young Haitian sugar cane cutters decide to join the Castro guerrillas, bringing their old Voodoo beliefs with them. One of them unwittingly exposes the other guerrillas to danger. Sentenced to die, his last wish is to have his lifelong friend be a member of the firing squad that will end his life.

Todo está oscuro (Everything Is Dark) Ana Díez / ICAIC–Alta Films–Canal Plus España–Igeldo Komunikazioa–Euskal Media–TVE–Teleset, 1997, Color, 93 min. *Music:* Pascal Caigne. *Cast:* Silvia Munt, Klara Badiola, Diego Achury, Valeria Santa, Kike Díaz de Rada.

Everything is indeed dark in this Cuban-Spanish-Colombian co-production. A successful Spanish businesswoman learns that her brother has been murdered in Bogotá, Colombia, and decides to travel to the place where the tragedy took place in order to identify the body. In the Colombian capital she becomes involved with a group of street urchins whom she suspects might be connected with the crime. She is then kidnapped and taken to a Bogotá slum where she gets involved in the lives of its inhabitants. There are no surprises for anyone in this "upper-class meets the poor" feature, and the only acting worth mentioning is that of Valeria Santa, who plays a street child called Jenny. Among its many defects, we could point to the lack of fluidity in the screen narration; the film is unconsciously jerky in its development and achieves only minor success in capturing the squalid reality of life in a Latin American slum.

Tulipa Manuel Octavio Gómez / ICAIC, 1967, B&W, 93 min. *Writing Credits:* Manuel Reguera Saumell, from his play *Recuerdos de Tulipa*. *Music:* Félix Guerrero and the anonymous French ballad *Titina*. *Cast:* Idalia Anreus, Daisy Granados, Omar Valdés, Alejandro Lugo, Teté Vergara, José Antonio Rodríguez, Alicia Bustamante, Ofelia González, Aramis Delgado, Raúl Eguren, Natalia Herrera and Ricardo Suárez.

Before the Revolution, Tulipa is a strip-tease dancer with a travelling show that does the provincial circuit. In spite of the disrespect and humiliation associated with that profession, Tulipa carries herself with honor and dignity, bringing elegance and artistry to her performance. When a younger dancer joins the troupe, Tulipa finds herself in a predicament: teaching someone all the tricks of her trade while knowing that this same person might someday take over her job. In spite of these tribulations, she does everything she can for her young protégé.

The film is opportune for this period of changing mores in that it shows that good people at times are forced to do work that is socially maligned. The thinly veiled criticism is of a system that forces people like Tulipa to do this type of work to earn a living.

La última cena (The Last Supper) Tomás Gutiérrez Alea / ICAIC, 1976, color, 120 min. *Music:* Leo Brouwer. *Cast:* Nelson Villagra, Silvano Rey, Luis Alberto García, José Antonio Rodríguez, Samuel Claxton, Mario Balmaseda, Idelfonso Tamayo, Julio Hernández, Tito Junco, Andrés Cortina and Mirta Ibarra.

According to the film's press book: "A wealthy and very religious owner of a sugar mill, a count of Havana (Nelson Villagra), is driven by his conscience to perform genuine acts of spiritual goodness. During Holy

La última cena

Rebellious slaves (slave in foreground is Tito Junco) get ready to do away with their tyrannical overseer (Luis Alberto García in stocks) in Tomás Gutiérrez Alea's *La última cena.*

Week, he visits his mill and gathers twelve black slaves. He washes and kisses their feet and then, in a supper similiar to the one Jesus gave to bid farewell to His disciples, he invites the slaves to join him at his own table.

"During the dinner on Holy Thursday, the count's behavior is alternately arrogant and humble. He converses with the slaves and tells them of an episode in the life of St. Francis, the moral of which is that perfect happiness lies in accepting pain and abuse with humility and joy. They eat and drink wine and, little by little, the initial tension is relieved. The wine helps the count regain his inner peace. He discovers that he feels at ease talking with his group of black men, and this astounds him: he becomes benevolent, happy and communicative. He even begins to speak ill of the overseer. Most of the slaves give way to these feelings and enjoy the occasion.

"On Friday morning, the count returns to his villa. At the sugar mill, the overseer rouses the slaves for work. The slaves tell him that nobody works on Good Friday. Some of the slaves who attended the supper given by the count are convinced that their master will not approve the attitude of the overseer and decide to resist. They hold the overseer hostage and send a message to the count to come to the sugar mill and pass judgment. When the count finds out the slaves have disobeyed the overseer, he is indignant and orders out an armed posse to control the situation. The count puts aside his benevolent and paternalistic attitude to act openly in accord with his real interests. Faced with the attack, some slaves kill the overseer and set fire to the sugar mill before fleeing.

"The count, with his mill in ruins, unleashes a cruel repression; he captures 11 of the 12 slaves who attended the supper and orders their heads cut off. Only one slave eludes capture. He escapes into the hills."

The film ends up being both an allegory and a satire on Christian values, which have managed to coexist with repressive slave owning economies thanks to the self-interested interpretations given to Jesus' words by capitalist slave owners like the count. The story is based on a historical incident in which a guilt-ridden count invited some of his slaves to a Holy Week supper. The recreation of an eighteenth century plantation, with its problematic relationships and daily injustices, is quite authentic.

La única (She's Unique) Ramón Peón / Proficuba (Productora Fílmica Cubana, S.A.; Salvador Fernández), 1952, B&W, 99 min. *Music:* Maño López and Julio Gutiérrez. *Cast:* Rita Montaner, Rafael Correa, Maritza Rosales, José Sanabria, Ángel Espasande, Miguel de Castillo, Enrique Montaña, Ray Tatú and Miguel Ángel Blanco.

Young Rita (Rita Montaner) works at a textile mill in this comedy, but she has high hopes for the future: she wants to take over the job of personnel director, currently held by a sour woman who bears the nickname "Vinegar." Rita polishes her manners and gets ready to make her move, but her plans have to be put on hold after a criminal gang burglarizes the company. Rita will not rest until she brings them to justice and becomes everyone's heroine.

Ustedes tienen la palabra (It's Up to You) Manuel Octavio Gómez / ICAIC, 1973, B&W, 103 min. *Music:* Leo Brouwer. *Cast:* Luis Alberto Ramírez, Salvador Wood, Omar Valdés, Idalia Anreus, Miguel Benavides, Rogelio Blain, Mario Balmaseda, Ruth Escalona, Raúl Eguren, Carlos Montezuma, Alfredo Ávila, Tito Junco, Ángel Toraño, Noel García, Luis Rielo, Samuel Claxton, Humberto García Espinosa and Luis Alberto García.

Eight years after the triumph of Castro's revolution, four men are accused of sabotaging a reforestation project by setting a fire that killed eight people and destroyed much of the forest. For added dramatic effect, the trial is set in the ruins of one of the greenhouses.

The four accused plead innocent, and the courtroom drama unfolds slowly as peasants, forestry workers and managers come forth to testify. After a detailed elucidation of events prior to the tragedy, the judges turn to the public in the makeshift courtroom and request a verdict from them, stating "ustedes tienen la palabra," or "it's up to you." The film gives a polished version of the workings of the revolutionary "people's courts" that were prevalent in the sixties.

Vals de La Habana Vieja (Waltz of Old Havana) Luis Felipe Bernaza / ICAIC–1988, color, 84 min. *Cast:* Silvia Planas, Ramón Veloz, Sara Rodríguez and Elena Bolaños.

Soledad Reina is the president of the Neighbors' Committee in a Havana building. She is a seamstress and her husband, Epifanio Glorioso, is a film projectionist at a local cinema. Soledad's dream is, of all things, to celebrate her daughter's fifteenth birthday in a very big way, no matter the cost, no matter the penury in which the expenditure will put the family, no matter what her husband Epifanio Glorioso thinks. The film is important as a social document, recording the curious practice of fifteenth birthday celebration in Cuban society, an affair whose overblown importance causes some bizarre behaviors in the general population.

Vampiros en La Habana (Vampires in Havana) Juan Padrón / ICAIC-Radio y Televisión Española, 1985, color, 80 min. *Animation:* Mario García-Montes. *Music:* Rembert Egües.

This is the best animated film ever to come out of Cuba. It tells the story of a vampire-scientist that is working on a formula that will help his vampire colleagues withstand the sun. After failing in Europe with his scheme, he comes to Cuba and completes his experiments on his nephew Joseph. The formula is successful and Joseph grows up in the streets of Havana as a normal child, playing in the sun like the rest of his friends and ignoring the fact that he is one of the undead.

"His uncle notifies the Vampire Group in Europe that he has devised the formula and that he wishes to donate it to all the vampires in the world. The European group has other plans for the formula: to establish a monopoly and sell it under the name 'Vampisol.'

"Elsewhere, the vampire mafia of Chicago (La Capa Nostra), whose business interests include underground beaches and clubs for vampires, is threatened by the marketing of Vampisol because it means that the vampires will begin going to real beaches.

"The European group and La Capa Nostra travel to Havana, one to steal the formula and the other to destroy it, while Pepito and his friends flee the tyrant Machado's police.

"The Europeans—a German, a Frenchman, an Englishman, an Italian and a Spaniard—broadcast an advertisement on Radio Vampire International, stating they have Vampisol. The Chicago vampires bring in specialists such as Sharpie (who fires silver bullets), Fadeout Johnson and a mediocre Wolfman to destroy the European group and its formula.

"After fighting for the formula, Pepito unintentionally ends up with the formula documents in his possession. His aim is to finish the work of his uncle (who has perished) and give it away, free of cost, to vampires. To do so, he must first confront the police and the two groups of vampires, who chase him all over Havana, until he is finally able to broadcast a song on Radio Vampire International whose lyrics are the manufacturing formula for Vampisol" (Press book).

Vaqueros del Cauto (Cauto Cowboys) Oscar L. Valdés / ICAIC, 1965, B&W, 30 min. *Music:* Leo Brouwer.

Life is rough around the Cauto River, Cuba's largest and most important waterway. This documentary traces the daily life of the cowboys of the region, their hopes and fears, and in the end it gives a sensible account of their psychological makeup.

Vecinos (Neighbors) Enrique Colina / ICAIC, 1985, color, 16 min.

A didactic documentary that reviews the norms that should be respected in the state-sponsored multiple family buildings. It also graphically explains how contempt for those norms can bring many problems for everyone. Scenes of daily life, with women scrubbing their balcony floors and throwing pails of water (which drench the lower floors), give a good idea of what life is like in one of these tenements.

Venir al mundo (Coming to the World) Miguel Torres / ICAIC, 1989, color, 79 min. *Cast:* Mario Balmaseda, Susana Pérez, Alberto Pujols and Miguel Navarro.

A gynecologist lives a perfectly blissful, structured existence, sticking to his cherished routine and avoiding all kinds of excitement. The problem begins when, inevitably, he falls for a beautiful medical student: his simple, uncomplicated life now becomes a vortex of conflict and constant tension, especially at home with wife and family. The director seems to be saying that love does not always lead to the wonderful, splendid experiences that romantic yarns might lead one to believe.

La vida en rosa (La Vie en Rose) Rolando Díaz / ICAIC, 1989, color, 86 min. *Cast:* Manuel Porto, Tony Cortés, María de los Ángeles, Santa, Lavinia Castro, Orlando Casín, Roli Peña, Elena Huerta, Odalys García, Lázaro Núñez, Luis F. Flores, Jorge Prieto and Bernardo Forbes.

A film about youth and the challenges that confront young people everywhere. Faced with lies and deception, a group of youngsters must make complex moral choices, such as accepting what fate and an adverse destiny have given to them or fighting to change their lot.

La vida es silbar (Life Is to Whistle) Fernando Pérez / ICAIC–Wanda Distribución España, 1998, color, 110 min. *Music:* Edesio Alejandro. *Cast:* Rolando Brito, Luis Alberto García, Jorge Molina, Bebe Pérez, Joan Manuel Reyes, Claudia Rojas, Isabel Santos and Coralia Veloz.

This is the story of three orphans struggling to make ends meet in present-day Havana. Amid the extreme poverty and grim ambiance of the institutions portrayed in the film, the three try to cope: Elpidio García is a musician torn by his desire to leave the island, leaving behind the memory of the one person that's meant the most to him, his mother who, by the way, was named Cuba. He has an American girlfriend spurring him on, while the plants she's given him are growing so fast that they are taking over his apartment. A second orphan, Julia, is not your normal, run of the mill Cuban, for she faints at the mere mention of sex. Mariana, on the other hand, is a dancer whose passion for men allows her imagination to undress them as they walk down the street. Mariana takes a vow of chastity to convince God that she should get the part of Giselle, the mad virgin, in an upcoming production. In the end, a scene of several people whistling, apparently with nothing else to do, underscores the feeling of futility given off by the film.

Una vida para dos (One Life to Share) Gerardo Chijona / ICAIC, 1984, color, 18 min.

Miguel Amántegui and Francisca (Panchita) Pérez are a loving couple of elderly Cubans living a peaceful retirement. To look at them (she, overweight and always smiling; he, white-haired and myopic) one would never suspect that they fought with the International Brigades in the Spanish Civil War (1936–1939) and again as partisans in the Second World War against the Germans. As they walk down the street with their arms around each other, it is clear that this is not only a tale of their heroic days and deeds, but also the story of a beautiful love affair that has lasted for many decades and is still going as strong as ever. This is a very well structured documentary. My only objection is that a story like theirs deserved quite a bit more than 18 minutes. One is left begging for more.

181 La Virgen de la Caridad

La Virgen de la Caridad (The Virgin of Charity) (1930). The bad guys are about to dispossess the poor farmer in this silent-film classic.

La Virgen de la Caridad (The Virgin of Charity) Ramón Peón / BPP Pictures, 1930, B&W, 71 min. *Writing credits:* Enrique Agüero Hidalgo. *Cast:* Diana V. Marde, Miguel Santos, Roberto Navarro, Estelita Echazábal, Mario Vasseur, Juan Antonio López, Sergio Miró, Julio Gallo, Ramón Peón, Francisco Muñoz, Matilde Mauri, Guillermo de la Torre, Ernesto Antón, Rafael Girón and Laura del Río.

This silent feature adopts a well-traveled story line. A poor farmer and a rich man (who left Cuba to make his fortune and has now returned) both seek to marry a wealthy rancher's daughter. The small farmer is not considered socially acceptable, whereas the other has made his fortune overseas. The evil, rich man doesn't play fair (how do you think he got rich?). To better reach his evil ends and be rid of his rival, he disputes the farmer's title to his lands (incidentally, the farmer's deed has been lost, depriving him of the necessary proof of ownership). A date is then set for the emigrant to wed the girl. The despairing farmer prays to the Virgin Mary at church; this appears to cause a workman's accident that uncovers a small patch of wall containing the misplaced deed. The formerly deedless farmer now rushes off to stop the wedding ceremony and to confront the emigrant, whose marrying plans will probably have to change. The story is indeed trite, but the film is remarkable for its elegant approach to an otherwise insipid subject. The views of the Cuban countryside are noteworthy.

Visa USA Lisandro Duque Naranjo / ICAIC–FOCINE (Colombia), 1986, color, 90 min. *Music:* Leo Brouwer, Alberto Barreto, Lucho Bermúdez, Laureano Martínez, Mario Oropesa and Adalberto Álvarez. *Cast:* Marcela Agudelo, Diego Álvarez, Gerardo Calero, Lucía María Castrillión Eguron Raúl Cuesta, Elios Fernández, Armando Gutiérrez, Vicky Hernández, Currea de Gellver Lugo and Lucy Tello Martínez.

This Cuban-Colombian co-production is the story of Adolfo (played nicely by Armando Gutiérrez, leading man in many popular soap operas), a D.J. working in a supermarket in Sevilla, in the western region of Valle del Cauca in Colombia. He courts the beautiful Patricia, but finds that her family rejects him because he is poor and has no discernible prospects for the future. He hatches a plan to better his chances: emigration to the U.S. There is a problem, though: his brother has gone to the U.S. and has remained there illegally, prompting the authorities to deny Adolfo the visa. Dejected, Adolfo decides to buy a fake passport and visa, and dragging Patricia behind him, we last see him on the way to the airport.

Viva la república (Long Live the Republic) Pastor Vega / ICAIC, 1972, B&W, 100 min. *Music:* Juan Márquez.

This is a full-length documentary that follows the life of the Cuban Republic, from the end of the independence wars to 1959. Using original clips, newsreels, political cartoons, photographs and materials supported by unimpressive background music, the director endeavors to give an unbiased overview of the events that led to the 1959 revolution. In the beginning we see some of the first newsreels produced, called "actualidades" at the time, with war footage produced by the Edison Company. One of these has Teddy Roosevelt's "Rough Riders" landing in Cuba. Especially absorbing are the clips showing ex-dictator Fulgencio Batista carrying out his affairs of state.

¡Viva papi! (Long Live Dad!) Juan Padrón / ICAIC, 1982, color, 5 min. 34 sec. *Animation:* Mario García-Montes. *Music:* Lucas de la Guardia.

A boy is sad because his dad is a locknut maker. He would have preferred a more glorified occupation for his father, something like airline pilot, locomotive engineer or knight in shining armor. In an effort to show that everyone is important, the cartoon demonstrates what would happen if there were nobody to make locknuts: the world as we know it would fall apart.

Vizcaya Under Full Headway America Mutoscope Company, 1898, B&W, 42.98 meters.

The Spanish Navy's second-class battleship *Vizcaya*, one of the most powerful warships in the world, came to pay a visit to New York early in 1898. It was built in Bilbao and put in the water in 1890, displacing 7,000 tons. Its engines produced 7,000 horsepower and it had 20 cannon and 10 heavy machine guns. Furthermore, it was manned by 492 experienced sailors. Its commander, Captain Eulate, hinted that his vessel could punch holes through New York's high-rise buildings.

This early silent, released in February of 1898, shows the Vizcaya steaming out to sea from New York harbor. Some months later the vessel would be destroyed in the naval battle of Santiago de Cuba.

Wreck of the Vizcaya American Mutoscope Company, 1898, B&W, 49.30 meters long.

This film was taken in July of 1898, the morning after the Battle of Santiago de Cuba. In this clash Spain's Atlantic Fleet was basically wiped out by a U.S. naval task force. This early silent shows the proud *Vizcaya* as a smoking, lifeless hulk, having been blasted to smithereens by Uncle Sam's boats. It makes a powerful contrast with the earlier American Mutoscope film *Vizcaya Under Full Headway*.

Y puro como un niño (And Pure as a Child) Mario Rivas / ICAIC, 1988, color, 8 min. 50 sec. *Music:* Daniel Longres.

For this short cartoon, a number of anecdotes have been selected from a book on Che Guevara's life written by his father. They all deal with Guevara's childhood. In line with the hero-worship tendencies of Cuban culture, the guerrilla fighter is portrayed as chaste, immaculate and principled.

Y todavía el sueño (The Persistent Dream) Humberto Padrón / EICTV, 1997, B&W, 11 min.

This documentary is in black and white because it uses archival footage to examine Cuba's contemporary reality, opposing it to the dreams and struggles of the early, socialism-building years. In spite of the many errors and setbacks, the dream of building a just society lives on.

Yambaó (Cry of the Bewitched) Alfredo B. Crevenna / Domino, 1956, color, 85 min. *Music:* Ian Andomian and Obdulio Morales. *Cast:* Xiomara Alfaro, Henri Boyer, Fedora Capdevila, Miguel A. Chequis, Martha Sean Claudet, Dandy Crawford, Bob Curtis, Rosa Elena Durgel, Ramón Gay, Olga Guillot, Isolina Herrera, Luis López Puente, José Martínez Silva, Celina Reynoso, Ricardo Román, Ninón Sevilla, Mercedes Valdés, Armando Velasco and Paulina Álvarez.

Yo soy, del son a la salsa 184

A Cuban-Mexican horror feature set in mid-nineteenth century Cuba. Everything is going nicely on the plantation: the master is successful, his wife is pregnant and the slaves are humble and productive. But wait, I hear some evil-sounding drums in the night ... somebody is up to naughtiness. Indeed, in the slave quarters a young slave woman is possessed by the enraged spirit of her murdered great-grandmother, who craves revenge for what the plantation owners did to her. The ensuing violence might induce chuckles in hardened contemporary movie enthusiasts. Besides, all those curvy, voluptuous slave women look too well-fed and manicured to be taken seriously.

Yo soy, del son a la salsa (From Son to Salsa) Rigoberto López / RMM Filmworks, 1997, color, 100 min. *Cast:* Rubén Blades, Willie Colón, Celia Cruz, Isaac Delgado (narrator), Tito Puente, Miguelito Valdés.

Although made in the U.S.A., this film merits inclusion in this Filmography due to its Cuban theme. "Cuban director Rigoberto Lopez's documentary, whose title roughly translates to 'From Son to Salsa,' explores the history of Caribbean/Afro-Cuban music from its conception during the 19th century to the days it was labeled mambo, then cha cha cha, and now 'salsa.' Packed with rhythm, spirit and knowledge, this film admires, respects and honors the legendary musicians who tell the tale. Narrated mostly by singer Issac Delgado, the film shines when Latin all-stars Tito Puente, Miguelito Valdés ("Babalú"), Rubén Blades, Willie Colón and Celia Cruz (interviewed by Puente) perform. Watching, one can feel the intense passion of these performers.

"For anyone interested in salsa, this film will answer any and all questions. But that comes at a price. 'Yo Soy, del Son a la Salsa' provides too much history and not enough music. Moviegoers get the feeling they're in a classroom doing book learning, when what they're yearning for are those moments when they can get up and dance" (José Martínez, *Boxoffice Online Review*).

Zip Xerep Juan Padrón / ICAIC, 1976, color, 5 min. 15 sec. *Animation:* Leonardo Piñero. *Music:* Lucas de la Guardia.

This is a short duration cartoon that attempts to satirize the stereotypical heroes, villains and themes in traditional stories. It's hard to tell what audience this is intended for.

Conclusion

In the end, Cuban film, like the nation that produced it, possesses a captivating power that, with most of us, the trials and tribulations of an ill-fated history seem to evoke. Year in and year out in Cuba's history, men and women, both young and old, have found in the ordeals of the Cuban nation the inspiration that made them feel that they were a part, however small, of the great world design that has the future on its side. From its courageous struggle for independence, through the arduous formative years of the republic to the revolution, it has been a source of inspiration for visionaries and idealists, and that inspiration has affected not only the powerful, but has touched the humblest in all walks of life. The short and calamitous life of Cuba as an independent nation and the unequal battles fought by its valiant citizens in the name of emancipation have created in many the conviction that to work for the good of a people, to take even a small step towards freeing it from its chains, is infinitely worthwhile — even if, when the dust clears, one finds that the dreams of utopia never materialized. It is the existence of that conviction in so many that has made it impossible for anyone in the early twenty-first century to be indifferent to the outcome of the Cuban experiment with socialism. Friendly or hostile, we have all known that its results, one way or another, would change the course of Latin American history.

Yet it could be argued that, if one examines the history of Cuba in its last forty years, the scale of individual achievement is disappointing. There are no scientists of the first order like Carlos Finlay; if the literature is interesting, there is no Martí, no Julián del Casal; there is no composer with anything near Ernesto Lecuona's talent, no performer with the charisma of Benny Moré. Outside of film, of which one may speak favorably, the revolution has added nothing to Cuban heritage which, ten years from now, the world will remember. But it is important to bear in mind that the main energies of the nation during that period have been devoted to the sheer struggle to build a new type of society. It is rare, under such conditions, for science or literature, art or music, to be produced that is not relevant to the survival of this daunting project. The essential Cuban achievement in this first generation of the revolution has been to make all of its people literate, to try to confer upon them a sense of common destiny, to bring a backward though self-important people into the world stage.

We might not know what Cuba can fully do for the heritage of mankind until, on the international plane, it has access to security, and draws therefrom the supposition that its people may take advantage of the physical and spiritual conditions which call to mind creative utterance in the arts and science. Those conditions are infrequently obtainable when, from the beginning, the very survival of its new social model has been in doubt. In times like these the collective mind of a nation is bound up with the daily task of fulfilling the requirements of a social experiment. It is only when Cuba passes from the fever of dream-realization to the temperature which leaves the creative mind at ease that one will be able to look for achievement, the sort to which only freedom of mind and heart can give birth.

Cuban socialism has been, for the most part, a doctrine on the defense against mighty enemies. A filmmaker in a nation that powerful neighbors agree to shun, because they reject the values it represents, tends in the nature of things to polemic rather than art. I don't mean to suggest that the two are incompatible. I do suspect that most filmmakers, as well as writers, artists and musicians, whose work is set in the context of the narrow outlook of polemic, are likely to fall into the superficial world of black and white, good vs. evil perspectives: they need to prove to their contemporaries that their views are legitimate. This would account for a good deal of the immature, self-indulgent imbalance of many a Cuban film in the early and middle years of the revolution.

It has to be remembered, as one examines the postulates of the revolution, that it came to a land staggering under political and social upheaval. It is a fact that much of the Cuban population, drained and tired of corruption, nepotism, graft and fraud, not only embarked on a great experiment of which it seems the only essence was sacrifice, but also allowed hindrances to political self-expression, accepted terror to be inflicted upon political and social dissent, and backed the uncontested leadership of a strongman whose infallibility was commonly accepted if not proclaimed. In spite of all of it, the truth remains that in Cuba, since the 1959 revolution, government corruption has generally and visibly decreased, social disorder is unknown and more men and women have access to health and education than ever before.

Summing up, some basic considerations can be made about the moral and ethical character of the Cuban social model and its cinematic image. Socialist development, in one form or another, was slated to be in Cuba's future. Pre-revolutionary Cuba shows a clear trajectory towards socialism, not only in the avant-garde social legislation of the '30s and '40s, but in the broad-spectrum sentiment expressed in a number of ways (in film with productions like *El Mégano*) by the island's population. Without socialism, bourgeois perspectives and the selfish dogma of private ownership were producing an unsustainable state of affairs. It is quite obvious that healthy competition between capitalism and the socialist principles espoused by workers and others has given rise to the economic and political progress of modern states in the West. In Cuba, this same rapprochement between the two systems seems inevitable. Before the advent of the revolution, the national situation produced a sorry state of affairs of neo-colonial oppression and racism. So capitalist Cuba could not help giving birth to socialist Cuba, but socialist Cuba has attempted to destroy by force the ground from which it grew. It can only be hoped that the expected rapprochement between the two systems rests on a popular, democratic foundation under the control of public opinion.

Whatever the future holds for Cuba, one thing seems clear: Film has become an integral part of its national ego, and it can only continue to document the dreams, ideals and painful disillusionments of the nation's quixotic citizens.

Bibliography

Adelman, Alan, *A Guide to Cuban Cinema,* Center for Latin American Studies, University of Pittsburgh, 1981, 68 p.
Adler, Renata, "Three Cuban Cultural Reports with Films Somewhere in Them," *A Year in the Dark.* Medallion Editions, Berkeley, 1971.
Agramonte, Arturo, *Cronología del cine cubano,* ediciones ICAIC (Instituto cubano del arte e industria cinematográficos), Havana, 1966, 212 p.
____, *Ramón Peón: apuntes biográficos de un cineasta,* author's edition, Havana, n.d., 15 p.
____, and Castillo, Luciano, "Enrique Díaz Quesada: El 'padre de la cinematografía cubana.'" *Cine cubano* # 151, Havana, January–March 2001, pp. 52–56.
Agüero Hidalgo, Enrique, "Cine cubano, cantera inagotable que aún está por explotar," *Cinema,* supplement, Havana, 1947.
____, "Hurgando en el pasado del cine cubano," serie de crónicas, *Cinema,* Havana, 1940.
Aguirre, Alberto, "El estilo del cine cubano," *Cuadro* # 7, Medellín, February–April 1979.
Aguirre, Mirta, "Ayer de hoy," *Unión,* Havana, 1980, 448 p.
____, *Crónica de Cine,* Letras Cubanas, Havana, 1988, 320 p.
Alfaro, Hugo, *Diez años de cine cubano,* Marcha. Montevideo. 1969, 22 p.
Almendros, Néstor, "The Cinema in Cuba," *Film Culture* vol. 2 # 3, New York, 1956.
____, *Días de una cámara,* Seix Barral, Barcelona, 1982, 328 p. (French version *Un homme à la caméra,* Hatier, Paris, 1980; English version *The Man With a Camera,* Faber and Faber, New York, 1985).
Álvarez, Carlos, Julio García Espinosa and Miguel Littin, "Cine latinoamericano y lucha revolucionaria hoy," *Octubre* #s 2-3, Mexico.
Álvarez, Santiago, "El cine como uno de los medios masivos de comunicación," *Cine Cubano* # 49, Havana, 1968.

_____, "I cinegiornali cubani," *Cinema e Lotta di Liberazione*, La nuova Sinistra, Samoná e Savelli, Roma, 1970.

_____, "Las noticias a través del cine," *Cine Cubano* #s 23-24-25, Havana, 1964.

_____, "El periodismo cinematográfico," *Cine Cubano* # 94, Havana, 1978.

_____, "Sinopsis de un filme sobre Cuba 1971," from an interview with Víctor casáus, *cine Cubano* #s 78-79-80, Havana, 1972.

_____, et al., *Cine y Revolución en Cuba,* Fontamara, Barcelona, 1975, 208 p.

_____, et al., *Literatura y Arte Nuevo en Cuba,* Laia, Barcelona, 1977, 296 p.

_____, et al., *Nuestro cine.* Escuela Internacional de Cine y Televisión/Centro de Información Cinematográfica del ICAIC. San Antonio de los Baños, Havana, 1986, 272 p.

_____, Julio García Espinosa,Tomás Gutiérrez Alea et al., "Cine cubano encuesta," *Cine* Cubano #s 54-55, Havana, 1969.

Alvear, Marta. "Interview with Humberto Solás." *Jump Cut* (Special Section, Cuban Revolutionary Cinema, Pt. 1), December 1978.

Amiel, Mireille, "L'intellectuel et la révolution: un interview avec T.G. Alea," *Cinéma 74* # 192, Paris, November 1974.

Ansara, Martha, "Octavio Cortázar, film director," *Cinema Papers* # 33, Australia, July–August 1981.

_____, "Tomás Gutiérrez Alea, film director," *Cinema Papers* # 32, Australia, May–June 1981.

Antolín, Matías, et al., "Cine Cubano," *Cinema 2002* # 46, Madrid, December 1978.

Antonio, Lauro, *Elementos para a historia do Cinema Cubano,* Enquadramento, Lisbon, 1975, 46 p.

Anuario Cinematográfico y Radial Cubano 1941–42, no. 2. Ramón Peón and Pedro Pablo Chávez, editors, Havana, 1942, 162 p.; *Idem 1942–43,* no. 3, editor Pedro Pablo Chávez, Havana, s.d., 126 p.; *Idem 1943–44,* no. 4, s.d., 143 p.; *Idem 1944–45,* no. 5, 1945, 127 p.; *Idem 1945–46,* no. 6, 1946, 191 p.; *Idem 1946–47, Cincuentenario del Cine en Cuba 1897–1947,* no. 7, 1947, 283 p.; *Idem 8th edition 1947–48,* no. 8, 1948, 159 p.; *Idem 9th edition, 1948–49,* no. 9, 1949, 174 p.; *Idem 10th edition 1949–50,* 1950, 152 p.; *Idem 11th edition 1950–51,* 1951, 162 p.; *Idem 12th edition 1951–52,* 1952, 154 p.; *Idem 13th edition 1952–53,* 1953 158 p.; *Idem 14th edition 1953–54,* 1954, 144 p.; *Idem 15th edition 1955,* 1955,158 p.; *Idem 16th edition 1956,* 1956,175 p.; *Idem 17th edition 1957,* 1957, 167 p.; *Idem 18th edition 1958,* 1958,147 p.; *Idem 19th edition 1959,* 1959, 125 p.; *Anuario Cinematográfico; y Tele Radial Cubano, 20th edition 1960,* 1960, 158 p.

Anuario Directorio de Cine, Radio y Televisión, 1951, vol. 1, Fernando López and Porta y Rojas (editors), Rolando Incera González, Havana, 1951, 158 p.

Arandia, Gisela, and Puri Faget, "El Cine, los Cineastas, la Crítica: una encuesta," cultural supplement to *El Mundo,* Havana, 18 January 1969.

Aray, Edmundo, *Santiago Álvarez, cronista del Tercer Mundo,* Cinemateca Nacional, Caracas, 1983, 416 p.

Arlorio, Piero, Federico de Cárdenas and Michel Ciment, "Situación y perspectivas del cine de América Latina," *Hablemos de Cine* #s 61-62, Lima, September–December 1971 ("Situation et perspectives du cinéma d'Amérique latine," *Positif* #139, Paris, June 1972; roundtable with Gustavo Dahl, Tomás Gutiérrez Alea and Fernando Solanas); "Banda sonora: entrevista con la delegación de cineastas cubanos," *Pantalla* #s 7 and 8, Lima, 1970.

Bibliography

Aufderheide, Patricia (ed.), *Latin American Visions*, International House of Philadelphia, 1989, 60 p.

Bendazzi, Giannalberto, *Cartoons, Il cinema d'animazione, 1888–1988*, Marchilio, Venice, 1988, 682 p.

Bernagozzi, Giampaolo, "Il cinema cubano." *Storia del cinema*, vol. IV, Marchilio. Venice. 1981.

Bernal, Augusto, and Carlos Tapia, "Del neorrealismo al subdesarrollo: entrevista con Tomás Gutiérrez Alea," From "Memorias en borrador" by T. Gutiérrez Alea, *Arcadia va al cine* # 13, Bogota. October–November 1986.

Biblioteca Nacional José Martí. *Índice de la revista Cine Cubano 1960–1974*, Orbe, Havana, 1979, 184 p.

Borges, Jacobo, et al., "En busca de un cine popular: conversación con Julio García Espinosa," *Cine al Día* # 17, Caracas, December 1973.

Boussinot, Roger, *L'Encyclopédie du Cinéma*, Bordas. Paris. 1980, 1,336 p.

Braun, Liz. "Music Is the Way of Life in Havana." *Toronto Sun*, 11 May 2001.

Brossard, Jean-Pierre, "Le cinéma cubain, quinze ans après," *Cinéma74* # 192, Paris, November 1974.

Brouwer, Leo, *La música, lo cubano y la innovación*, Letras Cubanas, Havana, 1982, 84 p.

Bullitta, Juan M., Federico de Cárdenas, Nelson García Miranda, Isaac León Frias et al., "Cine Cubano," *Hablemos de Cine* # 54, Lima, July–August 1970; "Cine Cubano (II)," *Hablemos de Cine* # 55-56, Lima, September–December 1970.

Buría Perez, Lázaro, and Rolando Díaz Rodríguez, "Un caso de colonización cinematográfica," *El Caimán Barbudo* # 85, Havana, December 1974; # 86, January 1975; # 87, February 1975.

Burton, Julianne, *Cinema and Social Change in Latin America: Conversations with Filmmakers*, University of Texas Press, Austin, 1986. 302 p.

____, "Cuba," *Les Cinémas de l'Amérique latine*, under the direction of Guy Hennebelle and Alfonso Gumucio Dagron. Pierre Lherminier, Paris, 1981, 544 p.

____, "Film and Revolution in Cuba: The First Twenty-Five Years," *Cuba: Twenty-Five Years of Revolution, 1959–1984*, under the direction of Sandor Halebsky and John M. Kirk, Praeger, New York, 1985.

____, "Special section: Twenty years of Revolutionary Cuban Cinema," *Jump Cut* # 19, Berkeley, December 1978; # 20, May 1979.

____, "Vingt ans de caméras cubaines," from an interview with Alfredo Guevara, *Afrique-Asie* # 205, Paris, 21 January 1980.

____, and John Hess, "Selected bibliography in English," *Jump Cut*, Berkeley, 22 May 1980.

Bykova, Irina, *Kino Ostrova Svobody*, Filmmakers' Union of the USSR., Moscow, 1982, 72 p.

Cabrera Infante, Guillermo, *Un Oficio del Siglo Veinte*, Ediciones Revolución, Havana, 1963, 546 p.; Seix Barral, Barcelona, 1973, 542 p.

Cancio Isla, Wilfredo, "Solás, en tiempo de sinceridad," *Revolución y Cultura* # 11, Havana, November 1988.

Canel, Fausto, "25 preguntas a Alfredo Guevara," *Lunes de Revolución*, Havana, 8 August 1960.

____, "Breve historia de un cine breve," *Lunes de Revolución*, Havana, 6 February 1961 ("Bréve histoire d'un cinéma bref," *Positif* # 53, Paris, June 1963; "Breve, storia di un cinema breve," *Cinema 60* #s 37-38. Rome, 1963).

Cano, Marcel, "Que viva Cuba," *La Méthode* #s 2-3, January 1961.
Capriles, Oswaldo, et al., "El cine cubano enfrenta el desafío industrial: Entrevista con Jorge Fraga y Tomás Gutiérrez Alea," *Cine al Día* # 19, Caracas, March 1975.
_____, et. al., "Resultados de una discusión crítica," *Cine al Día* # 12, Caracas, March 1971.
Cárdenas, Federico de, and Isaac León Frías, "El cine cubano hoy: entrevista con Alfredo Guevara," *Hablemos de cine* # 34, Lima, March–April 1967.
_____, and _____, "Reencuentro con Manuel Octavio Gómez," *Hablemos de Cine* # 75, Lima, May 1982.
Carpentier, Alejo, *Conferencias,* Letras Cubanas. Havana, 1987, 384 p.
_____, *Crónicas, Arte y Literatura,* Havana, 2 vol., 380 and 616 p.
Casáus, Victor, "Cine documental e imaginación poética: seis notas comunes," *Cine Cubano* # 102, Havana, 1982.
_____, "El género testimonio y el cine cubano," *Cine Cubano* # 101, Havana, 1982.
Casiraghi, Ugo, *Cinema cubano.* Quaderni della FICC (Federazione Italiana dei Circoli del Cinema), Rome, 1966, 78 p.
Castillo, Luciano, et al., "Entrevista con Humberto Solás: La voz de un hombre de éxito," *Formato 16* # 20, Panama. October 1987.
Catálogo de Filmes, 1961–1986, Estudios Cinematográficos y de Televisión de las FAR, Havana, 1986, 482 p.
Catálogo de Filmes Producidos por los Estudios-Cinematográficos de las FAR, 1962-1980, ECIFAR. Havana, 1980. 348 p.
Chanan, Michael, "Play it Again, or Old Time Cuban Music on the Screen," *New Left Review,* # 238, November/December 1999.
_____, *The Cuban Image: Cinema and Cultural Politics in Cuba,* British Film Inst./Indiana University Press. London-Bloomington, 1985, 314 p.
_____, *Santiago Álvarez,* British Film Institute, London, 1980, 72 p.
_____, *Twenty Five Years of Latin American Cinema,* British Film Institute/Channel Four Television, London, 1983, 40 p.
_____, et al., "Cuban Images: some notes," from interviews with Pastor Vega, Solás and Gutiérrez Alea, *Framework* # 10, London, Printemps, 1979.
Chávez, Rebeca, "Hablar de estas fotos: conversación con Santiago Álvarez," *Revolución y Cultura* # 11, Havana, November 1986.
_____, and Gerardo Chijona, "Filmar la espontaneidad: conversación con Jesús Díaz sobre su filme 55 hermanos," *Cine Cubano* # 96, Havana, 1980.
Chevaldonne, François, and Guy Gauthier, "Cuba, naissance d'un cinéma socialiste," and "Jeune cinéma cubain," *Image et Son* # 169, Paris, January 1964.
Chevassu, François, "El Otro Cristóbal: entretien avec Armand Gatti," *Image et Son* # 164, Paris, July 1963.
Chijona, Gerardo, "Cecilia o la búsqueda de lo nacional: entrevista con Humberto Solás," *Cine Cubano* # 102, Havana, 1982.
_____, "El cine cubano, hecho cultural de la Revolución," *La cultura en Cuba Socialista,* Letras Cubanas, Havana. 1982, 256 p.
_____, "Elpidio Valdés en el país del Iargometraje: una conversación con el realizador Juan Padrón," *Cine Cubano* # 98, Havana, 1980.
_____, "Entrevista con Humberto Solás, realizador de Cantata de Chile," *Cine Cubano* #s 91-92, Havana, 1977.
_____, "La última cena: entrevista a Tomás Gutiérrez Alea," *Cine Cubano* # 93, Havana, 1978.

Christensen, Theodor, "Estructura, imaginación y presencia de la realidad en el documental," *Cine Cubano* #s 42-43-44, Havana. 1967. *Cine Cubano* #s 42-43-44, French edition, Havana, 1967; "El cine cubano 1959/1969," *Cine Cubano* #s 54-55, Havana, 1969.

Cine Clubes: X aniversario, Muestra homenaje por el X aniversario del Círculo de Interés Cinematográfico de Plaza y del Movimiento Nacional de Cine Clubes, Casa de Cultura de Plaza/Cinemateca de Cuba, Havana, 1988, 20 p.

Cinema cubano 1959–1980: I film, i registi, XVII Mostra Internazionale del Nuovo Cinema, Pesaro, 1981, 24 p.

"*Cine Cubano* entrevista a los realizadores cuya obra reciente se integra en el ciclo dedicado a los cien años de lucha por la liberación," *Cine Cubano* # 68, Havana, April 1971. *Cine joven, I Muestra*, Asociación Provincial Hermanos Saiz. Havana, s.d., 26 p.

Cinema of the Third World, Auckland University Students Association, Auckland, 1972, 76 p.

Cinemateca de Cuba, *El cine cubano en la prensa nacional y extranjera* (1960–1977), Museo Numismático del Banco Nacional de Cuba. Havana, 1977, 110 p.

Cinemateca de Cuba (Maria Eulalia Douglas, coord.), *Manuel Octavio Gómez: la agonía de hacer cine*, Comité de Cineastas de América Latina/Universidad de los Andes/10I Festival del Nuevo Cine Latinoamericano, Havana-Mérida, 1988, 96 p.

Cinematografía Educativa (CINED), Títulos producidos hasta 1985, Ministerio de Educación. Havana, 1984, 44 p.

Colina, Enrique, "Al sur de Maniadero," *Cine Cubano* #s 58-59, Havana, 1969; *Pantalla* # 9, Lima n.d.

_____, "Entrevista a Manuel Octavio Gómez," *Cine Cubano* #s 56-57, Havana, 1969.

_____, "Entrevista a Santiago Álvarez," *Cine Cubano* #s 58-59 Havana, 1969.

_____, "Entrevista a Tomás Gutiérrez Alea sobre Hasta cierto punto," *Cine Cubano* # 109, Havana, 1984.

"Conclusiones de un debate entre cineastas cubanos," *La Gaceta de Cuba* # 23, Havana, 3 August 1963.

Crowdus, Gary, and Dan Georgakas. "Parting of the Ways: an interview with Jesús Díaz," see also "Parting of the Ways: a Cuban-American View" by Enrique Fernández. *Cineaste*, vol. XV # 4, New York, August 1987.

"Declaración de los cineastas cubanos," *Cine Cubano* #s 69-70, Havana, 1971.

Delage, Christian, *Révoltes, Révolutions, Cinéma*, under the direction of Marc Ferro, Editions du Centre Pompidou, Paris, 1989, 312 p.

Delmas, Jean, "Cinéma cubain: A Cuba, le cinéma de la révolution, entretien avec Saúl Yelin et Humberto Solás," *Jeune Cinéma* # 46, Paris.

Desnoes, Edmundo, and Tomás Gutiérrez Alea, "Memorias del subdesarrollo," *El Mundo*, Havana, 7 July 1968 (*Positif* # 98, Paris, October 1968).

Destanque, Robert, and Joris IVENS, *Joris Ivens ou la mémoire d'un regard*, Editions BFB, Paris. 1982, 352 p.

Díaz Torres, Daniel, "De La última cena a Los sobrevivientes: entrevista con el realizador Tomás Gutiérrez Alea," *Cine Cubano* # 97, Havana, 1980.

_____, "Entrevista con Pastor Vega," from "Notas acerca de una razón violenta," by Pastor VEGA, *Cine Cubano* #s 54-55, Havana, 1969.

_____, "La pantalla conflictiva," *Cine Cubano* # 103, Havana, 1982.

Díaz, Jesús, "Asaltar el cielo: función de la cultura revolucionaria," *Cine Cubano* #s 84-85, Havana, 1973.

———, "Para una cultura militante (tres notas sobre arte)," *Cine Cubano* #s 66-67, Havana, 1971.

———, "Provocaciones sobre cine documental y literatura," *Cine Cubano* # 101, Havana, 1982.

Díaz, Rodrigo, and Massimo Forleo, *Aspetti del cinema cubano*, Sulmonacinema '86, Sulmona, 1986, 128 p.

Doce, José, and Orlando Rojas, "Entrevista con Manuel Octavio Gómez," *Arte 7* #15, Havana, November 1971.

Douglas, María Eulalia, *Adenda al folleto de premios y distinciones nacionales e internacionales ganados por el cine cubano: relación de premios obtenidos de abril 1978 a Julio 1980*, Cinemateca de Cuba, Havana, 1980. 12 p.; *Adenda II*, Edición III Festival Internacional del Nuevo Cine Latinoamericano, Havana, 1981, 12 p.; *Adenda III*, IV Festival lnternacional del Nuevo Cine Latinoamericano, Havana, 1982, 12 p.; *Adenda IV*, V Festival Internacional del Nuevo Cine Latinoamericano, Havana, 1983, 12 p.; *Adenda V*, VI Festival Internacional del Nuevo Cine Latinoamericano, Havana, 1984, 8 p.; *Adenda VI*, VII Festival lnternacional del Nuevo Cine Latinoamericano, Havana, 1986, 16 p.

———, *Diccionario de Cineastas Cubanos, 1959-1987*, Cinemateca de Cuba/Universidad de los Andes, Havana-Mérida,1989, 180 p.

———, *Filmografía del cine cubano, 1959–1987, Producción ICAIC*, Cinemateca de Cuba, Havana, 1982, 101 p.

———, *Filmografía del cine cubano, julio 1980-septiembre 1981, Producción ICAIC*, Edición III Festival lnternacional del Nuevo Cine Latinoamericano, Havana, 1981, 12 p.

———, *Guía temática del cine cubano. Producción ICAIC, 195–1980*, Cinemateca de Cuba, Havana, 1983, 304 p.

———, *Premios y distinciones nacionales e internacionales ganados por el cine cubano (1960–1977)*. Cinemateca de Cuba, Havana, 1978, 108 p.

———, *Premios y distinciones nacionales e internacionales ganados por el cine cubano (Producción ICAIC) (1960–1986)*, Cinemateca de Cuba, Havana, [1989], 112 p.

———, and Carmen Lourdes Castro, *Homenaje a Humberto Solás*, Cinemateca de Cuba, Havana. 1987, 28 p.

———, and Héctor García Mesa, *Filmografía del cine cubano, 1959–junio 1980*, Cinemateca de Cuba, Havana, 1980, 90 p.

Duarte, Fernando, "Cinema Cubano," *Celulóide*, # 207, Rio Major, March 1975 (Portugal).

Dupeyron, Georges, "Le documentaire cubain" and "Premiéres années de cinéma cubain" by Jean Michaud, *Europe* #s 409-410, Paris, May–June 1963.

Duque Naranjo, Lisandro, "Con cuatro directores cubanos: Julio García Espinosa, Santiago Álvarez, Pastor Vega, Octavio Cortázar," *Cinemateca*, vol. 1 # 4, Bogota, May 1978.

The Edison Catalog, Thomas A. Edison, Inc. 1898.

Elwood, Philip. "A Moving Documentary of Musicians in Love with Life." *San Francisco Examiner*, 30 April 1998.

Engel, Andi, "Solidarity and Violence," *Sight and Sound* vol. 38 # 4, London, Fall 1969.

"Entrevista con Humberto Solás, realizador de Manuela," *Cine cubano* # 36, Havana, 1966.

"Entrevista con Julio García Espinosa," *Cine Cubano* #s 66-67, Havana, 1971.
Espinal, Luis, *Historia del Cine (1945–1970)*, Editorial Don Bosco, La Paz, 1981, 104 p. (first edition: 1972).
"Entrevista con Julio García Espinosa a su regreso de Vietnam," *Cine Cubano*, #s 60-62, Havana, 1970.
"Entrevistas con directores de largometraje, directores de fotografía, escritores, músicos.... "*Cine Cubano* #s 23-24-25. Havana, 1964.
"Es una apuesta, no sé si habré perdido: entrevista a Jesús Díaz," *Cine Cubano* # 113, Havana, 1985.
Évora, José Antonio, "La espina de la impaciencia," *Juventud Rebelde*, Havana, 8 March 1989 [S. Álvarez].
____, "De frente al proyector," *Juventud Rebelde*, Havana, 25 March 1988 [García Espinosa].
____, "El rábano por la raíz," *Juventud Rebelde*, Havana, 9 September 1988 [Tomás Gutiérrez Alea].
____, "Somos la primera pregunta," *Juventud Rebelde*, Havana, 11 December 1987 [Guevara].
Fanshel, Susan, *A Decade of Cuban Documentary Film, 1972–1982*, Young Filmmakers Foundation, New York, 1982, 48 p.
Fernández, Coca, Teresa. "Interview with Humberto Solás." *Granma*, 23 October 1968.
Fernández, Henry, David I. Grossovogel and Emir Rodríguez Monegal, "On Desnoes and Alea," *Diacritics: A Review of Contemporary Criticism* vol. 4 # 4, Cornell University, Ithaca, N.Y., winter 1974.
Fernández, Manuel, "Breve historia del cine cubano," *Cine-Guía*, Año II # 5, Havana, July 1954.
____, "La integración cultural de nuestro cine," as in "Profesión y estímulo: resortes claves del cine nacional" by Walfredo Piñera, *Cine-Guía*, Año VII # 5, Havana, July 1959.
Ferrari De Aguayo, Luisa, "Antecedentes para la historia del cine Cubano." *Cine Cubano* #s 23-24-25, Havana, 1964.
Filippi, Alberto, "Pesaro 68: la rivoluzione nei film cubani," *Cinema sessanta* # 69, Rome, 1968.
____, "Il vento dei Caraibi," *Ombre Rosse* # 6, Turin, 1969.
"Filmografia del cine cubano," *Cine Cubano* #s 23-24-25, Havana, 1964.
Firk, Michéle, "Articles et critiques," and "Temoignages," *Positif*, Paris, March 1970, 76 p.
____, "Cinéma et bureaucratie à Cuba: entretien avec Tomás Gutiérrez Alea," *Positif* # 85, Paris, June 1967.
____, "Cuba: polémiques," *Positif* # 70, Paris, June 1965.
____, "Naissance d'un cinéma," "Petit lexique du cinéma cubain en quinze réalisateurs," and other articles, *Positif* # 53, Paris, June 1963.
"Five Frames Are Five Frames, Not Six, But Five: An Interview with Santiago Álvarez," *Cineaste* vol. VI # 4, New York, 1975.
Fornet, Ambrosio, *Alea: una retrospective crítica*, Letras Cubanas, Havana, 1987, 364 p.
____, *Cine*, Literatura, Sociedad, Letras Cubanas, Havana, 1982, 276 p.
Fraga, Jorge, "¿Cuántas culturas?" *La Gaceta de Cuba* # 28, Havana, 18 October 1963.

____, "Ambigüedad de la crítica y crítica de la ambigüedad," *La Gaceta de Cuba* # 31, Havana, 10 January 1964.

____, "Nota sobre el cine, la cultura y los mambises," *Cine Cubano* #s 56-57, Havana, 1969.

____, Julio García Espinosa and Estrella Pantín, "Para una definición del documental didáctico," *Cine Cubano* #s 69-70, Havana, 1971.

Francos, Ania, "Cinéma cubain: Visite á l'Institut de Cinéma," *Cinéma 62* # 63, Paris, February 1962.

Frenais, Jacques, "Cuba: le mode d'expression propagandiste," *Cinema 77* # 220, Paris, April 1977.

Fundación Mexicana de Cineastas, *Hojas de Cine: Testimonios y documentos del nuevo cine latinoamericano*, vol. III: Centroamérica y el Caribe, Secretaría de Educación Pública/Universidad Autónoma Metropolitana, Mexico, 1988, 600 p.

Fusco, Coco (ed.), *Reviewing Histories: Selections from New Latin American Cinema*, Hallwalls Contemporary Arts Center, Buffalo, N.Y., 1987, 224 p.

Galiano, Carlos, *Festival internacional del nuevo cine latinoamericano*, 1979–1988, Centro de Información Cinematográfica del ICAIC, Havana, 1988, 200 p.

Garavito, Julian, et al., "Une semaine du cinéma cubain en France," *Cuba si*, Association France Cuba # 59, Paris, February 1977.

García Espinosa, Julio, "A propósito de Aventuras de Juan Quinquín," *Cine Cubano* # 48, Havana, 1968.

____, "Apuntes sobre el anticonformismo," *Cine Cubano* # 2, Havana, 1960.

____, "Cinco preguntas al ICAIC: responde Julio García Espinosa," *Cine al Día* # 12, Caracas, March 1971.

____, "Cine burgués: decadencia o muerte," *Revolución y Cultura* # 10, Havana, October 1985; *C-CAL, Comité de Cineastas de América Latina* # 1, Mérida, December 1985; *Cine Cubano* # 119, Havana, 1987.

____, "Cine dirigido," *Cine Cubano* # 4, Havana, December 1960–January 1961.

____, "Cine político," *Cine Cubano* #s 63-65, Havana, 1970.

____, "El Cine y la toma del poder," *Cahier des Rencontres Internationales pour un Nouveau Cinéma*, Montréal, 1974.

____, "La crítica y el público," *Cine Cubano* # 3, Havana, November 1960.

____, "Los cuatro medios de comunicación son tres: Cine y TV," *Uno por Uno, Cine y Medios de Comunicación en Ecuador* # 11, Quito, December 1977.

____, "En busca del cine perdido," *Cine Cubano* #s 69-70, Havana, 1971; *Cine al Día* # 14, Caracas, November 1971; *Cinemateca* # 1, Mexico, 1972; *Uno por Uno* # 1, Quito, August 1973.

____, "Galgos y podencos," *La Gaceta de Cuba*, # 29, Havana, 5 November 1963.

____, "Una imagen recorre el mundo," *Letras Cubanas*, Havana, 1979, 110 p.

____, "Una imagen recorre el mundo," *Octubre* # 6, Mexico, September 1979; *Revolución, Letras, Arte,* Letras Cubanas, Havana, 1980, 620 p.

____, "Impresiones a partir de Salvatore Giuliano," *Cine Cubano*, # 18, Havana, February 1964.

____, "Julio García Espinosa responde," *Primer Plano* # 4, Valparaíso, 1972; "Respuesta de Julio García Espinosa a la revista chilena *Primer Plano*," *Cine Cubano*, #s 81-82-83, Havana 1973.

____, "Meditaciones sobre el cine imperfecto ... quince años después," *Areíto* # 37, New York 1984. ("Meditations on Imperfect Cinema ... Fifteen Years Later," *Screen*, vol. 36 #s 3-4, London, 1985.)

_____, "Neorrealismo y cine cubano," *Nuestro Tiempo* # 2, Havana, November 1954.

_____, "Notas para una vinculación de las cinematografías cubana y latinoamericana," *El Caimán Barbudo* # 30, Havana 1969.

_____, "Nuestro cine documental," *Cine Cubano*, #s 23-24-25, Havana, 1964.

_____, "Pesaro y la nueva izquierda," *Cine Cubano*, # 49, Havana, 1968.

_____, "Por un cine imperfecto," *Cine del Tercer Mundo*, # 2, Montevideo, November 1970; *Cine Cubano*, #s 66-67, Havana, 1971; *Comunicación y Cultura* # 1, Santiago de Chile, July 1973; *Uno por Uno* #s 4-5, Quito, June 1974; *Octubre* # 4, Mexico, December 1975; *Cine Cubano* # 120, Havana, 1987 ("For an Imperfect Cinema," *Afterimage* # 3, London, Summer of 1971; "Für einen unvollkommenen Film," *Der lateinamerikanische Film heute*, Westdeutschen Kurzfilmtagen/Verlag Karl Maria Laufen, Oberhausen, 1976; "Pour un cinéma imparfait," *La Revue du Cinéma-Image et Son* # 340, Paris, June 1979).

_____, "Por un cine imperfecto," Rocinante/Fondo Editorial Salvador de la Plaza, Caracas, 1973, 72 p.; Miguel Castellote, Madrid, 1976, 80 p.

_____, "Pour un cinema imparfait," *Cinema et Politique, de la politique des autereus au cinéma d'intervention*, by Guy Hennebelle, Papyrus/Mayson de la Culture de Rennes, Paris, 1980, 376 p.

_____, "Vivir bajo la lluvia," *La Gaceta de Cuba* # 15, Havana, 1 April 1963.

_____, and Manuel Pérez, "El cine y la educación," *Cine Cubano* #s 69-70, Havana, 1971.

_____, and Mario Rodríguez Alemán, *Il documentario cubano dopo la rivoluzione*, IV Mostra Internazionale Cinema Libero, Porretta Terme, 1966, 20 p.

_____, *Tercer mundo, tercera guerra mundial*, Quaderno Informativo # 21. 6. Mostra Internazionle del Nuovo Cinema, Pesaro, 1970, 48 p.

_____, and Cesare Zavattini, *El Joven Rebelde*, Ediciones ICAIC. Havana, 1964. 132 p.

García Mesa, Héctor, "El cine negado de América Latina," *Cine Cubano* # 104, Havana, 1982; For*mato 16* #s 12-13, Panama, December 1982.

_____, "Incidence du cinéma francais muet á Cuba," *Le cinema francais muet dans le monde, influences réciproques*, Cinémathèque de Toulouse/ institut Jean Vigo, Perpignan, 1989, 288 p.

Gauthier, Guy, "Entretien avec Santiago Álvarez," *La Revue du Cinéma* # 243, Paris, 1970.

_____, and Robert Grelier, "Le cinéma cubain," *Image et Son* # 315, Paris, March 1977.

Georgakas, Dan, and Lenny Rubenstein (eds.), *The Cineaste Interviews, on the art and politics of the cinema*, Lake View Press, Chicago, 402 p.

"Girón: entrevista a Manuel Herrera," *Cine Cubano* #s 86-87-88, Havana, 1973.

Gómez, Manuel Octavio, "Los días del agua," *Arte 7* # 7 and # 8, Havana, March and May 1971.

_____, "El documental visto por los documentalistas," *Cine Cubano* # 6, Havana 1962.

_____, "Apuntes para la historia de un cine sin historia," *Cine Cubano* #s 86-87-88, Havana, 1973.

González, Moraima, "De la realidad de Nuevitas partimos: entrevista a Manuel Octavio Gómez," *Cine Cubano* # 96, Havana, 1980.

Gounzbourg, P., and R. Grilar, "Naissance d'un cinéma socialiste," *Miroir du Cinéma* #s 6-7, Paris, 1963.

Grelier, Robert, "Entretien avec Humberto Solás," *La Revue du Cinéma* # 240, Paris, 1970.
Guevara, Alfredo, "Alfredo Guevara responde a las aclaraciones," *Hoy*, Havana, 17 December 1963.
____, "El cine cubano 1963," *Cine Cubano* #s 14-15, Havana, October–November 1963.
____, "El cine cubano tiene diez años," *Bohemia* Año 61 # 5, Havana, January 1969; *Cine del Tercer Mundo* # 1, Montevideo, October 1969.
____, "El cine revolucionario cubano, factor de educación permanente," *Cine Cubano* #s 66-67, Havana, 1971.
____, "El cine y la Revolución," *La Gaceta de Cuba* # 27, Havana, 3 October 1963.
____, *La cultura y la Revolución*, Sindicato de Trabajadores CMQ, Havana, 1960, 24 p.; "La cultura y la Revolución," *Cine Cubano* # 4, December 1960–January 1961.
____, "Declaraciones de Alfredo Guevara," *Hoy*, Havana, 22 December 1963.
____, "En tensión hacia el comunismo," *Cine Cubano* # 95, Havana 1979.
____, "Habla Guevara," in INRA, vol. 1, year 1, Havana, 1960.
____, "Informe y saludo ante el primer Congreso Nacional de Cultura," *Diario de la Tarde*, Havana, 17 December 1962; *Cine Cubano* # 9, Havana, 1963.
____, "Una nueva etapa de cine en Cuba," *Cine Cubano* # 3, Havana, November 1960.
____, "Una obra de arte excepcional: la Revolución," *El Caimán Barbudo* # 34, Havana, September 1969.
____, "Para presentar cincuenta años de arte nuevo en Cuba," *Revolución, Letras, Arte*, Letras Cubanas, Havana, 1980, 620 p.; *Para presentar cincuenta años de arte nuevo en Cuba*, Letras Cubanas, Havana, 1981, 44 p.
____, "Realidades y perspectivas de un nuevo cine," *Cine Cubano* # 1, Havana, 1960.
____, "Reflexión nostálgica sobre el futuro," *Arcadia va al cine* # 18, Bogota, June–July 1988.
____, "Reflexiones en torno a una experiencia cinematográfica: I. El Cine Cubano tiene diez años; II. El Cine Cubano: instrumento de descolonización," *Cine Cubano* #s 54-55, Havana, 1969; *Cuadro* # 2, Medellín, 1970.
____, "Revisando nuestro trabajo," *Cine Cubano* # 2, Havana, 1960.
____, "Sobre el cine cubano," *Cine Cubano* # 41, Havana, 1967.
____, "Testimonios/Prolongando una discusión," *Cine Cubano* # 10, Havana, 1963.
____, et al., "El Cine Cubano," *Pensamiento Crítico* # 42, Havana, July 1970 [spec. edition].
____, et al., "Le cinéma cubain," *Bréches* # 7, Paris. December 1961.
Guía Cinematográfica 1955, Centro Católico de Orientación Cinematográfica de la Acción Católica Cubana, Havana, 1956, 456 p.; *Idem, 1956–1957*, 1957, 424 p.; *Idem, 1957–58*, 1958, 400 p.; *Idem 1958–59*, 1960, 332 p.; *Idem 1959–60*, 1961, 208 p.
Gumucio Dagron, Alfonso, *Cine, Censura y Exilio en América Latina*, Ediciones Film/Historia, La Paz, 1979, 15 p. (2nd edition: CIMCA/STUNAM/Federación Editorial Mexicana. La Paz-Mexico, 1984, 182 p.)
Gutiérrez Alea, Tomás, "12 notas para las 12 sillas," *Cine Cubano* # 6, Havana, 1962.
____, "El cine y la cultura," *Cine Cubano* # 2, Havana, 1960; *Cinecrítica* # 5, Buenos Aires, April–June 1961.

____, "Cómo se mira una película," *La Gaceta de Cuba*, Havana, 1 December 1962.

____, "Confesiones de un cineasta," *Araucaria de Chile* # 37, Michay, Madrid, 1987.

____, *Dialéctica del Espectador*, Union, Havana, 1982, 76 p.; Federación Editorial Mexicana, Mexico, 1983, 112 p. (*Dialética do Espectador*, Summus, Sao Paulo, 1984, 116 p.; "The Viewer's Dialectic," *Jump Cut* # 29, Berkeley, February 1984, and # 30, March 1985; *The Viewer's Dialectic*, José Martí Publishing House, Havana, 1988, 92 p.)

____, "Donde menos se piensa salta el cazador … de brujas," *La Gaceta de Cuba* # 33, Havana, 20 March 1964.

____, "Donde se habla de lo moderno en el arte y se dicen cosas que no fueron dichas en el momento oportuno," *Cine Cubano* # 9, Havana, 1963.

____, "Dramaturgia (cinematográfica) y realidad," *Cine Cubano* # 105, Havana, 1983; *Arcadia va al cine* # 4, Bogota, September–October 1983.

____, "El free cinema y la objetividad," *Cine Cubano* # 4, Havana, December 1960–January 1961.

____, "Memorias del subdesarrollo: notas de trabajo," *Cine Cubano* #s 45-46, Havana, 1967.

____, "No siempre fui cineasta," *Cine Cubano* # 114, Havana, 1985 ("I wasn't always a filmmaker," *Cineaste* # 1, New York, 1985).

____, "Notas sobre una discusión de un documento sobre una discusión (de otro documento)," *La Gaceta de Cuba* # 29, Havana, 5 November 1963.

____, and Ugo Ulive, *Las doce sillas*, Ediciones ICAIC, Havana, 1963, 136 p.

Guzmán, Patricio, and Pedro Sempere, *Chile: el cine contra el fascismo*, Fernando Torres, Valencia, 1977, 256 p.

____, *La insurrección de la burguesía*, Rocinante/Fondo Editorial Salvador de la Plaza, Caracas, 1975. 72 p.

Hernández, Andrés, "Filmmaking and Politics: The Cuban Experience," *American Behavioral Scientist* vol. 17 #3, Beverly Hills, January–February 1974.

Hinson, Hal. "My 20th Century," in *The Washington Post*, 4 Jan. 1991.

Hoffman, Hilmar, and Fritz Rumler, *Actualidades Cubanes (Castros Cuba in der cubanischen Wochenschau)*, Textliste der gleichnamigen Fernsehdokumentation, Oberhausen, 1970, 563 p.

Horvath, Ricardo, *Cuba, la oculta: vida cotidiana, comunicación y cultura*, Rescate, Buenos Aires, 1987, 208 p.

Hullebroeck, Joëlle, "Entrevista a Santiago Álvarez," *Corto Circuito/Court Circuit*, Paris, July–October 1989.

Humy, Nicholas Peter, and Ana M. López, "Interview: Sergio Giral on Filmmaking in Cuba," *Black Film Review* vol. 3 # 1, Washington, winter 1986-87.

ICAIC, *Instituto Cubano del Arte e Industria Cinematográficos*, Havana, 1960, 32 p.

ICAIC, "El nuevo cine latinoamericano," *Historia del* Cine *Mundial*, by Georges Sadoul, Siglo Veintiuno, Mexico, 1972, 830 p.

ICAIC Press Book for "La última cena." Havana: ICAIC, 1976.

ICAIC Press Book for "Vampiros en la Habana." Havana: ICAIC, 1985.

Jacob, Mario, "Reportaje a Santiago Álvarez," *Cine del Tercer Mundo* # 2, Montevideo, November 1970.

Jahnke, Eckart and Manfred Lichtenstein, *Kubanischer Dokumentarfilm*, Staatliches Filmarchiv der Deutschen Demokratischen Republik, Berlin, 1974, 228 p.

Johnson, William, "Report from Cuba," *Film Quarterly* vol. XIX # 4, Berkeley, c. 1966.
Kaplún, Mario, "Entrevista con Julio García Espinosa," *Dicine* # 27, Mexico, September-October 1988.
Kernan, Margot, "Cuban Cinema: Tomás Gutiérrez Alea," *Quarterly* vol. XXIX # 2, Berkeley, winter 1976.
Kovacs, Steven, "Lucía: Style and Meaning in Revolutionary Film," *Monthly Review* vol. 27 # 2, New York, June 1975.
Le Pennec, Françoise, "Cinéma de Cuba," *Cinéma 82* # 281, Paris, May 1982.
León Frias, Isaac, *Los años de la conmoción*, Universidad Nacional Autónoma de México, 1979, 296 p.
____, "Entrevista con Manuel Pérez," *Hablemos del Cine* # 70, Lima, April 1979.
López, Rigoberto, "Cine documental, cine directo, poesía de la realidad," *Cine Cubano* #102, Havana, 1982.
López, Roberto, "Hablar de Sara, de cierta manera," *Cine Cubano* # 93, Havana, 1978.
López Morales, Eduardo, "¿Crisis del Nuevo Cine Latinoamericano? Opina Julio García Espinosa," *Bohemia*, Havana, 17 and 24 June 1988.
Magín Hinojosa, Leonel, "Entrevista con Manuel Pérez," *Cine Cubano* # 100, Havana, 1981.
Manet, Eduardo, "El cine de Cuba," *Nuestro Cine* # 44, Madrid, 1965.
____, "De Hanoi a Haksat: Santiago Álvarez al regreso," *Cine Cubano* # 41, Havana, 1967.
____, "El solar, de la escena a la pantalla," *Cine Cubano* # 21, Havana, 1964.
____, "Tránsito: autopsia de un film," *Cine Cubano* #18, Havana, February 1964.
____, and Mario Rodríguez Alemán, *Tres guiones: Balada del Soldado, Divorcio a la Italiana, Casco de Oro*, ICAIC, Havana, 1967, 249 p.
Manrique Ardila, Jaime, *Notas de cine: confesiones de un crítico amateur*, Carlos Valencia Editores, Bogota, 1979, 112 p.
Marchi, Marie-Paule, *10th Festival du Cinema Latino-américain, Le Film Français*, supplement to # 2222, Paris, 2 December 1988, 16 p.
Mariñez, Pablo, "Entrevista con Humberto Solás," *Nuestro Cine* # 97, Madrid, May 1970.
Martin, Marcel, "Le Cinéma Cubain," *La Revue du Cinéma* # 360, Paris, April 1981.
____, and Paulo Antonio Paranagua, "Hommages: Humberto Solás," Festival international du film de la Rochelle, Cahier # 10, 1989.
____, and Paul-Louis Thirard, "Des havanes au Ranelagh," and "Cuba Notes," *Cinema 63* # 80, Paris, 1963.
____, et al., "Cuba: Petite Planéte du Cinéma" and other texts, *Cinéma 70* # 144, Paris, March 1970.
____, et al., "Quinze ans de cinéma cubain," interviews with Solás, Fraga and García Espinosa, *Ecran* # 54, Paris, January 1974.
Martinez, José. "Yo soy, del son a la salsa." *Boxffiice Online Review*, November 1997.
Martinez Torres, Augusto, and Manuel Pérez Estremera, *Introduzione al cinema cubano postrivoluzionario*, Quaderni del CUT # 8, Bari, 1970.
____, and Manuel Pérez Estremera, *Nuevo Cine Latinoamericano*, Anagrama, Barcelona, 1973, 232 p.
Massip, José, "La autenticidad y la contemporaneidad en la obra de arte de tema histórico," *Cine Cubano* # 114, Havana, 1985.

____, "David es el comienzo," *Cine Cubano* #s 45-46, Havana, 1967.
____, "Dos veces Guantánamo," *Cine Cubano* # 38, Havana, 1966.
____, "La Recuperación del pasado," *Cine y Liberación* # 1, Buenos Aires, 1972.
Matas, Julio, "Theater and Cinematography," *Revolutionary Change in Cuba*, under the direction of Carmelo Mesa-Lago, University of Pittsburgh Press, 1971.
Mesa Gisbert, Carlos D., and Pedro Susz K., "Cine Cubano," *Notas Críticas* # 45, Cinemateca Boliviana, La Paz, August 1983.
"Mesa redonda sobre Joris Ives," *Cine Cubano* #s 14-15, Havana, 1963.
Miccichè, Lino, *Il nuovo cinema degli anni 60*, E.R.I., Turin, 1972.
____, collaborating with Bruno Torri and Adriano Apra, *Teorie e pratiche del cinema cubano*, Marchilio Editori, Venice, 1981, 230 p. (coll. Nuovocinema Pesaro).
Monleón, José, "Notas sobre el cine cubano," *Nuestro Cine* # 72. Madrid, April 1968.
____, and Augusto M. Torres, "Entrevista con Manuel Octavio Gómez," *Nuestro Cine* # 91, Madrid, November 1969.
Mota, Francisco M., *Por primera vez en Cuba*, Gente Nueva, Havana, 1982, 112 p.
"La Muerte de un burócrata: entrevista con Tomás Gutiérrez Alea," *Cine Cubano* # 35, Havana, 1966.
Muestra del cine documental cubano, Instituto de Cooperación lberoamericana, Madrid, 1986, 96 p.
Muguercia, Alberto and Ezequiel Rodríguez, *Rita Montaner*, Letras Cubanas, Havana, 1985, 82 p.
Myerson, Michael, *Memories of Underdevelopment: the Revolutionary Films of Cuba*, Grossman Publishers, New York, 214 p.
Navarrete, José Antonio, and Félix Pita Rodríguez, *Testimonios de José Tabío*, Museo Nacional de Bellas Artes, Havana, 1985, 40 p.
Niota, Francisco, "Doce aspectos económicos de la cinematografía cubana," *Lunes de Revolución*, Havana, February 6, 1961.
Orovio, Helio, *Diccionario de la música cubana*, Letras Cubanas, Havana, 1981, 444 p.
Oroz, Silvia, *Gutiérrez Alea: as filmes que não filmei*, Anima. Rio de Janeiro, 1985, 192 p. *(Tomás Gutiérrez Alea: los filmes que no filmé*, Unión, Havana, 1989, 204 p.)
____, "Tomás Gutiérrez Alea: los filmes que no filmé," *Encuadre* # 6, Caracas, April 1986.
Otero, Lisandro, "Realidades del Cine en Cuba," *Excelsior*, Havana, 29 June and 1 July 1954 [T.G. Alea conference].
Padrón, Juan, *El libro del Mambí*. Editora Abril de la UJC, Havana, 1988, 152 p.
Palacios Moré, René, and Daniel Pires Mateus, *El Cine Latinoamericano, o por una estética de la ferocidad, la magia y la violencia*. Sedmay, Madrid, 1976, 200 p.
Paldy, Tomasné, and Sandor Peter (dir.). *A latin-amerikai filmművészet antológiaja*, Magyar Filmtudomanyi Intézet és Filmarchivum. Budapest, 1983, 588 p.
Paranagua, Paulo Antonio, *Cinema na América Latina: longe de Deus e perto de Hollywood*, L & PM, Porto Alegre, 1985, 104 p.
____, "Álvarez," "Cuba," "García Espinosa," "Gómez," "Gutiérrez Alea," "Solás," *Dictionnaire du cinéma*, under the direction of Jean-Loup Passek, Larousse, Paris, 1986, 888 p.
____, "Cuba: 30 años de documentales en la revolución," *Corto Circuito/Corut Circuit* #s 8-9, Paris, July–October 1989.

_____, "Cuba," *Le Tiers Monde en films,* CinémAction/Tricontinental coordinated by Guy Hennebelle, François Maspero, Paris, 1982, 224 p.

_____, "Nouvelles de La Havana: une restructuration du cinéma cubain," from "Une lutte cubaine contre les démons du dogmatisme," *Positif* # 328, Paris, June 1988 ("News from Havana: a Restructuration of Cuban Cinema," *Framework* # 35, London, 1988).

_____, "Renouveau du cinéma cubain?" *Positif* # 280, Paris, June 1984.

_____, *Semaine du cinéma cubain en France,* Ministère des Affaires Étrangères/Centre National de la Cinématographie, Paris, 1988, 24 p.

Partido Comunista de Cuba, *La lucha ideológica y la cultura artística y literaria,* Editora Política, Havana, 1982, 114 p.

Perdices, Enrique (dir.), *El cine en Cuba. Souvenir de la RKO Radio dedicado a la Convención Nacional de Empresarios.* Edited by the magazine *Cinema,* Havana, 1943, 40 p.

Pérez, Fernando, and Humberto Solás, "Grupo de creación: un reto artístico y organizativo," *Cine Cubano* # 122, Havana, 1988.

Perron, Gérard, "Les affiches de cinéma cubaines," *Lumière du Cinéma* # 9, Paris, November 1977.

Pick, Zuzana M., *Latin American Film Makers and the Third Cinema,* Carleton University, Ottawa, 1978, 260 p.

_____, *Le "Nouveau cinema" d'Amerique latine: développement culturel, économique and socio-politique depuis 1960,* Université de Paris I, 1979.

Pineda Barnet, Enrique, "David: ¿método o actitud?" *Cine Cubano* #s 45-46, Havana, 1967.

Piñera, Walfredo, "El estado y su responsabilidad ante el cinematógrafo," *Cine-Guía,* Año VI, Havana, May 1958.

_____, "Esquema filmográfico del cine nacional," *Cine-Guía,* año VIII # 12, Havana, February 1961.

_____, "Panorama Historique du cinémia cubain," *Revue Internarionale du Cinéma* # 10, Paris, 1951.

_____, "La verdad del cine nacional," *Cine-Guía,* Año VI # 8, Havana, October 1958.

Pino Santos, Oscar, "Las posibilidades de una industria cinematográfica en Cuba: consideraciones," *Carteles,* Havana, 30 November 1958.

Pogolotti, Graziella, *1000 carteles cubanos de cine,* Distribuidora Nacional de Películas, Havana, 1979, 28 p.

"Ponencia ICAIC al congreso de Educación y Cultura," *Arte 7* # 13, Havana, September 1971.

Portante, Jean, "Entretien avec le cinéaste cubain Humberto Solás," *Tageblan,* Luxembourg, 2 May 1987.

Primer anuario cinematográfico cubano 1940–41, con Los Consagrados de la Radio, Ramón Peón and Pedro Pablo Chávez, editors. Havana, 1940, 228 p.

Primer Plano, Valparaiso, vol. I # 2, Autumn 1972; # 3 Winter 1972; # 4 1972.

Pyhala, Mikko, "Kuuban Elokuva," and other articles, *Filmihullu,* 6/7O. Helsinki, 1970.

"¿Qué es lo moderno en arte? Referencia: el cine; mesa redonda," *Cine Cubano* # 9, Havana, 1963.

Quirós, Oscar, "Critical Mass of Cuban Cinema: art as the vanguard of society," *Screen,* 37:3, Autumn 1996.

Ramonet, Ignacio, "Le Cinéma Cubain," *Quinze ans de cinéma mondial 1960–1975,*

by Guy Hennebelle, Cerf, Paris, 1975, 432 p. (Portuguese translation: *Os Cinemas nacionais Contra Hollywood,* Paz e Terra, Rio de Janeiro, 1978, 246 p.)
____, *Cuba: Cinéma et Societé (1897–1971),* École Pratique des Hautes Études en Sciences Sociales, Paris, 1981.
Retrospective Xth anniversaire du cinéma cubain, Cinémathèque Française/Cinémathèque de Cuba, Paris, 1979, 20 p.
Ríos, Alejandro, "Veinte años sí son algo: Entrevista con Julio García Espinosa," *La Gaceta de Cuba,* Havana, January 1989.
Rodríguez Alemán, Mario, "Ayer y hoy en el cine cubano," *Mujeres,* Havana, 1 October 1967; and "El cine en la Revolución," November 1967.
____, "Bosquejo histórico del cine cubano," *Cine Cubano* #s 23-24-25, Havana, 1964.
____, *La sala oscura,* Unión, Havana, 1982, 2 vol., 396 and 380 p.
____, "Visión histórica de Ia evolución del cine en Cuba entre 1897 y 1958," *Diálogos y Enfoques* # 2, Centro de Información Cinematográfica, Havana, 1986, 61 p.
Roldán, Alberto, "Sobre la Ausencia," *Cine Cubano* #s 52-53, Havana, 1968.
Roman, José, "Del barroco americano y el ensayo fílmico," and "El culto de la antiestética" by Amílcar G. Romero, *Primer Plano* # 2, Valparaiso, Fall 1972.
Romano, Hélène J., *Évolution comparée du cinéma et des moyens de communication. Développement des communications de masse en Amérique latine, l' exemple du Mexique et de Cuba,* Université de Paris III, 1972.
Romualdo, Alejandro, et al., "El Cine Cubano en el Perú," *Pantalla,* Cine de Arte de la Universidad de San Marcos # 10, Lima, July 1970.
Saceiro, Miriam, "¿Qué fue la Cuba Sono Films?" *Bohemia* Año 76 # 26, Havana, 29 June 1984.
Sauvage, Pierre, "Cine Cubano," *Film Comment* vol. 8 # I, New York, 1972.
Schumann, Peter B., *Handbuch des lateinamerikanischen Films,* Verlag Klaus Dieter Vervuert/Freunde der Deutschen Kinemathek, Frankfurt, 1982, 326 p.
____, *Historia del cine latinoamericano,* Legasa, Buenos Aires, 1987, 368 p.
____, *Kino in Cuba 1959–1979,* Veriag Klaus Dieter Vervuert/Westdeutschen Kurzfilmtagen Oberhausen. Frankfurt, 1980, 416 p.
____, (dir.), *Kino und Kampf in Lateinamerika: Zur Theorie und Praxis des politischen Kinos,* Carl Hanser Verlag, Munich-Vienna, 1976, 264 p.
____, "Santiago Álvarez," *Möglichkeiten des Dokumentarfilms,* Westdeutschen Kurzfilmtage, Oberhausen, 1979.
Schwartz, Ronald. *Latin American Films, 1932-1994,* Jefferson, NC: McFarland, 1997.
Seguin, Louis, "Entretien avec Julio García Espinosa et Miguel Torres," *Positif* # 123, Paris, January 1971.
Serres, Jean, "Le cinéma révolution," *Le Technicien du Film* # 111, Paris, 15 December 1964.
Silberg, John. "Bitter Sugar." *Boxoffice Online Reviews,* October 1996.
"Sobre el cine y la literatura responden...." *Cine Cubano* #s 39, 40 and 41, Havana, 1967.
"Sobre un debate entre cineastas cubanos," and "Conclusiones de un debate entre cineastas cubanos," *Cine Cubano* #s 14-15, Havana, October-November 1963.
Solás, Humberto, "Alrededor de una dramaturgia cinematográfica latinoamericana," *Cine Cubano* # 105, Havana, 1983.

____, "¿Qué es Lucía? Apuntes acerca del cine," *Cine Cubano* #s 52-53 Havana, 1968.

____, "Reflexiones," *Cine Cubano* # 102, Havana 1982.

Solás, Sergio Benvenuto, "Miel para Oshún: Regreso a los albores." *Cine cubano* # 151, Havana, January–March 2001, pp. 33–35.

Steven, Peter, (ed.), *Jump Cut: Hollywood, Politics and Counter Cinema*, Between the Lines, Toronto, 1985; 400 p.

Sutherland, Elizabeth, "Cinema of Revolution — 90 Miles from Home," *Film Quarterly* vol. XVI # 2, Berkeley, winter 1961-62.

Talero, María Elvira, "Visión de Humberto Solás," *Cinemateca* # 2, Bogota, 1987.

Taylor, Anna Marie. "Imperfect Cinema, Brecht and the *Adventures of Juan Quin Quin*," in *Jump Cut*, #20).

____, "Lucia," *Film Quarterly* vol. XXIII # 3, Berkeley, 1975.

Tejada, Mario, "Introducción al cine documental cubano," from an interview with Octavio Cortázar, and from "Breve historia del cine cubano," by Augusto M. Torres and Manuel Pérez Estremera, *Hablemos de cine* # 64, Lima, April–June 1972.

Thirard, Paul-Louis, "Le cinéma cubain," *Image et Son* # 218, Paris. June–July 1968.

____, "Conclusions d'un débat entre les cinéastes cubains," *Positif* # 56, Paris, November 1963.

____, "Semaine du Cinéma Cubain," *Positif* #s 67-68, Paris, February–March 1965.

Thomas, Kevin. "'Sugar' Goes to Heart of Anti-Castro View." *L.A. Times*, 22 Novembert 1996.

Ulive, Ugo, "Biografía de Crónica Cubana," *Cine Cubano* # 10, Havana, 1963.

____, "Crónica del Cine Cubano," *Cine al Día* # 12, Caracas, March 1971.

____, "Historias de 12 sillas," *Cine Cubano* #6, Havana, 1962.

Vaillant, Fee, *Der Film Lateinamerikas: eine Dokumentation*, XXIX Internationalen Filmwoche, Mannheim, 1980, 614 p.

Valdés Rodríguez, José Manuel, "Algo en torno al cine y la República Cubana," *El Mundo*, Havana, 17, 19, 21 and 24 April 1960.

____, *El cine en la Universidad de la Habana*, Empresa de Publicaciones MINED, Havana, 1966, 488 p.

____, *Ojeada al Cine Cubano, 1906–1958*, Comisión de Extensión Universitaria. Havana, 1963, 16 p.

Vega Alfaro, Eduardo de la, *El cine de Juan Orol*, Filmoteca de la Universidad Nacional Autónoma de México, 1985, 104 p.

____, *Juan Orol*, Universidad de Guadalajara, Centro de Investigaciones y Enseñanza Cinematográficas, Guadalajara. 1987, 196 p.

Vega, Pastor, "El cine cubano y la voluntad creadora," *Cine Cubano* # 111, Havana, 1985.

____, "Conversando con Humberto Solás," *Cine Cubano* #s 42-43-44, Havana, 1967.

____, "Cuba: el cine, la cultura nacional," *Cine Cubano* #s 71-72, Havana, 1971; *Cinemateca* # 2, Mexico, June 1972.

____, "El nuevo cine latinoamericano: algunas características de su estilo," *Cine Cubano* #s 71-72, Havana 1971.

____, "Poética y política en De la guerra americana," *Cine Cubano* #s 60-62, Havana, 1970.

____, "Reflexiones," *Cine Cubano* #s 58-59, Havana, 1969.
Velleggia, Susana, *Cine: entre el espectáculo y la realidad,* Claves Latinoamericanas, Mexico, 1986, 184 p.
Verdecia, Carlos. "Nadie escuchaba." *The Miami Herald,* 18 Feb. 1988.
20 años de cine cubano, Centro de Información Cinematográfica. Havana, 1979, 56 p.
21 Muestra de CineJoven, Asociación Hermanos Saiz. Havana, 1989, 32 p.
Villanueva, Paulino, "El desarrollo del cine cubano en los últimos diez años," *Cine-Guía,* Año VIII # 12, Havana, February 1961.
Von Bagh, Peter, "Kuubalainen dokumenttielokuva," *Filmihullu,* 1/75, Helsinki, 1975.
Walfredo Piñera, "57 años de cine en Cuba," *Diario de la Marina,* Havana, 22 December 1953.
Waugh, Thomas (ed.), *"Show us life": Toward a History and Aesthetics of the Commited Documentary,* The Scarecrow Press, Metuchen, N.J., and London, 1984.
West, Denis, "Slavery and Cinema in Cuba: The Case of Gutiérrez Alea's The Last Supper," *The Western Journal of Black Studies* vol. 3 # 2, Indianapolis, c. 1979.
Zumbado, H., *Kitsch, kitsch ¡bang, bang!,* Letras Cubanas, Havana, 1988, 176 p.

Index

Abel, Dominique 60
Acapulco (theater) 32
Acebal, Sergio 17, 18
Acosta, Iván 172
Agramonte, Roberto 34
Agudo, Marcelo 22
Águila, Silvia 55
Alcalá, María Luisa 60
Alcalde, Oscar 47
Alejandro, Edesio 50, 70, 80, 103, 106, 180
Alfaro, Xiomara 183
Alfonso, Paco 34, 67, 166
Alhambra (Theater) 11, 18, 19, 46, 63
Alí, Jorge 71, 138, 174
Alí, Paula 133, 137, 145
Almendares (River) 11
Almendros, Néstor 137
Almirante, Enrique 56, 69, 114, 150, 174
Alonso, Alicia 31, 100, 101
Alonso, Manolo 34, 67, 167
Alonso, Manuel 24, 26, 27, 29, 34, 35, 37
Altolaguirre, Manuel 36
Altuna, Francisco 31
Álvarez, Enrique 133, 142
Álvarez, Paulina 21, 25, 183

Álvarez, Santiago 104, 117, 134, 140, 166
Álvarez Guedes, Eloísa 61, 160
Álvarez Guedes, Guillermo 63
Álvarez Tabío, Luis 25
Amaro, Blanquita 27, 30, 32, 34, 93
Amaya, Carmen 27
Anckermann, Guillermo 12, 15
Anckermann, Jorge 12, 13, 19
Angelo, Jean 27, 28, 35, 167
Anreus, Idalia 86, 87, 120, 142, 155, 160, 162, 165, 175, 177
Aragón, Delia 85
Aragón (Orchestra) 31
Aragón, Juan de 166
Arango, Arturo 119
Arenal, Humberto 40
Arenal, Jaqueline 133, 146, 153, 168
Arenas, Reynaldo 61, 62, 63
Arenas, Yolanda 75
Argentina, Imperio 24
Arias, Imanol 68, 69
Armendáriz, Pedro 35, 63, 136
Armstrong, Gillian 96
Arnaz, Desi 79, 109, 110, 111, 125
Arnaz, Desi, Jr. 124, 125
Arredondo, Enrique 22
Arredondo, Enrique, II 150, 169
Arrom, Juan José 29

Index

Arte y Cinema La Rampa (theater) 32
Arteaga (Cardinal) 37
Artigas, Jesús 12, 13, 14, 148
Arvizú, Juan 25
Assante, Armand 124, 125
Assante, Karen 125
Autocine Vento (theater) 33

Bacallao, Juana 116
Badías, Carlos 29, 31, 161, 166
Baliño, Carlos 11
Balmaseda, Mario 64, 82, 86, 92, 94, 113, 118, 136, 138, 145, 160, 164, 165, 175, 177, 179
Balmaseda, Simone 156
Banderas, Antonio 124, 125
Bardem, Javier 61, 62
Barnet, José A. 24
Barnet, Miguel 63, 99, 101
Barral, Manuel 38
Barral, Mario 37
Barral, Rolando 168
Barrio, Arturo "Mussie" del 21, 126
Batista, Fulgencio 23, 24, 26, 27, 28, 29, 34, 35, 36, 37, 38, 43, 56, 62, 65, 74, 75, 79, 83, 84, 85, 101, 106, 114, 129, 143, 144, 151, 169, 182
Bauzá, Mario 27
Beaudine, William 77
Belafonte, Harry 50
Benavides, Miguel 68, 73, 83, 85, 102, 113, 142, 143, 150, 152, 155, 160, 177
Benedek, Laslo 37, 52
Benguría, Xonia 67, 73
Benítez Rojo, Antonio 174
Bernaza, Luis Felipe 68, 83, 128, 151, 178
Betancourt, François 30
Birri, Fernando 165
Blain, Rogelio 85, 104, 113, 120, 150, 154, 159, 160, 177
Blanco Rico, Antonio 37
Blondell, Joan 106
Blue Ribbon Films 28
Bohemia (magazine) 12, 13, 53
Boitel, Pedro Luis 137
Bola de Nieve 39, 139, 161
Borbolla, Caledonio Jr. 23
Boti, Regino 21
Bouise, Jean 143, 169, 170
BPP Pictures 21, 22, 181

Bravo, Enrique Sr. 28
Bravo Adams, Caridad 27, 35
Brito, Julio 22, 24
Brito, Ramón 120, 129
Brito, Rolando 55, 56, 180
Brouwer, Leo 45, 52, 54, 57, 65, 68, 83, 85, 86, 93, 94, 104, 108, 113, 114, 118, 120, 123, 130, 134, 143, 146, 151, 155, 157, 159, 168, 174, 175, 177, 179, 182
Brull, Mariano 19
Brussels 22
Bunnet, Jane 171
Burke, Chris 84, 85
Burke, Elena 35, 139, 142
Burr, Raymond 52

Cabrera, Gina 34, 162
Cabrera, Lydia 24, 30, 36, 38
Cabrera Infante, Sabá 42
Caignet, Félix B. 20, 24, 29, 31, 34, 35, 36, 38, 161, 166
Cal, Mimi 28
"La Calandria" 27
Callejas, Félix 18
Camagüey 12, 16, 37, 136
Cambó, Ángel 23
Canal 4 (television station) 33
Canal 6 (television station) 33
Cancio, Salvador 28
Cané, Valentín 19
Cañedo, Roberto 162
Canel, Fausto 44, 146
Cao, Jorge 84, 153
Capablanca, José Raúl 18, 66
Caparrós, Ernesto 23, 24, 27, 28, 139, 166
Capote, Julio 131, 162
Capote, Raúl Fidel 81
Carbó, Sergio 129
Carbó Menéndez, José 28, 33
Cardona, René 36, 136
Cardoso, Onelio Jorge 43
Caribbean Film Company 16
Carmina, Rosa 36
Carpentier, Alejo 19, 23, 27, 28, 29, 30, 32, 35, 37, 60, 159
Carrillo, Isolina 31
Carteles (magazine) 17
Caruso, Enrico 17
Casals, Melchor 83, 107
Casals, Zulema 73

Index

Casanova, Delia 54
Casanova, Jorge 162
Casanova, Julio Alberto 56
Casasús, José E. 10, 11
Casaus, Víctor 60, 71, 144
Casín, Orlando 60, 83, 152, 172, 180
Cassavetes, John 52
Castelao, Emilio 25
Castell, Ana 101
Castell, Antonio 22
Castillo, Marcos 131
Cech, Vladimir 43
Centro Sperimentale di Cinematografia 41, 57, 151, 158
CEPLIC 35
Cernuda, Antonio 38
Cervera, Elvira 81, 102, 143, 156
"Chaflán" (Carlos López) 26, 93
Chanan, Michael 2, 87, 129, 154, 161
Chan-Li-Po 23, 24, 166
Chaplin (theater) 32
Chaplin, Charles 17, 22, 154
Chapotín, Félix 34, 139
Chibás, Eduardo 28, 30, 31, 34
CHIC Films 25
Chicharito 22
Chijona, Gerardo 46, 50, 115, 146, 180
Chocolate, "Kid" 115, 160
Chomón, Faure 38
Christensen, Theodor 41, 93
Cienfuegos 14, 38, 107
Cienfuegos, Camilo 64
Cine Club Estudiantil 37
Cine-club Visión 37
Cine Cubano (magazine) 40, 53
Cine Fans (magazine) 24
Cinelandia (magazine) 18
Cinema (magazine) 24, 28
Cinemateca de Cuba 22, 32, 40, 45
Cinemóvil 40, 45, 154
"Clavelito" 27
Claxton, Samuel 67, 72, 92, 118, 124, 133, 143, 144, 157, 160, 173, 174, 175, 177
CMQ (Radio Station) 23, 24, 27, 29, 31, 32, 33, 38, 166
Cobián, Juan 50
COCO (radio station) 24
Colina, Enrique 46, 179
Collazo, Bobby 25, 27, 30
Collazo, Fernando 127

Collazo, Luz María 156, 169
Colomo, Fernando 74
Colón, Antonieta 116
Colón, Willie 184
Communist Party of Cuba 19, 25, 98, 129, 137
Connery, Sean 74
Consulado (Theater) 33
Corrieri, Sergio 56, 71, 75, 113, 129, 130, 131, 146, 160, 161, 169
Cortázar, Octavio 50, 64, 84, 154
Cortés, Mapy 25
Couto, Armando 38
Cramer, Larry 171
Cremata, Juan Carlos 137
Crevenna, Alfredo B 38, 183
Cruz, Carlos 53, 63, 102, 115, 130, 145
Cruz, Celia 33, 52, 96, 124, 125, 184
Cruz, Vladimir 98, 115, 119, 146
Cruz, Xenia 142
Cruz Barrios, César 30
Cruz Barrios, Mario 30, 31
Cuba cinematográfica (magazine) 14
Cuba Sono Films 25, 26, 27, 29, 30, 31
Cueto, Rafael 19, 20

De Armas, Jesús 125, 126, 154
De Forest, Lee 20
De Foronda, Pituka 166
De La Cruz, René 60, 64, 72, 83, 113, 114, 118, 129, 138, 142, 146, 153, 158, 160, 165
De La Guardia, Lucas 56, 89, 91, 93, 126, 132, 168, 182, 184
De La Texera, Diego 173
De La Torriente Brau, Pablo 144, 158
De La Uz, Laura 106, 107
Delgado, Agustín P. 35, 36
Delgado, Aramis 55, 118, 120, 155, 175
Delgado, Carmen 73, 92
Delgado, Frank 53
Delgado, Idalberto 88
Delgado, Isaac 184
Delgado, Ricardo 19
Del Risco, Idalmis 53, 80, 153
Del Sol, Laura 163
Demicheli, Tulio 35, 36
Depp, Johnny 61
Desnoes, Edmundo 130, 131
De Vries, Sonja 99
Diario de la Marina (newspaper) 16

Index

Díaz, Aniceto 21
Díaz, Jesús 93, 95, 117, 145, 153
Díaz, Olallo 11
Díaz, Rolando 92, 130, 145, 159, 166, 180
Díaz Quesada, Enrique 6, 11, 12, 13, 14, 15, 16, 18, 19, 20, 146
Díaz Quesada, Juan 21
Díaz Torres, Daniel 46, 53, 103, 114, 115, 116, 143, 156
Diego, Constante 46, 71
Diego, Eliseo 38
Diestro, Aida 35
Díez, Ana 174
Dominican Republic 30, 60
Dotta, Pablo 87
Downey, Robert Jr. 61
Dridi, Karim 76
Duane, Darwin L. 156
Duane, Monse 156
Duplex (theater) 33
Duque Naranjo, Lisandro 182

Echazábal, Estelita 181
Echeverría, José Antonio 36, 37
Edison, Thomas Alba 9, 10, 11, 58, 77, 80, 133, 182
Egido (theater) 33
Eguren, Raúl 72, 86, 99, 102, 113, 129, 160, 165, 175, 177
Enright, Ray 106
Enyedi, Ildikó 58
Escuela de Ballet Pro-Arte Musical 22
Escuela Normal de Música de La Habana 22
Espasande, Ángel 67, 114, 118, 129, 177
Estefan, Gloria 97
Estenoz, Evaristo 12, 157
Estrada Palma, Tomás 11
Évora, César 54, 63, 66, 68, 89, 102, 112, 140
Exhibidor (magazine) 24

Fandiño, Roberto 61
Fangio, Juan Manuel 142, 143
Fariñas, Carlos 102, 108, 113, 129, 160, 169
Farré, Martha 90
Farrés, Osvaldo 24, 26, 28, 31, 168
Faz, Roberto 37
Fernández, Emilio "El indio" 30, 36, 162

Fernández, Erdwin 57, 165
Fernández, José 34
Fernández, Joseíto 20
Fernández, Leopoldo "Tres Patines" 21, 28
Fernández Bustamante, Adolfo 31, 127, 128
Fernández Retamar, Roberto 38
Ferro, José 59
Flores, Roberto H. 103
Florit, Eugenio 22
Flynn, Errol 63, 79, 80
Fornés, Rosita 35, 37, 138, 139, 145, 152, 156, 164
Fraga, Jorge 75, 83, 85, 92, 140, 141
Fraile, Alfredo 67
Franco Varona, Matías 18

Gabor, Zsa Zsa 38
Gabrial, Miguel 23
La gaceta teatral y cinematográfica 14
Galán, Natalio 72, 75
Gallardo, Cirilo 50
Gallardo, José 169, 170
Gallardo, Juan 50
Gálvez, María Cristina 71
García, Andy 97
García, Calixto 15
García, Luis Alberto 50, 56, 70, 72, 90, 92, 102, 107, 118, 126, 151, 175, 177, 180
García, Luis O. 171
García, María Eugenia 56
García, Pelayo 59
García, Ricardo 20
García Ascot, José Miguel 75
García Bogliano, Adrián 89
García Bogliano, Ramiro 89
García Caturla, Alejandro 24
García Espinosa, Humberto 88, 114, 138, 177
García Espinosa, Julio 36, 40, 41, 44, 46, 57, 75, 76, 114, 120, 128, 129, 151, 158, 159, 169, 173
García Márquez, Gabriel 67, 165, 174
García Menocal, Mario 13, 14, 15, 18, 27
García Montes, Mario 64, 91, 156, 178, 182
Garrido, Alberto 22, 26, 29, 34, 73, 93, 161

Garrido, Leticia 74
Gatti, Armand 42, 86, 143
Gattorno, Francisco 98, 140, 145
Gaztelu, Ángel 36
Gillespie, Dizzy 31, 137
Gilpin, Margaret 128
Giral, Sergio 43, 46, 124, 127, 134, 143, 152, 157, 173
Gispert, Jaime 18
Glimcher, Arnold 124, 125
Gómez, Jesús 46
Gómez, José Miguel 12, 157
Gómez, Manuel Octavio 42, 45, 86, 99, 105, 107, 136, 150, 155, 162, 165, 174, 175, 177
Gómez, Miguel Mariano 24
Gómez, Raúl 50, 154
Gómez Kemp, Ramiro 27
Gómez Urquiza, Zacarías 34
Gómez Yera, Sara 82
González, Carlos 101
González, Yolanda 127
González Betancourt, Miguel 89
González Freire, Natividad 38
González Gómez, Plácido 30
González Prieto, José 34, 73
Gramatges, Harold 30, 108
Granados, Daisy 54, 68, 69, 72, 74, 83, 90, 102, 112, 130, 137, 146, 153, 155, 160, 165, 169, 172, 175
Granados, María 88
Grau San Martín, Ramón 23, 29, 30, 31
Grenet, Eliseo 20, 22, 31
Grenet, Emilio 25
Grenet, Neno 126
Grupo de Experimentación Sonora 45, 100, 113
Guerra, Armando 70, 142
Guerra, Ramiro 25, 107
Guerrero, Félix 67, 73, 75, 175
Guevara, Alfredo 39
Guevara, Ernesto "Che" 56, 105, 108, 183
Guía Cinematográfica (magazine) 37
Guillén, Nicolás 21, 22, 23, 141
Guillén Landrián, Nicolás 70, 141
Guillot, Olga 30, 34, 183
Guines, Tata 171
Guirao, Ramón 23
Guiteras, Antonio 23, 24
Gutiérrez, Miguel 59, 70, 89, 114, 124, 152, 154, 173

Gutiérrez Alea, Tomás 6, 31, 34, 36, 41, 43, 44, 45, 46, 47, 67, 81, 83, 88, 97, 99, 102, 104, 108, 109, 128, 130, 134, 140, 151, 158, 168, 175
Gutiérrez Aragón, Manuel 72

Harlan, Richard 20
Haskins, Harry 18
Havana 9, 10, 11, 12, 13, 14, 15, 17, 18, 19, 20, 24, 25, 26, 28, 30, 32, 33, 34, 35, 36, 37, 38, 39, 40, 42, 43, 46, 52, 53, 54, 55, 56, 57, 59, 60, 62, 63, 64, 65, 66, 69, 70, 71, 72, 73, 74, 75, 77, 78, 79, 80, 82, 83, 84, 85, 86, 89, 90, 93, 94, 95, 96, 98, 99, 101, 102, 103, 104, 105, 106, 107, 109, 110, 111, 113, 119, 124, 125, 127, 128, 129, 131, 132, 133, 136, 137, 140, 142, 143, 144, 145, 146, 150, 151, 152, 154, 156, 161, 164, 166, 167, 168, 169, 171, 172, 175, 178, 179, 180
Hemingway, Ernest 36
Henríquez, Hernán 72, 125, 126, 154, 174
Henríquez Ureña, Max 19, 21
Hermann Dolz, Sonia 116
Hernández, Adalberto 119
Hernández, Andrés 54, 173
Hernández, Bernabé 90
Hernández, Broselianda 60, 72
Herrera, Evaristo 20
Herrera, Manuel 66, 100, 138
Herrera, Mequi 92
Hidalgo-Gato, Raymundo 172
Hijuelos, Oscar 124
Hoffman, Jerzy 45
Holland, John 137
Hoogesteijn, Solveig 163
Hopper, Jerry 37

Ibarra, Gladys 163
Ibarra, Mirta 50, 67, 74, 98, 101, 102, 104, 136, 143, 152, 164, 175
ICAIC (Instituto Cubano del Arte y la Industria Cinematográficos) 2, 39, 40, 41, 42, 44, 45, 46, 50, 52, 53, 54, 55, 56, 57, 58, 60, 61, 63, 64, 65, 66, 67, 68, 70, 71, 72, 73, 75, 76, 81, 82, 83, 84, 85, 86, 87, 88, 89, 90, 91, 92, 93, 94, 95, 96, 97, 99, 100, 101, 102, 103, 104, 105, 106, 107, 108, 109, 112,

Index

113, 114, 115, 116, 117, 118, 119, 120, 124, 125, 126, 127, 129, 130, 132, 133, 134, 136, 137, 138, 139, 140, 141, 142, 143, 144, 145, 146, 147, 148, 149, 150, 151, 152, 153, 154, 155, 156, 157, 158, 159, 160, 162, 163, 164, 165, 166, 167, 168, 169, 172, 173, 174, 175, 177, 178, 179, 180, 182, 183, 184
Ichaso, León 59, 60, 172
Instituto Nacional de Fomento de la Industria Cinematográfica Cubana 37
Ivens, Joris 41, 45, 84

Jiménez, Juan Ramón 24, 25
Jiménez, Yadira 30, 34
Jiménez Leal, Orlando 172
Joffre, Evelia 34
Johnson, Jack 15
Jorrín, Enrique 34
Juliachs, Erasmo 91, 93, 95, 96, 126, 132, 155
Junco, Jorgelina 167
Junco, Tito 72, 83, 154, 174, 175, 177

Kalatozov, Mikhail 42, 43, 169
Karmen, Roman 41, 45
Knight, Alden 136, 143, 144

Labrador Ruiz, Enrique 24, 34
Lagunas Gómez, Aurelio 27
Lam, Wilfredo 26, 28, 30, 34
Laplace, Víctor 67
Laredo Bru, Federico 24
Laván, René 59
Lay, Rafael 31
Lazo, Lilia 52
Lecchi, Alberto 142
Lecuona, Ernesto 13, 14, 17, 20, 21, 22, 23, 24, 31, 39, 127, 128, 161, 167, 186
Leduc, Paul 60, 116, 117
Lee, Hilda 172
Legrá, Adela 44, 64, 120, 122, 126, 158
Lente (magazine) 26
Lester, Richard 74
Lezama Lima, José 24, 25, 28, 29, 32, 35, 38, 43, 62
Lima, Noel 96, 149
Limonta, Mario 82, 83, 132, 160
Limonta, Mayda 69
Limonta, Rita 158

Littin, Miguel 54, 159
Lizaso, Félix 26
Llano, Fernando 17
Llauradó, Adolfo 54, 66, 67, 75, 81, 86, 102, 113, 114, 120, 124, 126, 144, 153, 155, 157, 160, 165
Llerena, Lilian 72, 108, 146
Longoni, Angelo 94
Longres, Daniel 64, 91, 95, 96, 119, 143, 156, 183
López, Alfredo 20
López, Carlos *see* "Chaflán"
López, Ivonne 67
López, Oscar Luis 24
López, Regino 16, 17
López, Rigoberto 184
López Nusa, Hernán 55
Loveira, Carlos 17, 18, 20
Loynaz, Dulce María 36
Lugo, Alejandro 34, 66, 69, 72, 92, 114, 129, 138, 143, 160, 165, 168, 175
Lumière Brothers 9, 10
Lusiardo, Tito 32
Lynn, Verónica 63, 107, 117, 136, 138, 151

Maceo, Antonio 15, 19, 95, 141, 142, 150
Machado, Gerardo 19, 20, 21, 22, 23, 121, 129, 134, 144, 179
Machado, Roberto 30
Machito 27
Madina, Raúl (actor) 116
Maetzig, Kurt 43
Magoon, Charles 12
Mahon, Barry 79
Mahon, Clelle 79
Maine (cruiser) 11, 13
Mañach, Jorge 19, 21, 22, 23, 29
Manet, Eduardo 85, 86, 143, 158
Mar, Aníbal de 23, 24, 26, 28, 166
Marcelo 34, 73
Marde, Diana V. 181
Marianao (theater) 33
Marinello, Juan 19, 27
Marker, Chris 41, 45, 86
Markle, Peter 84
Márquez, Juan 56, 149, 160, 164, 182
Martelli, Otello 41, 109
Martí (theater) 22
Martí, José 19, 23, 25, 26, 28, 36, 53, 73, 104, 134, 162, 186

Martínez, Julio 57, 83, 131
Martínez, Olivier 61
Martínez Casado, Juan José 34, 35, 131, 162, 168
Martínez Casado, Luis Manuel 24, 28, 86
Martínez Casado, Mario 129
Martínez Solares, Gilberto 35, 136
Martínez Villena, Rubén 19, 21, 23
Masferrer, Rolando 29
Massaguer, Conrado 19
Massip, José 83, 84, 103, 106, 107
Matamoros, Miguel 19, 20, 21, 22, 127
Matanzas 15, 16, 37, 57, 89, 136, 152, 164
Matthews, Herbert 37
Matthews, Tony 74
Medina, Raúl (director) 31, 34
Méliès, Georges 11
Mella (theater) 32
Mella, Julio Antonio 18, 19, 21, 129, 130
Mendieta, Carlos 23
Menéndez, Nilo 21
Milanés, Pablo 45, 99, 123, 140, 155, 159, 165
Minerva (magazine) 12
Miravalles, Reinaldo 53, 54, 72, 83, 88, 108, 113, 114, 145, 146, 151, 154, 156, 157, 159, 165, 168
Miravalles, Rodolfo 174
Miró, Sergio 27, 34, 181
Miroslava 35
Mistral, Jorge 35
Molina, Alberto 114, 154
Molina, Ángela 60
Molina, Enrique 84, 104, 106, 113, 115, 146, 154, 165
Molina, Humberto 93
Molina, Jorge 80, 89, 115, 180
Montalbán, Ricardo 38
Montaner, Rita 20, 25, 28, 30, 34, 38, 39, 127, 161, 177
Montezuma, Carlos 150, 154, 168, 169, 177
Montiel, Sarita 35
Mora, Blas 108, 114
Morayta, Miguel 36
Moré, Benny 28, 35, 116, 186
Moreno, Antonio 161
Moreno, Isabel 56, 60, 63, 136
Moreno, José Elías 116

Moreno, Marcos 116
Moreno, Nelly 174
Morín, Francisco 31
Morro Castle 10, 15, 133
Morúa Delgado, Martín 13, 157
Mulkay, Mijail 104, 133
Multicine (theater) 32
Mundo Cinematográfico (magazine) 37
Munt, Silvia 174
Mur Oti, Manuel 38
Musiak, Diego 107

Neo-realism 40, 41
Neptuno (theater) 33
New York 1, 2, 10, 16, 18, 27, 31, 53, 61, 62, 66, 78, 79, 91, 92, 125, 132, 133, 162, 166, 172, 183
Nieto, José 102
Nixon, Richard 36
Nolte, William 25
Nono, Luigi 112
Noticiario Royal News 27, 166
Noticiero Oriental 37
Nouvelle Vague 40, 42
Novás Calvo, Lino 23, 28
La Novela del Aire 27
La Novia del Mediodía (theater) 33
Nueva Trova 45
Núñez, Eslinda 54, 66, 68, 85, 120, 121, 130, 138, 143, 155, 169
Núñez, Lázaro 104, 180
Núñez, Nena 161
Núñez, Rolando 153
Núñez Jiménez, Antonio 36

Oates, Hilda 69, 102, 124, 150
Oliveros, Luis 150
Orígenes (magazine) 29, 37
Orlando, Felipe 24
Orol, Juan 26, 30, 35, 36, 38, 131, 132, 167
Oroná, Vicente 36, 37
Ortega, Juan J 31, 35, 36, 37
Ortiz, Fernando 20, 26, 30, 35, 151
Orts Ramos, Mario 21
O'Shea, Félix 22, 166
Osorio Gómez, Jaime 71
Otero, Adolfo 18, 28, 29

Padilla, Heberto 85
Padrón, Carlos 84

Index

Padrón, Humberto 183
Padrón, José 118
Padrón, Juan 46, 56, 57, 91, 93, 95, 96, 126, 132, 156, 178, 182, 184
Pais, Frank 37
Paley, William "Daddy" 77
Paramount Pictures 16
Paranagua, Paolo Antonio 1
París, Rogelio 52, 53, 67, 118, 139, 150
Pathé Films 10, 16, 17
Payret (theater) 13, 21
Paz, Senel 140
Pecoraro, Susú 107, 108
PECUSA Films 25, 26, 93, 161
Pedrosa, Manuel de la 34, 36, 38
Pelletier, Guy de 21
Peña, Lázaro 26
Peña, Sergio 75
Penn, Sean 61
Peón, Ramón 18, 19, 20, 21, 22, 25, 26, 34, 35, 39, 139, 161, 177, 181
Perdices, Antonio 21, 93, 161
Perdices, Enrique 24
Pérez, Fernando 46, 64, 70, 81, 106, 141, 142, 180
Pérez, Manuel 43, 45, 113, 160, 161, 165
Pérez, Marcelino 81, 141
Pérez, Susana 55, 70, 118, 142, 143, 165, 173, 179
Pérez Prado, Dámaso 29, 34
Perugorría, Jorge 55, 72, 84, 98, 102, 107, 119, 132
Piard, Terence 89
Piard, Tomás 89
Pineda Barnet, Enrique 43, 46, 56, 63, 100, 101, 129
Piñera, Virgilio 28, 37
Piñero, Federico 21, 22, 26, 27, 29, 34, 73, 93, 161
Piñero, Ignacio 22
Piñero, Leonardo 91, 126, 168, 184
Pirandello, Luigi 24
Planas, Mercedes 124, 173
Planas, Pedro Martín 88
Planas, Silvia 54, 85, 88, 120, 134, 145, 164, 165, 178
Planells, Salvador 35
Platt Amendment 11, 23
Polar Beer 27, 29
Pollack, Sydney 105
Pomares, Raúl 53, 56, 86, 90, 113, 114, 118, 124, 136, 137, 143, 150, 151, 153, 155, 156, 159, 160
Pomer, Julio 17
Pons, María Antonieta 26, 30, 167
Portell Vilá, Herminio 25
Portillo de la Luz, César 30, 31
Porto, Emilio 144
Porto, Manuel 55, 56, 67, 84, 118, 133, 164, 180
Portocarrero, René 28, 34, 37
Portuondo, Haydée 35
Portuondo, Omara 35, 68, 142
Powell, Julio 18, 19
Pozo, Chano 27, 31
Pozo, Diosdado del 167
Prats, Rodrigo 19, 167
Prío Socarrás, Carlos 23, 31, 33
Prochazka, Jan 43
Puente, Tito 125, 184
Pujols, Alberto 53, 60, 172, 179
Pulgarcito (magazine) 17
Pumarejo, Gaspar 33

Rabal, Liberto 138
Rabal, Paco 138
Radio Centro (theater) 32
Radio Reloj 30
Raggi, Tulio 53, 96, 149, 155, 168
Ramírez, Luis Alberto 64, 75, 154, 165, 174, 177
Ramos, José Antonio 21
Rampa, La (theater) 37
Rams, Martha 131
Rancho Boyeros (theater) 33
Ratti, Roberto 30
Raymat, Adelaida 57
Reade, Harry 72
Regina (theater) 20
Rentería, Lillian 54, 173
Rentería, Pedro 71, 113
Resortes 35
La Revista del cine (magazine) 23
Revuelta, Raquel 34, 56, 68, 75, 85, 112, 120, 138, 162, 168, 169
Revuelta, Vicente 55, 151, 168
Rex (theater) 33
Rey, Alejandro 74
Rey, Roberto 35
Rey, Silvano 142, 151, 175
Reyes, Consuelo 50
Reyes, Gilberto 83, 114

Index

Reyes, Joan Manuel 180
Reyes, José 89, 91, 96, 132, 174
Reyes, Sarita 82
Reyes, Víctor 29
Reyes Rodríguez, José 89, 91, 96, 132, 174
RHC-Cadena Azul 28
Rico, Alicia 93, 131, 161
Rivas, Mario 64, 96, 119, 183
Rodríguez, Agustín 22
Rodríguez, Alfredo 53
Rodríguez, Alina 53, 119, 127, 133
Rodríguez, Arsenio 27, 34
Rodríguez, Asenneh 85, 150
Rodríguez, Estelita 77, 78
Rodríguez, Francisco 11
Rodríguez, Julio César 67
Rodríguez, Nelson 54, 120, 141
Rodríguez, Pepín 53
Rodríguez, Silvio 45, 71, 99, 113
Rodríguez, Siro 20
Rodríguez Díaz, José 34
Rodríguez Feo, José 29
Roig, Gonzalo 12, 13, 17, 19, 22, 25, 28, 29, 31, 37, 161
Roig de Leuchsenring, Emilio 19, 25, 26
Rojas, Orlando 46, 50, 138, 140, 145
Rolando, Gloria 156
Roldán, Alberto 56
Roldán, Amadeo 19, 20
Román, Alberto 18
Romeu, Antonio María 20
Romeu, Gonzalo 63
Romeu, Mario 63
Roosevelt, Theodore 10, 182
Rory, Rosanna 63
Rosa, Orlando de la 27
Rosell, Rosendo 67, 168
Roumain, Jacques 81
Rubalcaba, Gonzalito 71
Rubens, Leo Aníbal 26
Ruiz, Rosendo, Jr. 30
Rulfo, Juan Carlos 50

Saderman, Alejandro 101, 113
Saladriga, Carlos 29
Salinas, Marcelo 21
Salvador, Jaime 26, 93
San Antonio de los Baños 35, 36, 46, 50

Sánchez Arcilla, José 22
Sánchez Galarraga, Gustavo 21, 24
Sandoval, Arturo 97, 138
Sandoval, Miguel 97
Sanguily, Manuel 14, 15, 148
Sant Andrews, Jaime 22, 32, 34
Santiago de Cuba 10, 13, 23, 30, 31, 37, 38, 83, 102, 119, 123, 150, 183
"Santo" 38
Santos, Isabel 50, 70, 117, 132, 164, 180
Santos, Pablo 12, 13, 14, 148
Sargent, Joseph 97
Sarol, José Antonio 36, 38
Schajowicz, Ludwig 27
Schnabel, Julian 61, 62
Schreyer, Wolfgang 43
Schub, Elizabeth 75
Schwartz, Ronald 2, 65, 87, 131, 155
Secada, Moraima 35, 142
Serpa, Enrique 37
Sevilla, Digna 136
Sevilla, Ninón 35, 38, 136, 137, 183
Sexteto Habanero 18, 20
Siboney Agency 38
Simons, Moisés 18, 161
Soberón Torchia, Edgar 89, 103
Solás, Elia 132
Solás, Humberto 43, 45, 46, 54, 65, 68, 85, 112, 120, 122, 123, 124, 126, 132, 140, 168
Soler Puig, José 43
Sonora Matancera (orchestra) 19, 33
Sopeira 22
Sotto Díaz, Arturo 55
Soviet Union 20, 21, 23, 28, 35, 40, 42, 46, 47, 57, 59, 66, 107, 119, 130, 142, 171
Stockwell, Dean 54
Suprem Films 18

Tabío, José 25, 29, 31
Tabío, Juan Carlos 46, 90, 97, 102, 119, 139, 153, 164
Tacón (theater) 9, 15
Tallet, José Zacarías 19
Tamayo, Claudio A. 104,
Tamayo, Idelfonso 55, 159, 173, 174, 175
Tamez, Gerardo 50
Taño, Aneiro 83
Taño, Tony 83, 85, 126

Index

Tarará (theater) 33
Tarraza, Juan Bruno 27
Tin Tan 34, 73
Torres, Gildo 85
Torres, Miguel 56, 73, 172, 173, 179
Tosquella, Max 22, 25, 27, 126
Touzet, René 29, 109
La Tremenda Corte 28
Tres Patines *see* Fernández, Leopoldo
Trinchet, Jorge 117
Tro, Emilio 29
Tropicana (nightclub) 26, 37, 115, 146
Tubau, María 10
Tuero, Emilio 127
Tuna Liberal 19

Ulive, Ugo 42, 73, 146
Ulla, Jorge 137
United Fruit Company 14, 169, 170
Urfé, Odilio 22

Valdés, Abelardito 25
Valdés, Bebo 75
Valdés, Juan 18
Valdés, Miguelito 109, 184
Valdés, Omar 54, 63, 99, 113, 118, 129, 165
Valdés, Oscar 43, 81, 93
Valdés, Oscar L. 56, 94, 160, 179
Valdés, Thais 50, 53, 83, 115, 137, 140, 146, 153
Valdés Rodríguez, José Manuel 21, 28, 31, 32
Valero, Antonio 119
Valero, María 29, 31
Valero, Noel 119
Van Dyke, W.S. 78
Varadero (beach) 17, 29
Vázquez, Pedro 18
Vega, Belkis 72, 167
Vega, Lilian 90
Vega, Pastor 45, 54, 83, 102, 103, 155, 160, 182
Velazco, Dulce 61
Vélez, Lupe 78

Veloz, Coralia 104, 159, 180
Veloz, Ramón 66, 178
Veloz, Ramoncito 118, 136, 144, 152, 164
Vergara, Teté 81, 86, 120, 158, 175
Veyre, Gabriel 9, 10
Víctor Víctor 59
Vidovszky, Lázló 58
Vilán, Mayte 59
Villagra, Nelson 65, 68, 72, 118, 154, 159, 160, 161, 165, 175
Villanueva, Larry 59
Villarondo, Guillermo 28
Villaverde, Cirilo 22, 32, 68, 69, 157
Villazón, Jorge 152, 153
Villoch, Federico 9, 13, 19
Villuendas, Enrique 11
Vitaphone (sound system) 22
Vitier, Cintio 25, 28, 35, 38
Vitier, José María 71, 74, 90, 98, 119, 146, 153, 165, 173
Vitier, Medardo 25
Vitier, Sergio 64, 66, 82, 95, 100, 124, 152, 174

Weyler, Gen. Valeriano 9
Willard, Jess 15
Wilson, Charles 106
Wilson, Ileana 55
Wilson, Richard 37, 63
Wong, Chino 131, 132
Wood, Patricio 56, 64, 67, 168
Wood, Salvador 56, 64, 114, 134, 138, 146, 150, 154, 157, 165, 169, 173, 177

Xiqués, Raúl 75, 88

Yarbrough, Jean 79, 109
Yevtushenko, Yevgeni 43

Zamacois, Eduardo 26
Zambrano, Benito 156
Zavattini, Cesare 41, 45, 114
Zayas, Alfredo 16, 18
Zinnemann, Fred 36

OHIO UNIVERSITY LIBRARY
Please return this book as soon as you have finished with it. In order to avoid a fine it must be returned by the latest date stamped below. All books are subject to recall after two weeks or immediately if needed for reserve.

CF